The Rise, Fall, and Legacy of Apartheid

The Rise, Fall, and Legacy of Apartheid

P. ERIC LOUW

PRAEGER

Westport, Connecticut
London

Library of Congress Cataloging-in-Publication Data

Louw, P. Eric.
The rise, fall, and legacy of apartheid / P. Eric Louw.
p. cm.
Includes bibliographical references and index.
ISBN 0-275-98311-0 (alk. paper)
1. Apartheid—South Africa. 2. South Africa—Race relations—History—20th century. 3. South Africa—Politics and government—20th century. I. Title.
DT1757.L683 2004
323.1196′068′09—dc22 2004017653

British Library Cataloguing in Publication Data is available.

Library of Congress Catalog Card Number: 2004017653
ISBN: 0–275–98311–0

First published in 2004

Praeger Publishers, 88 Post Road West, Westport, CT 06881
An imprint of Greenwood Publishing Group, Inc.
www.praeger.com

Printed in the United States of America

The paper used in this book complies with the Permanent Paper Standard issued by the National Information Standards Organization (Z39.48-1984).

10 9 8 7 6 5 4 3 2 1

Contents

Preface

As a member of the South African diaspora, I am constantly struck by how many educated people outside South Africa think they know what apartheid was, but actually have at most a partial grasp of the phenomenon. This book attempts to condense within one volume an enormous body of work on apartheid, by way of explaining what apartheid was, why it emerged, why it died, and its impacts on postapartheid South Africa.

An extensive body of academic and journalistic literature exists on apartheid. Much of the journalistic work is simplistic and one-dimensional and often encodes a selective self-righteous indignation, while the academic literature all too often slips into arcane meta-theory—more concerned with questions of methodological orthodoxy, intellectual nit-picking or point scoring than actually examining the phenomenon of apartheid. Some intra-Marxist debates and the discussion between the liberal and Marxist accounts of apartheid are cases in point. Instead of getting caught up in meta-intellectual debates, this book focuses on constructing a coherent narrative of apartheid. However, it seems useful to provide a brief outline of some key themes in the academic work done to date.

The academic literature on apartheid can be divided into three broad paradigms:

- Liberal
- Marxist
- Afrikaner nationalist

Within the Anglo world, analyses of Afrikaners and apartheid were dominated by the liberal paradigm until the 1960s. Liberals saw apartheid as the outcome of an Afrikaner politico-cultural peculiarity—Afrikaners were deemed to be an inherently racist and bigoted people who believed in white racial domination over blacks/white supremacy (*baasskap*). This was apparently associated with a "frontier tradition" (Afrikaner "primitivism")—in other words, Afrikaners were deemed never to have outgrown the racial prejudices they learned during the long years of black-white conflict on the Eastern Cape frontier, carried with them into the interior as *voortrekkers* (pioneers). Some liberals argued that inland Afrikaners were a backward people who had been cut off from the rest of Western civilization and so "missed out on" the Enlightenment. These inland Afrikaners were blamed for inventing apartheid as a backward-looking ideology (as opposed to forward-looking liberal democracy). A (false) binary opposition was thereby created between Anglos (representing liberal modernity) and Afrikaners (representing white supremacy and racism). Because liberals viewed ethnic mobilization as a backward anachronism in the modern world, they made no attempt to actually engage with Afrikaner nationalist thinking. Instead, liberal interpretations generally tended to simply reduce apartheid to an extreme form of (racist) segregation geared to keeping blacks in their place. Liberals were also inclined to draw (dubious) analogies between Southern U.S. rednecks and Afrikaners. Liberal interpretations of Afrikaners and apartheid can be found in the work of Walker, De Kiewiet, Macrone, Van den Berghe, De Villiers, and Thompson.[1] From this grew the notion—widely held by many Anglo South Africans (and many outside South Africa)—that Afrikaner nationalism was irrational, backward looking, and racist. In its extreme version, this view saw Afrikaners as fanatical villains, and likened Afrikaner nationalism to Nazism (a view also propagated by much liberal journalism).

Marxist and neo-Marxist historians challenged the liberal approach in the 1970s, shifting the emphasis to an examination of the evolution of capitalism in South Africa. Marxist revisionists like Wolpe, Legassick, Slovo, Davies, Bozzoli, and Yudelman argued that racism had been beneficial for the development of South African capitalism.[2] This Marxist paradigm pointed to the central role played by Anglo capitalists and British imperialists in developing the system of cheap migrant labor upon which racial capitalism was built, thereby dissolving the liberal paradigm's binary opposition between Anglos and Afrikaners. However, like liberals, the Marxists assumed that continuity existed between (preapartheid) segregation and apartheid—that is, early Marxist revisionists argued that both segregation and apartheid were "necessary" (functional) for reproducing the cheap black labor upon which South African capitalism was built. Later interpretations began to tone down the idea that segregation was "necessary."[3] The Marxist argument that apartheid served the interests of capitalism generated a liberal-Marxist debate in South African historiography given that the liberal school argued—in contradistinction to Marxist revisionists—that apartheid was dysfunctional for capitalist profit making.[4]

The liberal-Marxist debate ultimately revolved around the question of whether apartheid was organized around race or class. This debate was of more than academic concern because it influenced how South Africa's future was envisioned. Three positions emerged during the 1980s:

First, liberals argued that apartheid was a racialized state that hindered capitalist profit making. By ignoring class, and emphasizing race, (Anglo) liberals could efface their own complicity in apartheid. Instead, Afrikaner nationalism was seen to be an anachronism that has temporarily blocked South Africa's progress to a fully functional liberal capitalist state. Liberals effectively deployed a teleological argument in which capitalism represented "necessary progress"—in other words, capitalism would ultimately triumph over Afrikaner nationalism's "irrational" interference with liberal capitalist development. In what came to be called "the O'Dowd view,"[5] liberals suggested that "the market" would eventually undermine apartheid; consequently, there was no need for a revolutionary struggle to overthrow the system. Market economics and liberal reformism (of the Urban Foundation–type) would do the job and eventually improve the lives of all South Africans.

Second, Marxists/neo-Marxists, like Wolpe, Legassick, Bozzoli, and Davies, argued that South African capitalism had developed on the back of a racist state—producing a special form of capitalism, called racial capitalism. From this perspective, improving the lives of South Africa's black underclasses required an antiapartheid struggle to overthrow the race-based state. It was proposed that, because racial capitalism was an intermeshed phenomenon (i.e., race and class were conceptually collapsed), overthrowing apartheid would automatically translate into overthrowing the capitalist-induced misery of millions. This became the dominant view within the African National Congress (ANC)/South African Communist Party (SACP) and the United Democratic Front (UDF).

Third, a range of independent socialists and a few liberals argued that both racial and class interests were involved in creating apartheid[6]—that is, a mutual but nonessential relationship existed between race and class. From this perspective, overthrowing the apartheid state would not necessarily translate into an overthrow of South African capitalism or an improvement in the lives of most South Africans;[7] at most, it would create some black middle-class beneficiaries who would step into the shoes of displaced whites. From this viewpoint, anyone serious about socialism would need to organize outside of the ANC/SACP (and UDF) "national democratic struggle."

As will become clear from reading this book, I am broadly sympathetic to the third perspective.

Interestingly, both the liberal and Marxist paradigms spend much time engaging with each other, but little time actually engaging with Afrikaner nationalist *beliefs*. This book will engage with the Afrikaner nationalist paradigm, particularly in chapter 2. Connecting with Afrikaner nationalist thinking reveals two core concerns that underpinned the apartheid project (which the liberal paradigm ignores, and the Marxist paradigm only partially addresses). These two core concerns were:

- Anglos subjugated Afrikaners. Establishing an Afrikaner-controlled state was seen as a way to end both Afrikaner impoverishment (at the hands of Anglo capitalism) and the destruction of Afrikaner culture/language (by Anglo cultural imperialism).
- Afrikaners feared future subjugation at the hands of black people. Such subjugation was seen as the likely outcome of demographic shifts (triggered by World War II), combined with post–World War II international reconfigurations. Apartheid was designed to counter this threat of black subjugation.

The failure of the liberal and Marxist paradigms to seriously engage with Afrikaner nationalist thinking produced skewed explanations of apartheid. Understanding apartheid requires engaging with all three paradigms. Consequently, this book is eclectic in its use of sources, drawing on Marxist/neo-Marxist, social democrat, liberal, and Afrikaner nationalist sources. However, I was strongly informed by one member of the Marxist revisionist school, Dan O'Meara, who produced an especially valuable examination of the roots of apartheid. In 1983, O'Meara[8] published an analysis of Afrikaner nationalism in which he examined the economic and class underpinnings of this ideology. In the process, O'Meara shifted the focus away from (the liberal paradigm's) notions of irrational racist bigotry. His central thesis was that the "apartheid idea" was used by the National Party (NP) to cement a class alliance within which Afrikaner business interests dominated. However, one problem with O'Meara's thesis is that he overly minimized the role of Afrikaner intellectuals in the creation of apartheid. Further, another Marxist revisionist, Deborah Posel,[9] has disputed O'Meara's thesis, arguing that there were long-standing class struggles within Afrikanerdom, and that O'Meara overestimates the power of Afrikaner business interests within this struggle.

The Marxists/neo-Marxists—especially, O'Meara and Posel—made an enormous contribution to our understanding of apartheid. However, their overemphasis on economic imperatives/class meant that they ultimately failed to grapple with the cultural and symbolic "structures of feeling" within Afrikaner nationalism. This is where I diverge from the Marxist school. Class analysis is not enough. Afrikaner nationalism and apartheid cannot simply be understood in terms of economics and economic motivations. Ironically, the one thing that liberals, Marxists, and neo-Marxists appear to agree on is that economics are paramount. This is why both Marxists and liberals have so often misread Afrikaner nationalists and failed to understand what Afrikaners *believed* apartheid was about. In this regard, I agree with Hermann Giliomee, that in order to understand apartheid, one has to try and get into the heads of Afrikaner nationalists and take seriously what they believed about themselves, something Giliomee[10] does masterfully. So, like Giliomee, I hermeneutically grapple with Afrikaner nationalist texts. However, despite this "subjective dimension," I remain (simultaneously) sympathetic (unlike Giliomee) to the view that Afrikaner nationalism also had "material underpinnings." Consequently, this book explores the economic roots of apartheid, for which purpose the work of the neo-Marxist revisionists will be mobilized. On the other hand, because Afrikaner belief structures were not exclusively economically driven, the book also engages with Afrikaner nationalist thinking by "stepping inside" the Afrikaner "imagined community." Consequently, this book deploys a hybrid approach that will presumably not be to the liking of methodological purists.

Overall, the book simply tries to construct an accessible narrative, and tell the story of apartheid. It attempts to come to grips with the story of a sad country where, during the twentieth century, three "groups" vied for influence and power. A key feature of South Africa's twentieth-century journey was that two "national groups" (blacks and Afrikaners) defined themselves as having a right to the country. The problem is that they claimed the same country. Both constructed a (nationalist) worldview justifying their claims and the righteousness of their struggle for self-determination. They mutually constructed a zero-sum scenario in which the one group's dreams were the other group's nightmares, and then spent decades fighting over whose dreams would prevail. Anglos comprised the third "national group," busying themselves with running the economy, while blacks and Afrikaners pursued their nationalist dreams. These Anglos created racial capitalism, and ultimately therefore set the economic parameters within which Afrikaner and black politics functioned. Ultimately, these Anglo-made economic parameters have played a crucial role in influencing the success, or otherwise, of the nationalist struggles—and by the end of the twentieth century, the Anglo corporate sector seems to have been remarkably successful in narrowing the options available to both Afrikaner and black nationalists.

As we enter the twenty-first century, it appears the fighting may be over, but it is still unclear whether the endgame has been reached.

I would like to thank the following people for assisting me in locating information: Herman Giliomee and the library staff of Stellenbosch University, University of South Africa, University of Cape Town, and University of Queensland. Thanks to Grant Dobinson, Patchanee Malikhao, Nico Louw, and Rose Louw for assistance with maps and subediting.

Abbreviations

ANC—African National Congress
ANCYL—ANC Youth League
Armscor—Armaments Development and Production Corporation
AWB—*Afrikaner Weerstandbeweging*/Afrikaner Resistance Movement
AZAPO—Azanian People's Organization
BC—Black Consciousness
BEE—Black Economic Empowerment
CNO—*Christelik-Nasionale Onderwys*/Christian National Education
Cosatu—Congress of South African Trade Unions
CP—Conservative Party
EU—European Union
FAK—*Federasie van Afrikaanse Kultuurvereenigings* (Federation of Afrikaans Cultural Organizations)
FRELIMO—Front for the Liberation of Mozambique
GEAR—Growth, Employment, and Redistribution
GNU—Government of National Unity
IFP—Inkatha Freedom Party
IMF—International Monetary Fund
JMC- Joint Management Center
MDM—Mass Democratic Movement
MK—*Umkonto we Sizwe* (ANC Armed Wing)
MPLA—Popular Movement for the Liberation of Angola
NEPAD—New Partnership for Africa's Development
NEUM—Non-European Unity Movement
NGO—Non-Government Organization

NP—National Party
NSMS—National Security Management System
OSP—Office of the State President
PAC—Pan African Congress
RDP—Reconstruction and Development Program
Renamo—Mozambique National Resistance Movement
SABRA—South African Bureau of Racial Affairs
SACP—South African Communist Party
SADF—South African Defense Force
SAP—South African Police
SASO—South African Students' Organization
SSC—State Security Council
SWAPO—South West African People's Organization (Namibia)
TRC—Truth and Reconciliation Commission
UDF—United Democratic Front
UF—Urban Foundation
UM—Unity Movement
UN—United Nations
UNITA—United National Army for the Total Independence of Angola
UP—United Party
U.S.—United States
WHAM—Win Hearts and Minds
WICs—whites, Indians, coloreds
WTO—World Trade Organization
ZANU-PF— Zimbabwe African National Union-Patriotic Front
ZAPU—Zimbabwe African People's Union
ZAR—Zuid-Afrikaanse Republic (South African Republic)

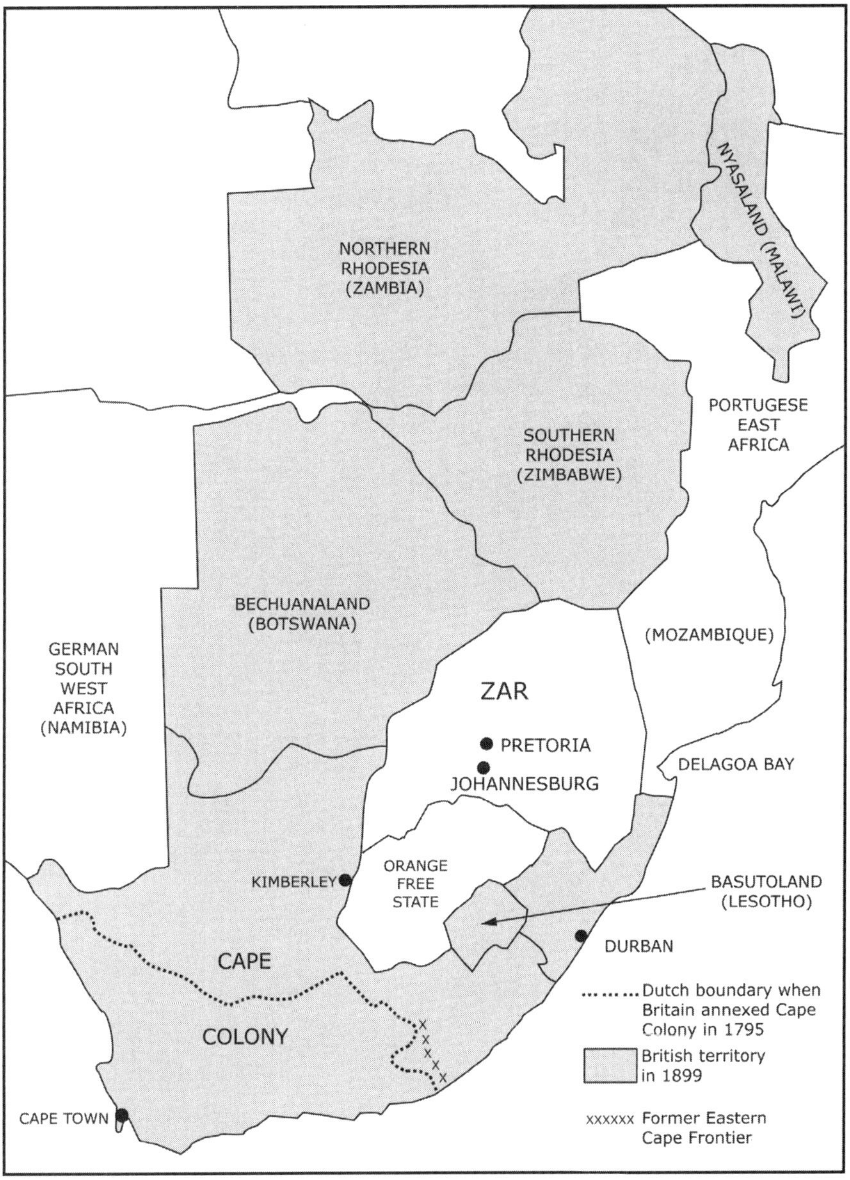

Map 1:
Southern Africa in 1899

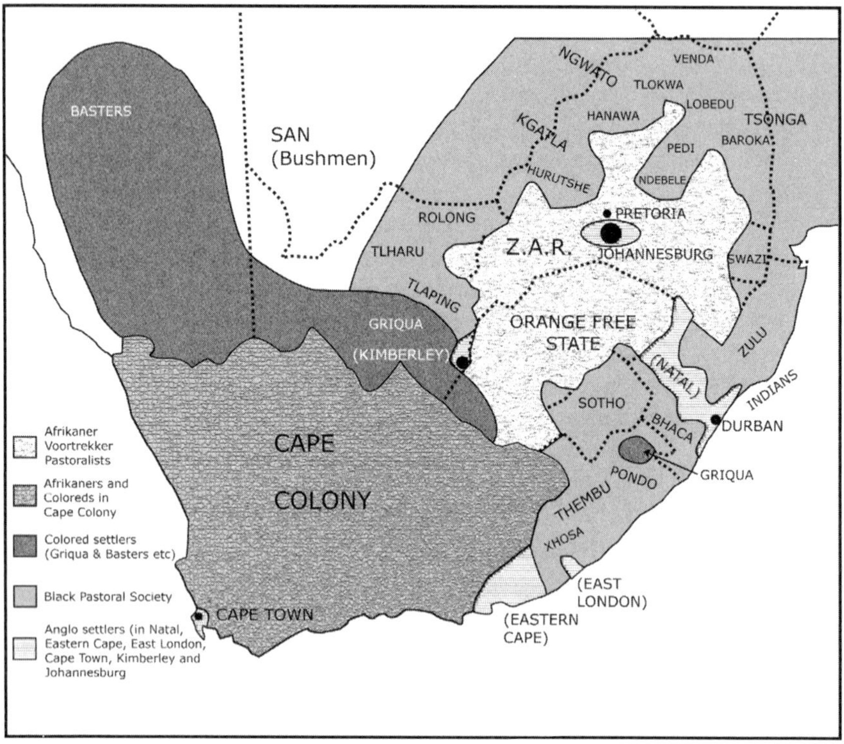

Map 2:
South Africa prior to the Boer War

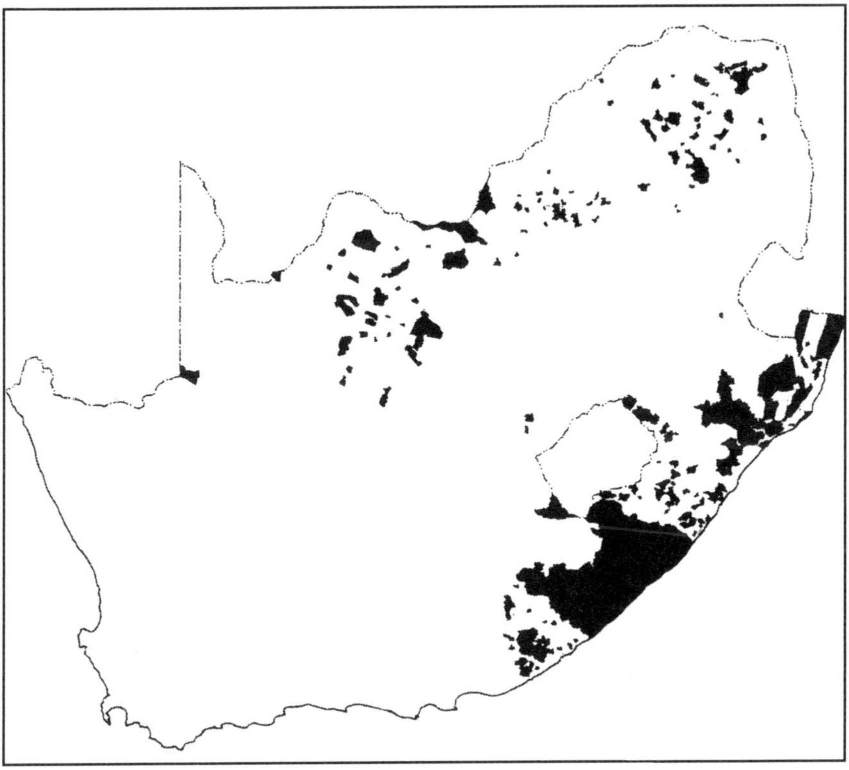

Map 3:
Black Reserves in 1913

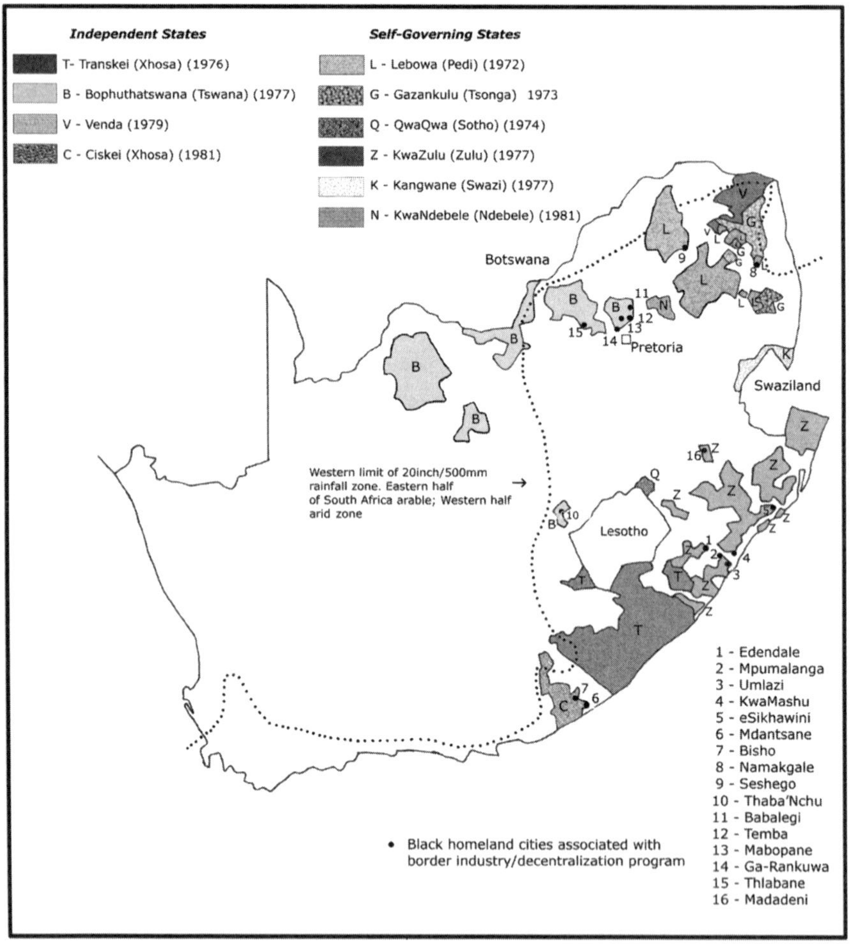

Map 4:
Black Homelands

CHAPTER 1

Milner's Model of Settler Capitalism

The outlines of the modern state we now call South Africa emerged during the first decade of the twentieth century. This South African state was a creation of the British Empire—its foundations laid by Lord Alfred Milner while he was British governor of the Transvaal and Orange River Colony following their annexation in 1900. As governor of these two northern conquests as well as high commissioner of Britain's other southern African territories, Milner began the process of transforming and reconstructing South Africa into a modern industrial capitalist state.[1] He established British hegemony over Southern Africa and planted settler capitalism at the heart of this British domain. From this was born the racial-capitalist state[2] as a peculiarly South African means of socioeconomic organization. Therein lie the roots of apartheid.

During the twentieth century, the British created many states to serve as the administrative fulcrums for politically and economically managing its far-flung domains. The boundaries of these states were determined by the need to create viable economic administrative entities.[3] This often threw together ethnically and culturally distinct people, sometimes with a history of conflict. The invention of South Africa as a unified modernizing state was precisely such a British creation. Designed to service the needs of mining capitalism, it brought together within one polity a diversity of people. Significantly, the majority of the people incorporated into this new British-built state were premodern pastoralists, who consequently needed modernization to become productive workers and consumers within the capitalist society being constructed.

As with other modernization projects, South Africans traveled through the traumatic transitions of urbanization, industrialization, mass education, media-ization, bureaucratization, democratization, and secularization,[4] and learned to imbibe the values of rationality, utility, efficiency, and individual responsibility.[5] But South Africa's different ethnic groups did not travel through these transformative stages simultaneously. Furthermore, in South Africa, the process of accumulating capital and constructing centralized political power was tied to ethnicity. Consequently, the story of South Africa's modernization process involved a complex multilayered pattern of interethnic interaction, exploitation, conflict, alliance building, and cooperation. Ultimately, the story of twentieth-century South Africa was about implementing three different (competing, yet interconnected) models of nation building and modernization, namely: an Anglo racial-capitalist model; Afrikaner nationalism's apartheid model; and the African National Congress's (ANC) postapartheid reconfiguration of racial capitalism, associated with the notion of "black empowerment."

The foundation model for twentieth-century South African nation building was racial capitalism because both the apartheid and postapartheid nation-building models effectively emerged as unintended consequences of Milner's post–Boer War reconstruction work. This involved planting Anglo modernity at the heart of Britain's Southern African hegemony. Milner and his team—called the kindergarten—brought with them from England an Anglo-liberal worldview derived from John Locke's[6] argument that good governance involved building secure environments wherein individuals could compete to improve their lot. This worldview emerged from sixteenth-century struggles of northwestern European burgher/bourgeois middle classes to free themselves from feudalism. Locke argued that individuals had the right to expect the state to protect their property, and the right to be treated as equal before the law (i.e., feudal nobles and monarchs were no longer to be regarded as superior). Initially, this did not mean that all individuals were regarded as equal, because early liberal societies were premised upon class differences, and slaves were regarded as property to be protected. But it did mean that the Rule of Law applied—that is, no one was subject to arbitrary laws; laws/policies now emerged from a prescribed legislative process (not the capricious will of nobles); and all laws were equally applicable to everyone (including lawmakers). This form of government freed the middle classes from laws unhelpful to wealth creation. Locke believed the best guarantee for securing the rights to life, liberty, and property was liberal democratic government, wherein legislators were elected to represent the interests of the electors. Milner was steeped in this worldview[7] when he set about building a governance structure and a functioning capitalist economy in South Africa. However, due to South Africa's fraught and complex ethnic mix, the original Anglo liberal-capitalist model was modified into racial capitalism—and so the journey into apartheid was initiated.

A WAR TO ESTABLISH CAPITALISM AND A MODERN STATE

Britain fought the Boer War (1899–1902) to secure British hegemony across Southern Africa and establish the conditions for a modern capitalist state. The British first arrived in South Africa in 1795, when they seized the Dutch colony in Cape Town[8] to prevent it from falling into Napoleon's hands. During the nineteenth century, the Cape Colony was Britain's core Southern African possession. Until the discovery of diamonds in the 1860s and gold in the 1870s/1880s, Southern Africa remained an economically insignificant, sparsely populated, unpromising backwater, overwhelmingly populated by Afrikaner[9] and black pastoralists. These pastoralists had for a century jostled and vied with each other over territory as the empty land was gradually settled. Only in the 1880s was the settlement frontier closed (when all available arable land was finally occupied). These pastoralist demographics were dramatically altered by nineteenth-century diamond and gold rushes, which drew European, Australian, and American migrants to new urban centers like Kimberley and Johannesburg. Anglos dominated both this migrant flow and the mining-capitalist economy being built. Britain quickly annexed the diamond fields to the Cape Colony, but was unable to gain control of the richer goldfields lying inside the Afrikaner-controlled ZAR (South African Republic). They would need to fight a war to secure these goldfields.

The diamond industry radically transformed Britain's Cape Colony, attracting foreign capital, entrepreneurs, and migrants. It stimulated agriculture, a transport industry, and foreign trade, plus dramatically improved government tax revenues, customs receipts, and stamp duties, thereby creating the basis for government spending on railways and harbor construction. The discovery of diamonds made Southern Africa, for the first time, economically attractive to Europeans. This led to the British acting in 1879 to entrench white hegemony across the region by crushing the last two South African black polities with any power, namely the Zulus and Pedi. Kimberley became a resource base for funding the projection of British power into the interior, and became the seedbed for a modern industrial South Africa dominated by Anglo capitalists.[10] In the midst of a simple pastoral society peopled by Afrikaners and Griqua-coloreds[11] grew a modern city with a complex division of labor and class stratification. The Kimberley crucible produced the mining companies from which grew an indigenous South African capitalism, and the corporate know-how and capital later used to develop the Witwatersrand goldfields. Significantly, the Kimberley crucible also gave birth to a racially divided labor force, within which black migrant workers lived in closed compounds and provided cheap labor, facilitating the rapid capital accumulation achieved by companies like (Cecil Rhodes's[12]) De Beers.[13] Johannesburg ultimately grew into a larger and more complex society than Kimberley, but Kimberley provided the original template for racial capitalism—the template Anglo mining capitalists redeployed to the Witwatersrand goldfields.

The Witwatersrand gold industry abruptly planted modern capitalism into the Afrikaner-ruled ZAR during the 1880s, aggressively challenging Afrikaner pastoralist society. The 1890s saw Johannesburg grow into a significant center of mining capitalism as fortune seekers flooded in from around the world. Anglos economically and culturally dominated the new city in the heart of the Boer Republic. The Randlords (mine owners) were Anglos, or Europeans assimilated into Anglo South Africa. So too were the artisans, shopkeepers, engineers, managers, and clerks who made up the complex new stratified urban world built by the migrants. Black migrant workers served as an unskilled labor force. Johannesburg's growth also impacted upon some rural areas by providing a market for agricultural products. This produced changes within Boer[14] pastoral society, generating the start of Afrikaner urbanization and proletarianization in the 1890s, as surplus Boers were driven off the land.[15]

The growth of Johannesburg's gold-mining industry led to the Boer War—a war about who would control Southern Africa and what modernization and development model would be deployed to harness the newfound wealth. For the British, Witwatersrand gold created the problem that the formerly poor ZAR was transformed into a potential hegemonic rival in the region. Britain could no longer single-handedly dictate Southern African policy from the governor general's Cape Town residence. Gold also made Southern Africa a prize worth having, creating resources for building a self-funding British power base in Africa, as an important link in Britain's expanding Indian Ocean empire. Cecil Rhodes, who had emerged as Kimberley's wealthiest man, a key investor in Johannesburg mining, and prime minister of the Cape Colony, was quick to seize the opportunities this wealth offered for realizing his imperial dreams of a British Cape-to-Cairo empire. Rhodes established a private "Rhodesian" fiefdom over today's Botswana, Zimbabwe, Zambia, and Malawi.[16] He also agitated for the ZAR to be brought under British control, and his agents worked to rouse Johannesburg's Anglo *uitlander* (foreigner) population to campaign against Afrikaner rule. Both Rhodes and Milner wanted the ZAR to become British, but Governor General Milner found Rhodes a liability, who hindered rather than helped British scheming to achieve this result.

For ZAR Afrikaners, gold created both opportunities and problems. On the one hand it gave them, for the first time, the resources and tax base to build a viable state. On the other hand, they were a pastoral folk, ill prepared to manage the speed of the transformations generated by mining capitalism. In the 1880s, these Boers were a pioneer community, descended from people who had been trekking inland from the original Dutch colony at Cape Town for 200 years. Inland Afrikaners were, like the black tribes surrounding them, pastoralists. Theirs was a rural society with little division of labor, no middle-class merchants, professionals, or intellectuals. The Boer economy consisted of small-scale self-sufficient farming units that included the farmer, his family, servants, and retainers. The self-sustaining nature of this economic activity restricted capital accumulation, making it difficult for the ZAR state to develop a tax base with which to support a state bureaucracy.[17] While Afrikaners in and around Cape Town knew about trade, capital, and credit, inland Afrikaners, like their black tribal neighbors, did not initially have the experience, skills, or political infrastructures to equip them for the arrival of mining capitalism. Once gold began generating tax revenues and customs dues, the ZAR government under President Paul Kruger began constructing a state bureaucracy, which was facilitated by importing Cape Colony Afrikaners, Hollanders, and Germans. One such import from the Cape was Jan Smuts, who would one day become prime minister of South Africa.

For ZAR Afrikaners the question was how to manage the new economic forces unleashed in their midst by gold mining. Their concern was to ensure that Johannesburg did not unleash migrations that would swamp their Afrikaner world. There was the perceived threat that so many Anglos would migrate to this new city that the ZAR would by default eventually be absorbed into the British Empire. This was a core Afrikaner concern of the ZAR descendants of *voortrekkers* (pioneers) who had left the Cape Colony in the 1830s precisely to escape British rule and establish their own independent Boer republics. The ZAR's solution to this "Anglo problem" was to deny *uitlanders* (foreigners) the vote, ensuring that no matter how many Anglos migrated to Johannesburg they would not gain control of the ZAR Parliament. Ultimately, Britain used this *uitlander* vote issue to provoke the Boer War.

Another important cause of war was that the ZAR hindered the full flowering of racial capitalism (transplanted from Kimberley) by impeding black labor flows to Witwatersrand mines. ZAR Afrikaners had an understanding of black-white relationships that was quite different from views held by Johannesburg's Anglo capitalists. For mining capitalists, blacks were simply a potential source of cheap labor needed for the labor-intensive mining method being developed. As far as Anglo entrepreneurs were concerned, Johannesburg needed many black workers because a large force of unskilled menial labor was crucial to make Witwatersrand mining economically viable.[18] Effectively, blacks needed to be induced to leave behind their premodern pastoral lives and become modern workers in the emerging urban economy. From within the (Locke-derived) worldview of the Anglo entrepreneurs, good governance involved building environments wherein they, as middle-class businessmen, could make a profit.

Their liberal expectation was for government legislation that was helpful to wealth creation and capitalist modernization. This required a state with a legislative program to break up black (and Boer) premodern pastoralism in order to create the modernized labor force required by the mines. Central to the Anglo worldview was the creation of a unified state with authority over everyone, governed by the Rule of Law, wherein all laws applied equally to every individual. Modernization consequently involved breaking up South Africa's "feudal" patchwork of semiautonomous communities and overlapping sources of authority, and (forcefully) integrating people into a single unified society, governed by one set of laws. This would create the conditions for concentrating people into industrialized cities where they were subject to the processes of cultural homogenization (modernization).

However, inland Afrikaners had a different understanding of the world based upon the idea of communities governed by different codes, worldviews, and authority structures living side by side in a hodgepodge patchwork of relationships. Interactions between such communities were governed by a complex set of power relationships involving both violence and negotiations. Inland Afrikaners had for generations lived in such a hodgepodge world, among and alongside other communities (e.g., coloreds, Khoisan, and Griquas, and later, various black tribes), but never integrated with them. They fought wars with some of these groups, subjugated some (as slaves or servants), negotiated sharecropping deals with some, and negotiated "boundary treaties" with others.[19] Inland Afrikaners saw no need to have a single-authority structure and regarded the homogenizing effects of Anglo-run modernization as positively dangerous because breaking up Southern Africa's various (premodern) communities and integrating these people into a single unified society would spell the end of Afrikaner self-determination and a separate Afrikaner identity. The origins of the Great Trek in the 1830s lay in this clash of worldviews. Consequently, the ZAR Afrikaners had no intention of allowing Anglo capitalists to dominate their government, impose their Anglo worldview on the ZAR, undermine their (pastoral) way of life, or build a large modernized black working class in Johannesburg. As far as the majority of ZAR-burghers were concerned, the ZAR was an Afrikaner state, and so should be used to promote Afrikaner interests. And in the 1890s, the interests of these still overwhelmingly pastoralist Afrikaner burghers did not coincide with the wealth-creation-at-all-costs motivations of the Anglo capitalists.

The result was that ZAR legislation got in the way of profit maximization on the mines. Most crucially, the ZAR state impeded the rapid creation of a black working class assimilated into a modern urban economy. In large measure, this occurred because of the nature of the ZAR state and Afrikaner conceptions of nationhood. The ZAR was a weak state, consisting of a checkerboard of white-black feudalistic relationships. Afrikaner colonization of the ZAR left tracts of land in black tribal hands. In such "black areas," the Pedi, Swazi, Venda, Tswana, and Ndebele continued to live in semiautonomous polities as premodern pastoralists. Afrikaner pastoralists treated some tribes as a subject people from whom they could extract labor tithes and *inboekelinge* ("apprentices" seized during warfare, bought, or bartered).[20] However, some tribes (such as the Swazi) were treated as allies, and many *inboekelinge* were Swazi war booty, passed on to their Afrikaner allies.[21] Even within the areas of Afrikaner settlement, black servants and retainers lived culturally autonomous lives in black *kraals* geographically separate from Boer homesteads. Blacks consequently lived as a semiautonomous feudal caste, living alongside and parallel to Afrikaner society, but not being assimilated into that society. Because Afrikaners and their black retainers interacted daily, cultural exchanges occurred in both directions; however, the different groups retained their autonomy within an entanglement of semifeudal interactions. So although black people supplied labor to white farmers, they also kept their own cattle and grew their own crops. Their relationship to Boer society was thus a (premodern) neofeudal one, based on negotiated tithing and sharecropping. This was very different from the modern labor relations mining capitalists brought to the ZAR. For Afrikaner pastoralists, the arrival of mining capitalism was unwelcome because Johannesburg threatened to destabilize the patchwork of rural feudalistic relationships they had put into place across the ZAR by drawing labor away from their farms (and the autonomous black polities) and by transforming (modernizing) black pastoralists. These Afrikaner pastoralists constituted the bulk of the ZAR's electorate, and they elected Kruger as their president—a man promising to protect their interests.

During the 1890s, Kruger's government facilitated the growth of a hybrid economy and society—the rural feudalistic checkerboard built upon pastoralism was protected, but simultaneously a modern urban capitalist economy was allowed to grow on the Witwatersrand. This capitalist economy also began spilling out into the rural areas around the Witwatersrand, where pastoralism gave way to modern agriculture (supplying food to the goldfields). Gold mining necessarily stimulated a transport industry, foreign trade, and a tax base for Kruger's government, which saw this new source of wealth as an opportunity to improve the lot of Afrikaners. The growth of a modern (Anglo-run) economy on the Witwatersrand was consequently to be managed to the benefit of Afrikaners. An example of this "state management" of modernization was the building of the Pretoria-Delagoa Bay railway, which came to symbolize the grievances of the mining entrepreneurs in three ways. First, the construction and operation of this rail project was given to a Dutch consortium. Second, this railway connected the Pretoria-Johannesburg area to the only Southern African port not in British hands. Kruger's government rejected lobbying to extend the Cape Colony's railway to Johannesburg. When this Cape rail extension was allowed, it was granted to the same Dutch consortium. Third, freight rates and tariffs were gerrymandered to the benefit of the Dutch consortium. Effectively, gold mining was being used as a cash cow to fund ZAR development projects and channel wealth into Afrikaner/Dutch hands. This was achieved by setting up a system of government-licensed concessions to ensure that some of the wealth generated by gold mining flowed into Afrikaner hands. These concessions were geared to building a non–Anglo-controlled industrial base in the infant state. But because the ZAR market was so small, these industries could only survive if protected by tariffs, which dramatically drove up the costs of Witwatersrand mining and the general cost of living in Johannesburg. Not surprisingly, the concession system, tariffs, and taxation became a core source of *uitlander* grievance against the ZAR government. These grievances became enmeshed with the fact that *uitlanders* were disenfranchised—so violating the liberal credo of no taxation without representation. Kruger's concession in 1892 of proposing a second Parliament for *uitlanders* was deemed insufficient. Anglo *uitlander* negativity toward the ZAR was further exacerbated by daily interactions with a state bureaucracy, and police (called Zarps) who were seen as "foreign." Anglos were especially upset by the fact that these Zarps and bureaucrats insisted on using Afrikaans for all state business, a language that Anglos considered culturally inferior.

The mine owners wanted a government based on liberal (Lockean) principles that would facilitate profit maximization. Milner, as British governor general in Cape Town, wanted the ZAR removed as a rival power center. Rhodes wanted the ZAR to be part of his dream of a British Cape-to-Cairo empire. The coincidence between these three sets of interests generated a momentum toward war—a war to make Southern Africa British, turn South Africa into a modern capitalist state with Johannesburg as its economic heart, and begin the process of sweeping away premodern black and Boer pastoralism. In preparing the ground for war, Southern Africa's Anglo press—much of it owned by mining capitalists like Rhodes—promoted the view of Boer backwardness and inferiority. Kruger's government was painted as both incapable of providing the necessary conditions for modern development and dangerous because of its sympathy for Germany. The Boer state was demonized for its:

- Afrikaner patronage,
- promotion of employing white labor rather than black labor,[22] and
- inability[23] to intervene "correctly" in tribal areas to create subordinate black populations from which cheap labor could be drawn.[24]

The Anglo press's "ideological creativity"[25] successfully built a groundswell of Anglo public opinion in favor of war against a backward "peasant" state that was a hindrance to modern development.

In reality, the ZAR was gradually modernizing—constructing a bureaucracy and enacting legislation necessary for modernization. In fact, after the Boer War, the British retained many ZAR laws.[26] Infrastructures like transport and education were built and skilled people imported (from the Cape, Holland, and Germany) to build the required urban middle class of managers, bureaucrats, professionals, and teachers. Kruger's government also developed an industrialization policy (based on tariff protection), and allowed the capitalization of agriculture in a gradualist/reformist way to feed the growing urban population.[27] With the resources made available by the discovery of gold, there is no doubt the ZAR would have successfully completed its modernization process without British intervention.[28] However, because the ZAR was modernizing on its own terms, the process was not to the liking of Johannesburg's mining entrepreneurs or the British colonial authorities. Among the features of ZAR modernization most riling Anglos was Kruger's state interventionism to promote Afrikaner economic and cultural interests. The ZAR also operated a multi-tiered "checkerboard" system consisting of a modern urban sector, modern rural sector, (premodern) Boer pastoral sector, and (premodern) black pastoral sector. This was premised upon a complex cultural patchwork understanding of social organization that underpinned Afrikaner thinking. This patchwork notion—which involves communities simultaneously interacting while retaining cultural distinctness—also supported the Netherlands' *verzuiling* (pillarization) model of social organization. This *verzuiling* conception cut across the worldview of the Anglo entrepreneurs who saw "progress" as necessarily involving the replacement of premodern behaviors with urban/modern behaviors in order to build the large (modern) working class they required. This included educating (assimilating) premoderns into behaviors appropriate to modern capitalism—that is, destroying the kaleidoscope of cultures, codes, and authority structures existing in the ZAR. For Afrikaners, Boer and black pastoralism and black tribal cultures needed to be allowed to survive alongside and parallel to the modern economy. Within this Afrikaner vision of modernization there would be pockets of (premodern) people not incorporated into the central capitalist economy. The problem with this model was that it meant black labor could not be controlled. This was, in fact, one of the mine owners' complaints against Kruger's government—the ZAR would not intervene to retrieve black workers who deserted Johannesburg's mining compounds. The Afrikaner version of modernization—which allowed modern and premodern societies to coexist—was unacceptable to Anglo entrepreneurs because it meant less control over workers, and would have dramatically slowed down South Africa's modernization by creating fewer (and therefore more expensive) workers and reducing the number of potential consumers. Essentially, the ZAR violated the Anglo (Lockean) conceptualization of how liberal states should behave to facilitate the unfettered growth of modern capitalism. Kruger came to be seen as an obstacle to modernization and the exploitation of resources for profit maximization. If South Africa was to be modernized, regime change was needed.

The Boer War was about regime change—that is, implementing a political framework within which capitalism could prosper. This involved building a strong state and the Rule of Law, creating a modern bureaucratic and taxation system to facilitate capitalist development, creating the conditions and regulatory framework for capitalist entrepreneurs to prosper, building a metropolis (Johannesburg) to serve as a commercial and industrial center for capitalism, deconstructing the existing cultural and authority structures in order to reconstruct and transform (modernize) the population, and coercing the (pastoral) rural population to relocate to the cities (as workers).[29] Milner's project was about creating the conditions for destroying Southern Africa's existing social forms in all their complexity and variety[30] in order to build a modern (Anglo-ruled) capitalist state. To facilitate this modernization project, ZAR Afrikaner power had to be broken so a strong (Anglo imperial) state could be built with enough power to radically transform Southern Africa.

MILNER AND HIS KINDERGARTEN

Lord Milner was governor general of Britain's Southern African possessions from 1897 to 1905, and went on to become a British cabinet minister. When Britain annexed the ZAR in 1900 (renaming it the Transvaal), Milner moved to Johannesburg. Transferring the seat of British power from Cape Town to Johannesburg was symbolic of the importance Milner attached to transforming Johannesburg into the commercial and industrial hub of British Southern Africa. The new governor general's residence of Sunnyside sat atop the Witwatersrand (ridge of white waters), commanding views across the high veld toward Pretoria, where Britain's main garrison was stationed. At Sunnyside, Milner gathered around him a group of young graduates from Oxford and Cambridge. What came to be called Milner's kindergarten[31] consisted of Lionel Curtis, J.F. Perry, Patrick Duncan (later Sir), John Buchan (Lord Tweedsmuir), Geoffrey Robinson, Hugh Wyndham, Lionel Hichens, Richard Feetham, John Dove, Robert Brand (later Lord), Philip Kerr (later Lord Lothian), and Dougal Malcolm, together with close associates of Milner like Leo Amery. Members of the kindergarten, drawn from the heart of the English establishment, were chosen because they embodied the values of late-nineteenth-century British imperialism and so could be relied upon to enact Milner's dream of making South Africa British.

Set to the task of post–Boer War reconstruction, Milner and his kindergarten were to irrevocably transform South Africa. They drew the administrative boundaries in terms of which South Africans were governed for half a century, and created bureaucratic and taxation structures (modeled upon

Britain's) and an efficient civil service, police force, and judicial system. These became the foundation for South Africa's unified system of government. The kindergarten framed the legislative backbone upon which modernization, capitalist industrialization, and urbanization was built. They also established a customs union, common native policy, and system for governing black people and controlling black labor. This Milnerist system for black governance became the backbone of apartheid's administrative system. The kindergarten also installed the black migrant labor system (which saw Mozambique, Lesotho, Swaziland, Botswana, and Malawi become the key sources of mine labor). This migrant labor system underpinned racial capitalism throughout the twentieth century. Milner's kindergarten did not invent racial capitalism, but they drew together the various pieces of the jigsaw—for example, Theophilus Shepstone's (Natal) segregation system, Cecil Rhodes's (Cape) Glen Grey Act, labor practices developed in Kimberley by Rhodes's De Beers company, and labor practices developed in Johannesburg by the Randlords—and from these created the foundations for a racial-capitalist state.

Milner's original reconstruction project had two core goals: to make Southern Africa British, and to create the conditions for capitalist modernization. Milner clearly considered himself a "social engineer" engaged in a modernist development program (which he called building a "progressive community").[32] For Milner, modernizing and British-izing South Africa were necessarily interrelated, because a thriving capitalist economy would make South Africa a self-funding part of Britain's Indian Ocean empire and make South Africa a valuable partner within Britain's imperial trading network. Power was centralized at Sunnyside to achieve these goals, with Milner building a strong imperial state able to aggressively intervene to reconfigure the socioeconomic order. Milner even wanted, but could not achieve, suspension of the Cape Colony's constitution to facilitate his interventionist schemes.[33] He imported Anglos to staff the new governance machinery, thereby ensuring that Anglo values were encoded into the new state.

Having fought the Boer War to remove Afrikaner power and seize the goldfields, Milner's first postwar task was to create the conditions for mining capitalism to thrive. Milner's policy for economic reconstruction was summed up in his notions of "lift and overspill."[34] By "lift," he meant modernization and the destruction of Boer (and black) pastoral society. "Overspill" referred to using the wealth generated by mining expansion to fund the wider modernist development project.

On becoming governor of the two annexed Boer states (renamed the Transvaal and Orange River Colony/ORC), Milner enacted a political economic program consisting of ten elements.[35] The kindergarten's first concern was to restart gold mining. The key problem faced was finding enough cheap labor because black people, who had returned to the rural areas during the war, were not keen on returning to mining. To overcome this problem, Milner brought 50,000 Chinese laborers to Johannesburg. This unleashed a storm of protest among white South Africans and in Britain. By 1908, British control of the rural areas was sufficient to ensure that black labor flowed to the mines, thus beginning repatriation of the Chinese. But Chinese labor generated the initial "overspill" Milner sought for his development program.

The kindergarten's second task was to resettle Afrikaners. A repatriation department was established to relocate 200,000 Afrikaner farmers and their families. At the end of the war, half were in concentration camps for women and children and 24,000 were in prisoner-of-war camps overseas. Blacks who sided with the Boers were also imprisoned in concentration camps and needed resettlement. The farms they returned to were no longer productive units because buildings, crops, and seed stocks had been burned, livestock killed, and implements removed. Consequently, the repatriation department not only had to resettle people, but also help them reactivate farming, plus feed them in the interim. During the repatriation process, Milner and John Buchan traveled extensively in the rural areas, interacting with Afrikaners. Both concluded from these interactions that Afrikaners needed to be Anglicized, and thus would become a "great colonizing force" for the empire.[36] It was a fateful conclusion, feeding into the rise of Afrikaner nationalism and contributing to a chain of events leading to apartheid.

Third, the Inter-Colonial Council was created to mesh Transvaal and ORC government structures in pursuance of Milner's ideal of eventually unifying British Southern Africa from the Cape to the Zambezi.[37] Fourth, in 1903, Milner convened a conference of representatives from all of Britain's Southern African colonies (including Rhodesia) to promote the ideal of union. This conference achieved a common customs union with an external tariff giving preference to British goods. It agreed that the black population of British Southern Africa was insufficient to meet labor demands, and indentured Asian labor should be imported. As a result, Milner established a Native Affairs Commission (1903–1905) to examine ways of coordinating native policy and labor issues across all of Britain's colonies. This commission established segregated black reserves (later called homelands), and created the basic framework for the future governance of black South Africans.

Fifth, Milner took over the privately owned Transvaal and ORC railways, merging them under the control of the Inter-Colonial Council. Milner put great energy into improving the subcontinent's transport system, believing this to be vital for economic development. He also built branch lines that, by facilitating the transport of agricultural products to the cities, created the conditions for capitalizing agriculture.

Sixth, Milner founded nominated Transvaal and ORC legislative councils, whose task was to liberalize the legal framework, thereby facilitating the growth of capitalist enterprise. No leading Afrikaners accepted nomination onto these councils.

Seventh, a system of local government and town planning was established, modeled on British municipal traditions. The kindergarten invested considerable energy into establishing good municipal government on the Witwatersrand to create the infrastructure for Johannesburg to grow into the country's leading city and economic heart of Britain's African empire. This included establishing the Rand Water Board. Milner was especially eager for Johannesburg to become a British city by attracting large numbers of Anglo settlers. He saw this as the key to maintaining British hegemony over Southern Africa.

Eighth, much effort was put into establishing a system of British law and order in the Transvaal and ORC by creating a network of magistrates and establishing, under Baden-Powell, the South African Constabulary, which operated in both colonies. This constabulary, under the control of the Inter-Colonial Council, became the foundation of the South African police. A network of district commissioners was established to govern rural black people in the "reserves" set aside for them. These reserves became the basis of apartheid's homeland system. The kindergarten also constructed an efficient "pass system" (internal passports for blacks). In this regard, Milner said:

> If aboriginal natives are to come and go in large numbers in search of labour and to reside for considerable periods in the midst of a white community, there must be some passport system, else the place will be in pandemonium. . . . It is absolutely essential to have some reasonable arrangements by which the incoming native can be identified, and his movements traced. Nor is it unjust, indeed it is necessary, that when he has freely entered into a contract he should be bound to observe the terms of it.[38]

The network of district commissioners, magistrates, and police stations created an effective system for controlling black labor. This, together with migrant labor from neighboring countries (like Mozambique), ensured an abundant supply of cheap workers. Milner knew that deep-level mining of Witwatersrand gold was only economically viable if large quantities of cheap labor were available, and that is precisely what the ZAR failed to provide because it allowed pastoralism to coexist with capitalism and because the Transvaal was too small as a political/economic unit.[39] Milner was clear about the problem he faced if the labor required for capitalist development was to be made available. As he said: "As regard native labour for the mines, the greater development of which is a condition of all other industrial development, the difficulty is that, while natives can be found in abundance to do surface work, the number of those willing to go underground is limited."[40]

Essentially, a strong state was required with the capability to destabilize Southern Africa's premodern rural societies in order to generate the required flow of labor to the cities. For Milner, this was the core reason a united South Africa was necessary,[41] and why he and his kindergarten agitated for a united (federated) South Africa under the British flag. But even before Union, Milner established a network of native commissioners who set about disarming blacks and imposing taxes.[42]

Ninth, Milner placed great store in modernizing and capitalizing South African agriculture through kindergarten-established departments of agriculture. Agricultural experts and veterinarians were imported and experimental farms established. In this regard, Milner wanted to see Boer pastoralism destroyed, rural Afrikaners modernized, and large tracts of rural South Africa settled by Anglos. The capitalization of agriculture necessarily spawned a large surplus rural population of Boers and blacks who migrated to slums in the ever-growing cities, where they joined the proletariat and lumpen proletariat that Milner's modernization project was creating.

Tenth, the kindergarten created a system of free elementary secular education for whites designed to equip them to run a modern state and economy. Teachers and school administrators were imported from Britain. Two new training colleges for teachers and a technical college were established, and Milner convened a conference to try and unite the education departments of all four colonies into a single efficient administration for Anglicization. Separate schooling that emphasized manual training was provided for black children. This was based on Milner's view that:

> Much more should be done for the education of the natives . . . I do not mean that they should be educated like Europeans, for their requirements are very different, but that they should be trained to develop their natural aptitudes for their own good and that of the community. Undoubtedly the greatest benefit that could be bestowed upon them or South Africa generally would be to teach them habits of regular and skilled labour.[43]

At heart, Milner's political economic agenda was about creating a unified modern state as the fulcrum for a thriving mining industry. Hence, during Milner's governance, taxation policy explicitly benefited the accumulation of mining capital. He anticipated that mining would fund the growth of a wider urbanization and industrialization process upon which British civilization could be embedded into South Africa. For Milner, modernization, British migration, and imperialism were part of the same "progressive" and "civilizing" dynamic. As he said:

> The Transvaal possesses an amount of mineral wealth . . . which will ensure the prosperity of S. Africa for the next fifty years; and other resources, both industrial and agricultural, which properly developed, should make it a rich country, humanly speaking, for ever. Economically, all that is required is that a very small

proportion of the substantial but exhaustible riches of the mines should be devoted to developing the vast permanent sources of wealth which the country possesses, and which will maintain a European population twenty times as large as the present, when all the gold has been dug out. No doubt it is not economic measures alone which will achieve that result. A social change is also necessary, viz. the introduction of fresh blood, of a body of enterprising European settlers, especially on the land, to reinforce the Boer population, who have been too few, and far too easy-going, to do even the remotest justice to the vast natural capabilities of the soil, on which, for the most part, they have done little more than squat.[44]

Ultimately, twentieth-century South Africa was built upon Milner's conception of constructing a modern capitalist society ruled by a white oligarchy and dominated by Britons. Milner framed his vision thus:

Our welfare depends on increasing the quantity of our white population, but not at the expense of its quality. We do not want a white proletariat in this country. The position of the whites among the vastly more numerous black population requires that even their lowest ranks should be able to maintain a standard of living far above that of the poorest section of the population of a purely white country. But, without making them hewers of wood and drawers of water, there are scores and scores of employments in which white men could be honorably and profitably employed, if we could at once succeed in multiplying our industries and in reducing the cost of living . . . However you look at the matter, you always come back to the same root principle—the urgency of that development which alone can make this a white man's country in the only sense in which S. Africa can become one, and that is, not a country full of poor whites, but one in which a largely increased white population can live in decency and comfort. That development requires capital; we have got the capital, but it also requires a large amount of rough labour. And that labour cannot, to any great extent, be white, if only because, pending development and the subsequent reduction in the cost of living, white labour is much too dear.[45]

With this goal in mind, Milner set about constructing British hegemony over the subcontinent, which included economically tying Portuguese-ruled Mozambique into the new order he was building. Milner's new socioeconomic order grew into racial capitalism—a socioeconomic system constructed upon a racial/ethic hierarchy. Milner's project required forcefully reconfiguring Southern African society by breaking alternative sources of power, destroying any bolt-holes to which disaffected labor could flee, disrupting premodern pastoralism, and ensuring a continuous flow of migrant labor from the peripheries to the economic heartland (Johannesburg). Because this development model required subordinating both blacks and Boers, Milner retained after the Boer War a considerable British garrison of 25,000 soldiers paid for by the British and Indian governments.[46] This garrison, together with the South African Constabulary, was an important dimension of Britain's new hegemony during the early twentieth century—being required while black pastoralists were transformed into a migratory proletariat.

From the point of view of reconstructing South Africa into a modern capitalist state, Milner was successful. However, in addition to his economic reconstruction agenda, Milner had a "cultural program" that consisted of two elements, namely, British colonization and Anglicizing Afrikaners.

Milner's dream was to create a federal South Africa under the British flag. Within this new state, Anglos were to be politically and economically dominant. To achieve this, Milner believed that 60 percent of the white population should be British, which required a large-scale migration program.[47] As he said: "It is our duty to provide for the influx of a selected British population, who will do much to consolidate S. African sentiment in the general interests of the Empire."[48]

Milner believed that once he kick-started the economy, there would be no difficulty attracting Anglo migrants to the cities and that most South African Anglos would always be urbanites. However, he also deemed it important to settle Anglos in the rural areas in order to break up the Boer rural hegemony and modernize agriculture.[49] He wanted 40 percent of the rural population to be Anglo. Milner specifically wanted Anglo migration to happen quickly so he could achieve an Anglo majority in the Transvaal before granting self-government. Land Boards were created to acquire the land and bring settlers.[50] For his land-settlement scheme, Milner was especially keen on Canadians, Australians, and lowland Scots.[51] This was part of his wider project of building the empire as a global federation of Anglo civilization.[52] Milner's land-settlement scheme ultimately failed because he was unable to attract large numbers of Anglos to Africa, and by 1906 it was clear that Afrikaners would remain the demographic majority within the white community. So although Milner achieved Anglo economic and political dominance in South Africa, he failed to plant a large Anglo population in Africa. For this reason, members of the kindergarten (who remained in place after Milner left) had to adjust their plans for building a unified British-dominated South African state, because they now had to achieve British control on the basis of Anglos only constituting 40 percent of white South Africans.

The other half of Milner's cultural program was the Anglicization of Afrikaners, which is discussed below. The kindergarten's cultural agenda was ultimately unsuccessful, but while trying to implement it, Afrikaner nationalism was inadvertently kindled. This was to have enormous consequences for South Africa's future.

The third element of Milner's reconstruction program involved constructing a new political system. Milner's original conceptualization was to implant Westminster democracy in South Africa. As with Britain's other newly federated dominions of Canada and Australia, only white males were enfranchised. However, Milner agreed with Rhodes's dictum of "equal rights for all civilized men," in terms of which Westernized nonwhites would be given the vote if they met education and property qualifications. (This system had operated in the Cape Colony since 1854.) Milner specifically advocated modernizing blacks and coloreds and their assimilation into the South African society he was building, saying:

> For all our sakes it is of profound importance that the general standard of native civilization be immensely raised. Even as a purely material question, it is one of great importance . . . [because] the mere mechanical value of the native who has risen to some state of civilization is enormously greater than that of the man still on bedrock.[53]

In 1903 Milner had told a white audience that, as a result of his modernization project, some natives would "rise to the level of your shoulder."[54] He hypothesized it would take centuries to "civilize" South African natives and the numbers would never be large. But Milner argued that the few who were Westernized/Anglicized should be incorporated into the political system in accordance with Rhodes's dictum, saying he was "in favour of that wider extension of popular liberties which is what the triumph of the British ideas in this county means."[55] Significantly, Milner never saw this as challenging the white oligarchy he was building. He was clear that "the white man must rule because he is elevated by many steps above the black man; steps which it will take the later centuries to climb."[56] Milner opposed what he called the two "extremes"—those who advocated enfranchising all blacks, which he described as "detestable," and those who wanted blacks to be "wholly unrepresented."[57] Instead, Milner proposed allowing Westernized blacks to elect some (white) representatives to Parliament, or alternatively establishing a separate Native Council which would deal "with all matters affecting Natives."[58] He suggested that a Native Council could legislate for native reservations (later called homelands), plus make recommendations to the White Parliament about legislation affecting blacks in white areas. Under Milner's model, blacks would qualify for the vote by passing property and education tests that he proposed should be set higher for blacks than whites.[59] This model was later held up as an alternative to apartheid by Anglos governing Rhodesia and Nyasaland,[60] where an electoral system based on property, income, and education qualifications restricted the franchise to the (mostly white) middle classes.[61]

However, when South Africa was finally unified in 1910, Milner's franchise model was not adopted. Both Milner and his kindergarten dropped any notion of extending even the Cape's limited black franchise to the rest of South Africa because they feared this would undermine their primary purpose of securing British imperial hegemony over Southern Africa. Milner realized that political "generosity" toward black people was the one thing that could unite Afrikaners and Anglo South Africans against imperial governance. It was not worth the risk. Hence, the new South African state became unambiguously a white oligarchy, and outside the Cape Province only white males could vote within a South African Westminster parliamentary system.

ANGLICIZING SOUTH AFRICA

Milner's objective was to build a unified modern state that would be an asset to the British Empire. Securing this state for Britain required making Anglos dominant, economically and culturally. As a start, English became the sole official language in the newly conquered Transvaal and ORC. The new civil service, courts, police service, and schools established by Milner were staffed by Anglos and run exclusively in English. Milner's nation-building project included three cultural dimensions—making English the official language, mass Anglo migration to South Africa, and the Anglicization of Afrikaners through a state-run education system. As Milner said in 1901:

> On the political side I attach the greatest importance of all to the increase of the British population . . . If, ten years hence, there are three men of British race to two of Dutch, the country will be safe and prosperous. If there are three of Dutch to two of British, we shall have perpetual difficulty . . . Next to the composition of the population, the thing which matters most is education. In the agricultural parts of the Cape Colony this needs to be completely overhauled . . . In the new colonies the case will be easier to deal with provided we make English *the language of all higher education*. Dutch should only be used to teach English, and English to teach everything else. Language is important, but the tone and spirit of the teaching conveyed in it is even more important . . . I would attach especial importance to school history books[62] (emphasis in original).

For Milner, the Boer War was about making South Africa British, and as far as he was concerned, the war was not over when the fighting stopped. As Milner said, "It is no longer war with bullets, but it is still war . . . we now hold the winning cards, but it is not true we have won the game, and we cannot afford to lose a single trick. We are fighting for something immensely big."[63] Milner's first instinct was to Britishize South Africa by encouraging Anglo mass migration (especially to the Transvaal) so as to demographically swamp Afrikaners. He assumed it would be easy attracting Anglo settlers to the cities, but was concerned about the rural areas:

> The difficulty is to place any number of them [Anglos] on the land. The majority of the agricultural population will always be Dutch. This does not matter, provided there are some strong English districts and that, in most districts there a sufficient number of British to hold their own. A mere sprinkling is no use. They only get

absorbed, and become more Dutch than their neighbours. The only way to achieve this is by large purchase of land on the part of the Government with a view to reselling . . . to suitable settlers.[64]

Milner's goal was to settle Anglos in such a way that Anglo and Afrikaner populations would integrate to form a single British community. By importing enough Anglo settlers and Anglicizing Afrikaners through education, "homogenization" would be achieved on British terms. The result would be a unified white (Anglo) community that would thereafter rule Britain's African empire as a white oligarchy.[65]

Milner's policy was to create "one British race out of two white races" by "denationalizing"[66] Afrikaners—that is, assimilating "backward Afrikaners" into "progressive British" culture.[67] The outcome would be to integrate Afrikaners into Milner's "family of nations," which was to be "a consortium directed by the British race."[68] He attached great importance to education as an assimilation mechanism. For Milner, winning over Afrikaner children to the English language and English ways of thought would have the same effect as an influx of Anglo migrants.[69] Afrikaner children were forced to use English at school (reminiscent of how Welsh children were forcibly Anglicized). Until he left in 1905, Milner consistently rejected the idea that English and Dutch should be equal, and enforced Anglicization in the schools.[70]

Afrikaners resented Milner's Anglicization of the civil service, courts, and police. However, the enforced English schooling stirred especially deep hostility. The result was a backlash organized by elected parents' committees and the Dutch reformed churches. Starting in 1904, 200 Dutch-language primary schools—called CNO (*Christelik-Nasionale Onderwys*/Christian National Education) schools[71]—were established in the Transvaal and ORC to offer an alternative to Milner's schools. From this phenomenon grew a new ideology calling itself "Christian nationalism." Teachers who were imported from Holland to run these schools brought with them Dutch notions of *verzuiling* (pillarization), which fed into Christian nationalism, promoting the idea that every cultural group had the right to use its own language, cultural institutions, and cultural spaces. This was encapsulated in the notion of "own-ness" (*eiesoortigheid*), which promoted the idea that all cultural groups are equally valuable because they have been created by God. Hence, every people (*volk*) had a right to exist; every people should take pride in their "own-ness" and fight to preserve it, while at the same time respecting the rights of others to their separate identities/"own-ness." This notion of "own-ness" was to underpin apartheid ("apartness"). Significantly, "Christian nationalism" was the in-house term deployed by the National Party (NP) to describe its apartheid policy.

Milner's Anglicization policy was intended to "denationalize" Afrikaners. Instead, it became one of the roots of Afrikaner nationalism and apartheid—that is, the notion that Afrikaners had a God-given right to preserve their cultural autonomy and "separateness" from others. Because "own-ness" was born from a struggle to resist Anglicization, its original meaning encoded the idea of linguistic/cultural difference (rather than racial difference). But by the time "own-ness" became encoded into apartheid, its meaning had broadened to also include racial difference.

THE MATURING OF RACIAL CAPITALISM

The kindergarten shaped the foundations for a racial-capitalist state, creating the fulcrum for a social order with the following features:

- Society was organized to service the needs of an Anglo-owned mining industry (especially gold mining). This industry was organized around the principle of maximizing profit.
- The economy depended upon cheap black labor to facilitate industrialized deep-level mining.
- To guarantee an abundant supply of black labor, a migrant labor system was built covering all Southern Africa. Since alternative forms of labor-intensive employment were a potential threat to labor flows to the mines, these were curtailed and managed; for example, Boer sharecropping practices were destroyed and "surplus labor" was driven out of farming districts. The 1913 Land Act, which created "black reserves," finally sealed this closure.
- Autonomous black polities, which provided alternatives to joining the migrant system, were perceived as dangerous; hence, they were turned into "reserves" administered by district commissioners. These reserves came to be overwhelmingly populated by women, children, and old people because males became migrant workers.
- A pass system regulated the flow of blacks into "white areas."
- This socioeconomic order was overwhelmingly owned and managed by Anglo settlers, committed to their British Empire links. Until the early 1960s, these Anglos called Britain "home."
- Racial capitalism built an ethnic ranking system within which Britain's class system was ethnicized. In British South Africa, the following class-race ranking emerged: British-born Anglos constituted an elite. Thereafter came Anglo colonials, followed by non-Anglo whites (e.g., Afrikaners), Indians, and coloreds. Next came Westernized/Anglicized blacks, and then premodern blacks. The premodern category was itself ranked, with some tribes being considered "superior" because they had "fought bravely" (significant for a "martial" people like the English), for example, Zulus and Matabele were judged "superior" to Tswana or Shona.
- Politically, the Union of South Africa—as the culmination of the kindergarten's efforts—was a white oligarchy. Outside of the Cape Province, only whites were enfranchised.[72] Afrikaners constituted 60 percent of the electorate. This meant that South Africa's Anglo corporate elite spent the first half of the twentieth

century striving to identify and promote "moderate" Afrikaner leaders prepared to retain and manage the kindergarten-built system. Postapartheid South Africa saw Anglo corporates engage in a similar exercise geared toward "moderate" black leaders (see chapters 8 and 9).

In 1906, Lord Selbourne replaced Milner as high commissioner, but continued to rely on Milner's kindergarten to carry on the process of reconfiguring Southern Africa's sociopolitical landscape. Selbourne initiated a significant shift in British policy, namely, incorporating one section of the Transvaal/ORC Afrikaner population into an alliance with the British ruling group. A group of large landowners had emerged in late-nineteenth-century Boer society, forming an upper class. Selbourne brought about a *rapprochement* between these Afrikaner "notables" (represented by Louis Botha and Jan Smuts's *Het Volk* Party) and the British government.[73] By incorporating this Afrikaner "rural aristocracy"[74] into an alliance with Anglo Randlords, the foundations were laid for 40 years of Anglo-imperial hegemony over South Africa. It was during this period that the seeds were planted for both Afrikaner and black nationalism—forces that would shape South African politics in the second half of the twentieth century.

During the twentieth century's first four decades, racial capitalism grew, mutated, and matured under the prime ministerships of Louis Botha, Jan Smuts, and J.B. Hertzog. Although they were Afrikaners, Botha, Smuts, and Hertzog did not fundamentally challenge the dominance Anglo settlers exercised over South Africa's socioeconomic order. In fact, during their reign, a startling Anglicization of South Africa took place[75]—with 350,000 settlers (including 40,000 East European Jews) added to Anglo South Africa between 1904 and 1936. Smuts, in particular, came to strongly associate with Anglo South Africans and the British Empire, and was also closely aligned to Anglo corporate interests. Hertzog was an Afrikaner nationalist, but also a pragmatist who recognized the extent of Anglo power. Hertzog consequently opted to work within the empire's framework to try and improve the Afrikaners' lot.[76] In the process, he did much to stabilize racial capitalism and make it function more effectively.

Under Smuts and Hertzog, the core dynamic driving the political system was how to deal with Afrikaner urbanization and proletarianization. It was, in particular, Smuts's failure to grasp the way in which urban modernization was changing and radicalizing the Afrikaner worldview that led to his United Party's (UP) 1948 defeat by D.F. Malan's National Party (NP).

Milner's modernization program impacted upon Afrikaners in two ways: first, northern agriculture was capitalized during the first two decades of the twentieth century, creating a class of Afrikaner agrarian capitalists;[77] and second, large-scale Afrikaner urbanization resulted from the destruction of

Boer pastoral society.[78] Afrikaners driven into the cities were overwhelmingly proletarianized;[79] for example, in 1907 they constituted 17.5 percent of mine workers, but by 1936 they constituted 75 percent.[80] Most of these urbanizing Afrikaners were impoverished; many lived in mixed-race slums. But urbanization also built a small Afrikaner middle class. This later group, transformed by embourgeoisement,[81] became the leaders of the NP. They were the unintended children of Milner's modernization program who turned to anti-Anglo nationalism in response to the Anglicized cities and ethnic ranking system Milner left as his legacy. In 1948, these nationalists persuaded a majority of Afrikaners to vote for the NP.

When the NP came to power, they inherited a functioning racial-capitalist system built between 1900 and 1939.[82] Racial capitalism, primarily constructed around the needs of a mining industry that required cheap labor, served the purpose intended for it by Milner's kindergarten—it underpinned Britain's hegemony over Southern Africa until 1948. Racial capitalism was a socioeconomic order constructed upon an ethnic ranking system. At the top were Anglo mining corporates, beneath which emerged secondary industry primarily owned by an indigenous Anglo middle class. This secondary industry, which grew especially rapidly during the 1930s, was only viable because of tariffs used by the state to create employment opportunities (through its "civilized labor policy") for poor Afrikaners.[83] Further, Hertzog's Keynesian state interventionism built a significant state-owned industrial sector (e.g., the Iron & Steel Corporation), also used to create working-class jobs for Afrikaners. Taxing the mining industry, which Smuts and Hertzog's legislation had ensured was highly profitable, paid for Hertzog's Keynesian interventions. Phasing out highly paid British artisan miners and replacing them with Afrikaner workers supervising black migrant labor had enhanced mining profitability.[84] As a result, Afrikaners became an intermediary ranked group between Anglos (capitalists, managers, professionals, and small businessmen) and blacks (migrant workers).

The creation of an Afrikaner working class, ranked as intermediaries within racial capitalism's ethnic class ranking system, emerged as an offshoot of Milner's destruction of Boer pastoral society. This drove Afrikaners into the cities and towns where, without the skills required by modern urban capitalism, many became destitute slum dwellers. By 1929 (*before* the Great Depression), 28 percent of Afrikaners had become a "very poor"[85] lumpen proletariat. The growth of the "poor white problem"[86] and significant Afrikaner unemployment became a threat to both the state and corporate sector because Afrikaners had the vote and had demonstrated a capacity for political militancy. The dangers of this militancy were most clearly seen during the 1922 Rand revolt,[87] when a wage cut drove Afrikaner and Anglo workers to seize the Witwatersrand and raise both the red flag and *vierkleur* (the ZAR's flag).[88] Smuts's government deployed 20,000 soldiers to regain control of the Witwatersrand, and bombed white working-class suburbs (becoming the first government to use an air force against its own civilians). The upshot of Smuts's action was that he was seen as too close to the Anglo corporates, precipitating an alliance between Hertzog's nationalists and Cresswell's Labour Party. In 1924, this pact alliance defeated Smuts's government, and Hertzog became prime minister. This nationalist-socialist pact government was instrumental in bringing racial capitalism to maturity because, under Hertzog, the system was stabilized by building a Keynesian interventionist state. Hertzog's state:

- Successfully guaranteed the supply of black migrant labor to the mines (and northern farmers), thereby building a tax base to pay for its Keynesian policies.
- Refined the administration of "black reserves," and increased the size of these reserves.
- Made urban segregation compulsory; this segregation legislation was driven by middle-class concerns about poor Afrikaners and nonwhites living together in slums that had grown up since the Boer War.
- Created working-class employment for Afrikaners in the state-owned railways, Iron & Steel Corporation, and secondary industries that mushroomed thanks to tariff protection.
- Facilitated the growth of an Afrikaner middle class by employing Afrikaners in the civil service and as teachers.
- Tamed trade unions through an industrial conciliation system that delivered material benefits to white workers.
- Made Afrikaans a second national language (1925), replaced the British flag with a South African flag (1928), made *Die Stem* a national anthem alongside "God Save the King" (1934), and secured dominion status within the British Empire through the Statute of Westminster (1931). Malan's NP argues this only served to obscure Britain's de facto hegemony.

Effectively, Hertzog's successive governments (1924–1939) mobilized Afrikaner nationalist symbolism, while cementing a deal between the state and Anglo corporates to tame the potential threat posed by Afrikaner poverty and militancy. Under the circumstances, mining capital was only too happy to pay the taxes funding Hertzog's Keynesianism,[89] which secured rather than challenged the kindergarten's basic racial-capitalist model.

Despite Hertzog's delivery of symbolic value and jobs, many Afrikaners felt a deep alienation from this new modernizing South Africa, which De Klerk describes thus:

They had been a defeated people. Their traditional society, in the process of defeat and post-war reconstruction, had been shaken to its foundations . . . They had . . . gathered in fringe areas of the cities. They had already formed a wage-earning class; and alongside but also below them, another had been forming. It was black. The dominant white [Anglo] classes of the cities were no comfort, because they too were strange. The cities were still citadels of Anglo-Saxon culture and British economic power. The new immigrant Afrikaners were, in fact, strangers in their own country: hesitant, fearful of using their own language in shops and businesses, and confined very largely to the humbler areas and jobs. They were without the fine schools supported by the English churches, the institutions and amenities generally which the English took for granted . . . They were exposed to the rivalry of non-white S. Africa. The increasing competition from black Africans, which took place primarily in the cities, affected them . . . [while] the established English middle class lived and worked in areas where the problems of color were items in the daily newspapers. In spite of all the leaders of the Union so far having been ex-Boer War generals, South Africa was still a British country.[90]

As De Klerk notes, both Afrikaners and blacks shared "the common experience of being indigenous have-nots in cities of 'foreign' haves."[91] The alienation this produced was to feed the fires of nationalism, especially evident among the small emergent Afrikaner middle class who set up the NP (and Broederbond). This middle class was comprised of urbanites who had passed through the trauma of Milner's modernization and witnessed the poverty of fellow Afrikaners. A number of middle-class *dominees* (church pastors) and intellectuals had grappled firsthand with the poor white issue, including the two men who became NP prime ministers, D.F. Malan (who had been a pastor) and Hendrik Verwoerd (who had been a social work professor concerned with the issue of poor Afrikaners). They harbored resentments over the Boer War, the concentration camps, Milner's attempts at Anglicization, and the concentration of wealth in Anglo hands. And, despite being middle class, they daily experienced both the impact of being ranked second class within racial capitalism's ethnic ranking system, and the racist contempt Anglos felt toward Afrikaners. From this mix was born radical Afrikaner nationalism, quite different from Hertzog's gentile nationalism. (Hertzog was prepared to negotiate accommodationist deals with Anglo South Africa.) This new radical nationalism first emerged among young academics, journalists, and lawyers, and was thereafter popularized within Afrikaans universities by the Afrikaans Student Union and sections of the Afrikaans Press.

This new radical nationalism was institutionalized in D.F. Malan's ("purified") NP in 1933. But the NP proved unable to persuade the majority of Afrikaners to defect from Hertzog, who cemented a United Party (UP) alliance with Smuts. However, then came World War II, which transformed South African politics by providing the NP with three issues they could use to persuade most Afrikaners to vote for them.

First, the way Smuts became prime minister in 1939 was a godsend to the NP. When Britain declared war on Germany, Hertzog argued for South African neutrality, while Smuts argued that South Africa was part of the British Empire and should fight alongside Britain. When Hertzog lost the parliamentary vote, he dissolved the government and asked the governor general to call an election (confident he would win an election on the neutrality issue). However, the governor general, Sir Patrick Duncan (who had been in Milner's kindergarten), instead made Smuts prime minister. Smuts declared war, effectively dissolving five years of (UP) "fusion" work by Hertzog and Smuts to build Anglo-Afrikaner unity. The NP argued that the governor general's actions demonstrated Britain's power reigned supreme over the democratic will of Afrikaners, and Duncan's actions helped rekindle Afrikaner republicanism.

Second, during World War II, Britain relied upon its dominions to manufacture munitions, vehicles, and rations. In South Africa, this generated a major industrial boom, causing a dramatic increase in the demand for industrial workers. To meet this demand, Smuts's government relaxed pass-law enforcement from 1942, which produced a wave of black migration to the cities—106,000 of the 125,000 new workers added to South Africa's working class during World War II were black. Moreover, during the war, many blacks moved into skilled and semiskilled jobs previously performed by whites.[92] For the Afrikaans working class, this was deeply troubling because it meant increased competition for jobs. It also raised the number of blacks to 44.6 percent of South Africa's total city population by 1946. At the start of World War II there were more whites than blacks in South Africa's cities, but by the end of the war, urban blacks outnumbered whites in some cities for the first time. The NP blamed Smuts's government for this migration phenomenon, which they regarded as a demographic threat to white South Africa. The NP's 1948 apartheid policy promised to remove this threat by stopping black migration to the cities and returning these black people to their "homelands."

Third, the Atlantic Charter[93] deal struck between the United States and Britain initiated a post–Second World War world in which European empires were to be dismantled and replaced with a U.S.-led global trading system that would tie together postcolonial independent states organized as liberal democracies. This heralded the threat of pressures for majoritarian democracy in South Africa, which would spell the end of the white oligarchy. Intellectuals like Verwoerd recognized the danger this posed to Afrikaners, and so conceptualized apartheid as a form of internal decolonization to try and accommodate Atlantic Charter demands while simultaneously securing a territorial base for an Afrikaner republic. Apartheid was put forward as a mechanism to secure Afrikaner political and cultural rights in a changing world that looked increasingly threatening.

The 1948 election was fought between Smuts's UP (advocating "South Africanism") and Malan's NP (advocating apartheid). Nelson Mandela claimed that the NP fought the 1948 election on the slogans of "kaffir in his place" and "coolies out of the country." There never were such slogans.[94] The election was fought over something else—Afrikaners perceived the UP's "South Africanism" to mean a continuation of *de facto* Anglo domination within a unified state structured to serve Anglo corporate interests. Worse still, a UP state would serve the interests of a rapacious Anglo business sector demanding ever-greater quantities of labor. This encouraged black migration from South Africa's "reserves," Mozambique, and British Africa. Such migration seemed to herald a new-looking industrialized South Africa, which would be increasingly urbanized, with cities demographically dominated by black people. So under a UP government, Afrikaners believed they would not only be politically dominated by Anglos, who owed loyalty to a "foreign" queen, but would now also be demographically swamped by black migration. This migration did not pose a cultural threat to Anglos because they were part of global Anglo culture and had the resources to "buy" their cultural autonomy. But the NP persuaded Afrikaners that it was a real threat to their culture.

By 1948, there were three Afrikaner worlds—a large working class, a small middle class, and farmers. The NP successfully mobilized its Afrikaner nationalist and apartheid rhetorics to unite these three constituencies, all of which felt culturally and economically subjugated by Anglo racial capitalism. Afrikaner workers felt exploited by Anglo capitalists and threatened by black migrants who drove down the price of labor by competing for jobs. The farmers felt threatened by the way industry drew away their labor, and the Afrikaner middle classes felt stifled by a dominating and overbearing Anglo bourgeoisie and Milner's ethic ranking system.

The NP promised to invent a new kind of state—based on apartheid—which would tame rapacious Anglo business, stop (and even reverse) black migration, and create economic opportunities for Afrikaners by overturning Milner's ethnic ranking system. Ultimately, the NP's apartheid policy was the outcome of decades of traumatic transformation experienced by Afrikaners as a result of the kindergarten's program of modernization and Anglo nation building. Apartheid promised to deliver to Afrikaners an end to this trauma.

CHAPTER 2

The Theory of Apartheid

Apartheid grew out of Afrikanerdom's painful encounter with modernization and British imperialism. Until the late nineteenth century, South Africa was an unimportant, mostly semidesert area on expanding margins of the Western world. The discovery of gold changed that, because it created the possibility of capitalist development. Consequently, South Africa joined the list of peripheral societies to endure the "tidal wave" of capitalist modernization driven by British imperial expansion.[1] With the Boer War, the full weight of Britain's industrial might was unleashed upon Afrikaners to bring about regime change. In the wake of this war, Lord Milner imposed capitalist modernity and urbanization upon South Africa's Boer and black populations. Nationalism was the result of the painful rude awakening Afrikaners experienced as rapacious Anglo capitalism and Anglo sociocultural hegemony tore their world apart and reconstructed it anew, in ways that seemed not to serve their interests.

With the destruction of Afrikaner pastoral society and the loss of political power, Afrikaners were driven into the cities in ways paralleling how enclosures forced English peasants into Britain's cities from the sixteenth to nineteenth centuries. But whereas England's enclosures, urbanization, and industrialization created resentments and turmoil based on class differences, in South Africa the situation was more complex—because racial capitalism generated resentments based not only on class differences, but also on culture and race. Urbanizing Afrikaners found themselves driven into cities dominated economically and culturally by "foreign" Anglos,[2] where they encountered Anglo racism and poverty. The use of Afrikaans, or even an Afrikaans accent was a huge liability in the labor market. To make matters worse, Afrikaners found themselves competing with black migrant laborers Anglo capitalists were importing from across Southern Africa. Because these migrant workers left their families at home in the reserves where traditional subsistence economies sustained them, they could charge less for their labor than Afrikaners, who had to support their families living in the poor urban ghettos. Therefore, Afrikaners came to believe that the blacks had an unfair advantage in the labor market, and this translated into the perception that "capitalist English [were] using blacks to get the better of Afrikaners."[3] These were the perceptual roots of apartheid laid down by intellectuals like Verwoerd[4] decades before the National Party (NP) came to power.

By the 1930s, a new kind of Afrikaner intelligentsia (the first generation to have grown up in cities) emerged in the universities (at Stellenbosch, Pretoria, Potchefstroom, and Bloemfontein) and at *Die Burger* newspaper. This emergent Afrikaner petit bourgeoisie were modern urbanites created by Milner's socioeconomic revolution. Together with many Calvinist church pastors (whose work brought them into daily contact with urban Afrikaner poverty), this intelligentsia concluded that the problem of urban poverty was "getting out of hand . . . [and that] soon a considerable part of Afrikanerdom would, economically and spiritually, be beyond redemption."[5] Consequently, this petit bourgeoisie became radicalized, reflecting the dislocation and anger of the wider urban Afrikaner community they lived among. Some—like future prime minister Malan—gathered in Cape Town's coffeehouses to discuss Afrikanerdom's socioeconomic problems, while on Afrikaans campuses a new nationalism and anti-British imperialism began to be formulated. The *Afrikaanse Nasionale Studentebond* (Afrikaner Student Union) and speakers like P.J. Meyer[6] popularized this nationalism among students. The journal *Inspan* (official organ of the Federation of Afrikaans Cultural Organization/FAK and *Reddingsdaadbond*)[7] disseminated the emergent nationalist and apartheid concepts countrywide.

Many intellectuals—Hendrik Verwoerd, Werner Eiselen, Nic Olivier, Geoffrey Cronje, Nico Diederichs, Barney van Eeden, P.J. Schoeman, P.J. Coertze, and F.J. Language—helped formulate this emergent nationalist worldview during the 1930s–1940s. Also at this time, intellectuals in the South African Association for Racial Studies (*Suid-Afrikaanse Bond vir Rassestudie*/SABRS),[8] chaired by Mrs. E.G. Jansen, played a key role in formulating the apartheid concept. A Cape group (at Stellenbosch University and *Die Burger*) was especially productive; its formulations for excluding blacks from the political system (i.e., apartheid) deployed secular social science reasoning and never mobilized racist concepts.[9] The northern intellectuals—for example, Cronje and Diederichs[10]—on the other hand, were more inclined to mobilize racist concepts or divine sanction.[11]

Diederichs—who would one day become South Africa's president—laid the basic theoretical cornerstone of this radical Afrikaner nationalism with his *Nationalism as a Worldview and Its Relationship to Internationalism*.[12]

He expounded a vision of Afrikaner (Christian) nationalism that was infused with the *verzuiling* (pillarization) logic of Dutch Calvinist theologian Abraham Kuyper.[13] According to Diederichs's "theologized politics,"[14] God, not humans, created nations.[15] And these nations had nothing to do with material manifestations like race, color, physiology, or territory;[16] but rather with "spiritual" attitudes and a "way of living." Further, nations had—in terms of Kuyper's *verzuiling* logic of *sowerieiniteit in eie kring* (sovereignty in one's own sphere)—a (God-ordained) right to exist as separate entities.[17] By extension, Afrikaners had a right to exist as a separate nation, to refuse Anglo assimilation, and to refuse a "British-designed" South Africa that lumped Afrikaners (as a minority) in with other ethnic groups.

Cronje[18] also played an important role in stimulating the logic of nationalist "apartness" (apartheid) with his books, *A Home for Future Generations*[19] and *Justified Racial Separation*.[20] He was highly critical of Anglo imperialism and capitalism for impoverishing Afrikaners[21] and exploiting, repressing, and detribalizing blacks.[22]

Cronje argued that Afrikaners needed to build a cultural-political "space" separate from Anglos, blacks, coloreds, and Indians. The alternative was that Afrikaans culture would be swamped by a combination of Anglo cultural imperialism and the sheer weight of numbers of black migrants being imported by Anglo capitalism. Cronje's thesis was that Afrikaners found themselves (in a polity created by Anglo imperialism) as a minority group surrounded by a majority who were culturally and racially different. He argued that given these circumstances, Afrikaners could never allow blacks to fully develop economically or politically because this would necessarily imply black domination over the Afrikaner minority. He acknowledged that curtailing black development was unjust and unchristian, but argued that as long as Afrikaners lived in the same polity as a black majority they had no choice but to repress black development. Cronje's Christian national solution to this dilemma was total partition—that is, apartheid would completely separate blacks and whites. Once this was done, argued Cronje, whites would no longer need to suppress black interests and could actually then assist blacks to develop their full potential in their separate black polities.[23]

By 1943, a basic concept of apartheid was in place,[24] and a conceptualization was solidified at a 1944 People's Congress in Bloemfontein.[25] By 1947, a merged Cape and northern conceptualization of apartheid was being popularized by *Inspan*.[26] Apartheid was proposed as an alternative to both integration (creating a single South African nation) and segregation. Apartheid theorists spent much time explaining why apartheid (partition) was superior to segregation[27] because the NP's key opponent was Smuts's United Party (UP), which advocated segregation. Apartheid theorists argued that the UP's policy was unsustainable because it involved placing whites and blacks into a single polity on the basis of white supremacy—that is, whites simultaneously segregated themselves from blacks while continuing to both

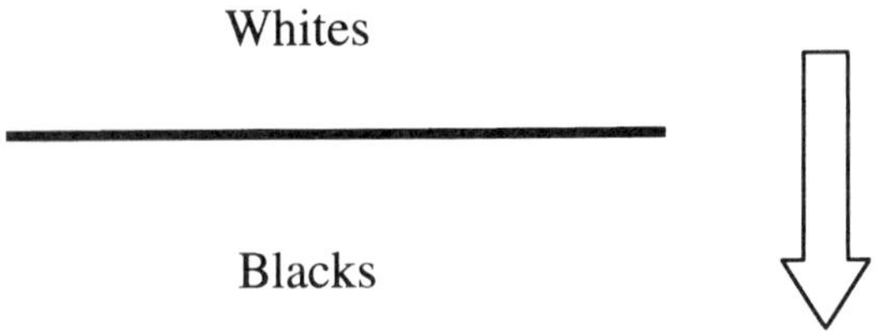

Figure 2.1:
"Horizontal Domination" (White Supremacy)

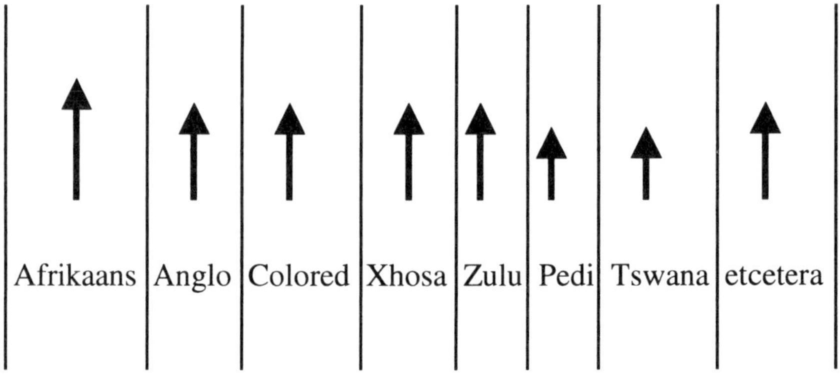

Figure 2.2:
"Vertical Separation" (Apartheid/Partition)

rule over blacks and exploit them economically. Eiselen called this a form of "caste-society"[28] based upon a "master-people complex."[29] Apartheid (apartness) was proposed as a radical partition alternative to the UP model—in other words, the goal would become total partition (apartheid) instead of semidetachment (economic integration and residential segregation within a unified polity). It was proposed that apartheid would separate people "vertically" rather than "horizontally"[30] (see figures 2.1 and 2.2).

The UP's policy was seen to involve "horizontal domination" or white supremacy (*baasskap*), in which whites ruled over blacks in accordance with the old British imperial model. It was argued that such domination was dangerous because it caused bitterness, frustration, and resentment, and would breed resistance and racial conflict. The UP's segregation/white domination model was deemed unsustainable. Apartheid was proposed as a "rational" alternative because it involved separating ethnic groups so each could develop separately in its own "cultural space." In 1948, the NP advocated that its apartheid policy would end racial conflict, whereas the UP's policies would breed future conflict through the dangerous mixture of *baasskap* together with encouraging mass black migration into the cities (to feed capitalism's labor needs). Further, apartheid was deemed to be more just than old-style UP segregation because it (vertically) "freed" blacks to develop their own politico-cultural identity.[31] This was seen as an improvement to the UP's patronizing logic of expecting blacks to assimilate into Western culture in order to become "acceptable" within a socioeconomic system dominated by whites. This apartheid idea served Afrikaner interests in two ways. First, its logic of cultural partition offered a means for Afrikaners to secure an autonomous space free of both Anglo domination and the potential domination of a black majority within a unified state. Second, it was argued, apartheid (or "apartness") involved ending white supremacy—that is, each group would be free of the domination of others, and hence able to develop in its own way. The practice of apartheid never matched this theory, but the theory provided Afrikaners with a way to rationalize and justify repressive actions by referring to an "ideal" future state.

However, the Afrikaner petit bourgeoisie who developed the apartheid idea went beyond theorizing. They also organized themselves into a network of nationalist structures such as the *Broederbond* (Brotherhood), the Federation of Afrikaans Cultural Organizations (*Federasie van Afrikaanse Kultuurverenigings*/FAK), *Reddingsdaadbond*, the Institute for Christian National Education (*Instituut vir CNO*), and the White Workers Protection Association (*Blanke Werkers Beskermingsbond*).[32] Within this network, the *Broederbond* was especially important[33]—becoming the core fulcrum wherein petit bourgeois Afrikaners circulated new Christian national concepts and discussed ways to overcome obstacles to Afrikaner advancement in Anglo-dominated cities. This nationalist petit bourgeoisie learned to successfully present themselves as patriots who would lead the Afrikaner *volk* (people)[34] out of its bondage to Anglo imperialism and end Afrikaner poverty and humiliation derived from being treated as inferior by Anglos. By 1948, the message had widespread resonance.

The Afrikaner nationalist intelligentsia, Malan's NP, and the *Broederbond* formulated a radical program rejecting:

- racial capitalism's ethnic ranking (placing Anglos on top),
- British imperialist hegemony, and
- the ethnic "*mengelmoes*" ("hodgepodge/mess") created by Anglo capitalism's importation of black migrants[35] from across Southern Africa.

Their solution was a radical nationalist reordering of South Africa geared toward achieving an Afrikaner republic free of British imperialism. Afrikaners were to "take back their country" from the English, use state interventionism to end the socioeconomic subjugation of Afrikaners, and end the ethnic hodgepodge threatening Afrikanerdom with erasure through assimilation in a unitary state. Significantly, although their (nationalist) proposals rejected Anglo capitalist hegemony, they did not propose a (conservative) return to Boer pastoralism because this intelligentsia was an urban petit bourgeoisie. All key Afrikaner nationalists of the 1940s—D.F. Malan, E.H. Louw, T.E. Donges, N.J. van der Merwe, C.R. Swart, J.G. Strijdom, and H.F. Verwoerd—were products of Milner's urbanization and a generation once removed from the pre-Milner world of rural Afrikanerdom.[36] Consequently, they developed a radical vision retaining the basic outlines of Milner's modernizing urban-industrial revolution.

The 1930s–1940s Afrikaner nationalist intelligentsia successfully constructed an Afrikaner "imagined community."[37] They creatively mobilized Afrikaners by furnishing "maps" of this community and narratives of a heroic past,[38] promoted Afrikaans as a vernacular language for nation building, and provided a future-oriented moral purpose that created a sense of destiny and "place" for Afrikanerdom among other nations.[39] Their nationalist narratives explained the pain of Milner's racial capitalism in ethnic terms; mobilized opposition to British imperialism and Anglo hegemony; and formulated a plausible-sounding plan for capturing the state, asserting Afrikaner sovereignty over this state and ending the threat of being swamped by black migrants. Significantly, this nationalist intelligentsia relied heavily upon the newly emergent Afrikaans print media to mobilize and construct their Afrikaner "imagined community." *Koers* (Directions) became a major theoretical journal of Christian nationalism, circulating ideas for discussion in the *Broederbond* and on university campuses. *Inspan* popularized these ideas. The *Huisgenoot* (Home Enjoyment) became a widely read, nationally circulated family magazine, while *Burger Boekhandel* (Citizen Books) churned out Afrikaans books. The *Huisgenoot* and *Burger Boekhandel* did much to construct a sense of Afrikaner identity, rooted in the deliberate use of Afrikaans (rather than English or Dutch). The newspaper *Die Burger* (The Citizen) became the voice of Malan's NP in the Cape Province, *Transvaler* its Transvaal voice, and *Volksblad* (People's Newspaper) its Free State voice.

However, this nationalist intelligentsia reached beyond the print media and, in the 1930s, organized *kultuurpolitiek* (cultural politics). This involved building parallel cultural organizations like the *Voortrekkers* (Afrikaner version of Boy/Girl Scouts); *Noodhulpliga* (First Aid League—Afrikaner version of St. John's Ambulance); and a campaign to stop discrimination against Afrikaans that called on Afrikaners to "Never shop where you are not served in Afrikaans," "Pay no accounts not issued in Afrikaans," and "Do not patronize firms not advertising in Afrikaans." Further, the *Broederbond* used its "cultural wing," the *Afrikaanse Taal-en-Kultuurvereniging*/ATKV (Language and Cultural Union), to organize the

1938 *Eeufees* (centenary celebrations) of the Great Trek.[40] The result was an extraordinarily successful cultural campaign of mass ethnic mobilization that did much to lay the foundations for the NP's 1948 electoral victory. The four-month-long *Eeufees* involved reenacting the Great Trek. Replica wagons converged on Pretoria from across the country. *Eeufees* liaison committees were formed in every town and city to arrange welcome celebrations when the wagons passed through. Men, women, and children dressed as *voortrekkers* (pioneers) and renamed streets after *voortrekker* heroes. The result was first-rate politico-cultural theatre, broadcast nationally by the new Afrikaans radio service. The *Eeufees*—constructed around the nation-building message of *volkseenheid* (people's unity)—did much to popularize Afrikaner nationalist themes, build grassroots nationalist networks (tied to the FAK), and popularize the Afrikaans radio service.[41] The *Eeufees* culminated in laying the foundation stone for Pretoria's Voortrekker Monument on 16 December 1938 (the 100th anniversary of the Blood River Battle); more than 100,000 Afrikaners gathered for this event. Eleven years later, the 40-meter-high Voortrekker Monument, ringed by 64 granite ox wagons, was completed. At its heart is a cenotaph, situated so that on 16 December each year a shaft of sunlight falls on the words "*Ons vir jou Suid-Afrika*" (We pledge ourselves to South Africa). The *Eeufees*, and the monument, provided Malan's nationalists with a wealth of patriotic symbolism to draw upon. Every year during the apartheid era, an NP-led rededication to Afrikaner nationalism took place at the Voortrekker Monument on 16 December.

Although the *Eeufees* popularized Afrikaner nationalism's core themes, it was World War II that provided Malan's nationalists with both the opportunities to build political alliances (needed to win power) and the "evidence" (the declaration of war) to demonstrate that Botha, Smuts, and Hertzog had delivered *de facto* Anglo hegemony antithetical to Afrikaner interests. Smuts's declaration of war drove Hertzog out of the Smuts-Hertzog UP alliance and into a tense alliance with Malan. Significantly, Hertzog brought his moderate Afrikaner nationalist constituency with him into the new "reunited" NP. When Hertzog withdrew from politics in 1940, Malan's radical nationalists retained Hertzog's political machinery and his constituency. From this they built the NP, which won the 1948 election.

THE ROOTS OF APARTHEID

Malan's NP advocated apartheid during the 1948 elections. At its heart, apartheid represented a radical nationalist program for ending Anglo hegemony and reconfiguring the racial-capitalist socioeconomic order introduced by Milner half a century earlier. Reductionist explanations have tended to portray apartheid as white racism (directed at blacks), a form of white supremacy, or segregation, but it was far more complex than this, as can best be revealed by unpacking its six roots.

First, the desire for "apartness" (apartheid) was rooted in a deep Afrikaner resentment toward Anglos.[42] Malan's primary concern in the 1940s–1950s was to regain control of the country from Anglos.[43] He was not especially concerned with the "black issue," and it is not even mentioned in his autobiography,[44] which concentrates exclusively on his passion for uniting Afrikaners against Anglo domination.[45] Formulating a policy toward blacks was never center stage under Malan, and only started to become significant from 1955 under Prime Minister Strijdom.[46] During the 1930s–1950s, the NP and *Broederbond* were more focused upon creating "own-ness" (*eiesoortigheid*) in relation to Anglos than in relation to blacks. The NP's key objective in the 1950s was to end the Afrikaner sense of humiliation in the face of Anglo political, economic, and cultural subjugation. The aim was to rerank Afrikaners upward within Milner's racial-capitalist order and end the "consuming sense of inferiority" that Afrikaners felt in the face of "the dismaying affluence of the English"; the playing of "God Save the King" and the screening of the Union Jack in cinemas and concert halls; the use of English in the courts and for public notices; and the fact that Anglos treated Afrikaners as inferior, regarded Afrikaans as a "kitchen language," and forced Afrikaners to use English.[47] Resentment bred the nationalist desire for "apartness" (apartheid). In this sense, Afrikaner nationalism shares many of the "antiforeigner"[48] sentiments of black nationalism. Consequently, much of the 1950s was about Afrikaner cultural assertiveness targeted at Anglos (not blacks)—for example, halting Anglo migration, pouring resources into Afrikaner educational institutions and cultural spaces, funding the development of Afrikaans as a modern industrial language, enforcing bilingualism, and forcing Anglo schoolchildren to learn Afrikaans. South African Anglos experienced a sense of political impotence, second-classness, subjugation, and much alienation during the 1950s. Many migrated to Rhodesia, Britain, and Australia, carrying with them deep resentments toward Afrikaners and apartheid. This alienation translated into a problem for the NP because, not surprisingly, South African Anglos "conveyed unsympathetic views[49] on Afrikaners to foreign diplomats, journalists and businessmen, who rarely could speak or read Afrikaans."[50]

Ultimately, one of the deepest roots to Afrikaner nationalism's desire for apartness was the sense that, without a state protecting an Afrikaner cultural/linguistic space, Afrikaners would disappear in the face of Anglo cultural dominance. Symbolic of this was Milner's enforced Anglicization program, which profoundly impacted on the psyche of Afrikaners punished for speaking Afrikaans at school. They remembered this for the rest of their lives, passing on their resentments to their children and grandchildren.[51] That Milner's Anglicization program spawned Christian

National Education (CNO) is highly significant in the story of apartheid, because CNO helped spawn Christian nationalism and the Kuyperian logic of own-ness/*verzuiling*. Initially, the desire for own-ness was developed in relation to Anglos, but later expanded to include blacks.

Second, apartheid fed off powerful Afrikaner anti-imperialist sentiments, which, in fact, made Afrikaner nationalists grasp the full significance (and dangers) of postwar black anticolonialism.[52] As Cronje said:

> The Boer people have themselves gone through the crucible of imperialist and capitalist domination and exploitation. They still show the wounds and bruises of it all. Their national life and culture have been disrupted. As a nation they almost perished because they served the interests of other people. They know what it means to see "own-ness" destroyed, but they also know what it means to promote through their own efforts a national revival and restoration . . . the Boer nation can therefore understand the sufferings of the Bantu [blacks]. It is the same imperialism and capitalism, having them believe that the foreign is better than what is their own, which seeks to destroy their tribal life.[53]

Afrikaner nationalists effectively merged Christian nationalism's call for "own-ness" with an anti-imperialist Republicanism. The *Broederbond*, in particular, promoted anti-imperialism, having originally been created in the wake of the 1926 Balfour declaration granting South Africa dominion status.[54] The *Broederbond* saw this declaration as dangerous because it disguised de facto Anglo hegemony; and *Broeders* (members of the *Broederbond* were called *broeders*/brothers) worked to expose Hertzog's sellout to British imperialism. The *Broederbond* focused its energy into persuading Afrikaner workers that "foreigners" and "imperialism" threatened "the small man."[55] And because many of the *Broederbond*'s petit bourgeois members were educators, they could easily diffuse such ideas. "Like the 'educated elite' of colonial Africa, the Afrikaner petty bourgeoisie identified 'imperialism' as the source of all its ills"[56] and they successfully taught the next generation of schoolchildren to share this anti-imperialism. From this emerged the notion of establishing an independent Christian National Republic—an idea driven especially vigorously by *Die Transvaler* under Verwoerd's editorship.[57]

Malan's autobiography spelled out his life's passion as geared to uniting Afrikaners in order to mobilize sufficient political power to drive British imperialism out of South Africa.[58] Yet, when the NP came to power, it restrained its anti-imperial instincts, and under Malan and Strijdom the NP made no moves to establish an independent republic, nor engaged in the removal of Anglo place-names or symbols of British imperialism (e.g., statues of English kings and queens). The only name the NP changed was Roberts Heights—the site of Britain's post–Boer War military garrison in Pretoria.[59] Only minor symbolic changes were made, for example, President

Kruger's statue and the ZAR Parliament's republican coat of arms were restored in Pretoria's Church Square in 1954 (Milner had removed these). In 1957, "God Save the King" and the Union Jack ceased to have standing in South Africa. This NP restraint was motivated by both their notion of "own-ness" (which meant respecting Anglo cultural spaces) and a desire not to drive Anglo capital out of the country. Ultimately, the NP only declared a republic 13 years after coming to power. It was inaugurated in Pretoria's Church Square in a ceremony steeped in the symbolism of Afrikaner anti-imperialism.

Third, apartheid was grounded in Kuyper's *verzuiling* worldview of "sovereignty in one's own sphere." Effectively, Afrikaner nationalists developed a worldview diametrically opposed to liberal capitalism. Christian nationalism/*verzuiling* effectively represented an attempt to halt the way capitalist urbanization eroded cultural differences by homogenizing different ethnic groups and assimilating them into a unified South African (Anglo-dominated) culture. Apartheid grew out of a worldview hostile to the way capitalist modernization destroyed small cultures and languages (such as Afrikaans), or what Cronje referred to as "denationalization." Du Plessis maintained that the only people benefiting from liberal capitalism were Anglo employers, arguing liberals only wanted blacks to migrate to the cities so they could exploit them.[60] He asserted that the process of urbanization and semi-assimilation in South Africa's cities relegated blacks into second-class roles within segregated ghettos. Du Plessis feared that if this capitalist-driven process went on long enough, semi-Westernized blacks would become South Africa's demographic majority, and this would politically swamp Afrikaner (and white) society.[61] Apartheid, geared to stopping this process, consequently rejected the liberal capitalist worldview, giving precedence to economic development, efficiency, and profit making. For Afrikaner nationalists, their cultural survival took precedence over profits. They blamed liberal capitalism for eroding the Afrikaner's culture, language, and sovereignty. Apartheid theorists like Diederichs, Cronje, and Du Plessis argued that unbridled capitalism and its associated worldview of liberal cosmopolitanism would eventually replace Southern Africa's rich ethnic diversity with bland cultural homogeneity, because Southern Africa's multiplicity of small ethnic groups (including Afrikaners) would not survive the assimilationist pressures of Anglo capitalism. Cronje understood that his apartheid plan flew in the face of capitalist logic and stressed that capitalist arguments should never be allowed to stand in the way of the "apart-making"[62] process (partition/apartheid). Ultimately, the underlying spirit of Afrikaner nationalism's vision that "cultural diversity" should take precedence over "economics" is best captured by General Christiaan de Wet's speech in which he said he would rather stand on a dung heap[63] surrounded by his own people than be in a British palace.[64]

Built into apartheid's worldview was a nationalist opposition to Anglo capitalism, which was seen to throw together people who did "not belong together" and undermine cultural diversity/sovereignty in the name of profit making. The homogenizing urban world built by Anglo capitalism was seen as responsible for turning Afrikaners into a poor and threatened ethnic minority within a (British-made) unified nation state. Interestingly, in seeking a political solution to this state of affairs, Malan's NP rejected all the main ideologies of their day—liberalism, communism, and fascism. In its 1944 "Economic Plan for SA," Malan's NP described communism, national socialism, and laissez-faire capitalism as the "three extremes" it wished to avoid.[65] Instead, Afrikaner nationalists proposed the locally grown ideology of Christian nationalism (apartheid/partition), which promoted a "love of one's own, especially one's own language, history and culture."[66] Afrikaner culture was deemed to be intrinsically enmeshed with Christianity, in particular as represented by the three Calvinist "sister" churches[67]—*Nederduitse Gereformeerde Kerk*/NGK, *Nederduitse Hervormde Kerk,* and *Gereformeerde Kerk.*[68] During the 1940s, the NP cemented an alliance with these churches through the Broad Church Committee, originally created to fight for Afrikaans female factory workers. F.W. de Klerk's father, Jan, played a leading role in this alliance building. This NP-church alliance became a central feature of Christian nationalism, as was evident in the NP's core slogan, displayed for decades at NP meetings—"Believe in God. Believe in your People. Believe in Yourself."

The NP saw itself as engaged in a struggle against three "foreign," "materialist," and "godless" ideologies that contradicted Christian nationalism's Kuyperian principles:

- Encoded into apartheid's founding texts[69] was a rejection of godless capitalism, which (because it was driven by a single-minded pursuit of profit) was seen to ignore the "higher callings" of community/cultural identity and community service, and to divide the nation into classes (which undermined the unity and welfare of the *volk*).[70] Under Malan, Strijdom, and Verwoerd, this variant of anticapitalism was a powerful subtext of Afrikaner nationalism. It began to weaken during Vorster's premiership, and was finally abandoned by P.W. Botha's NP.
- Fascism was rejected as unchristian, and during the 1940s, Malan's NP fought an intense struggle for its very political survival against the pro-Nazi *Ossewabrandwag*/OB (ox wagon guards). For a while, it was unclear which of the two—Malan's Christian nationalists or the OB—would emerge victorious.
- Communism was passionately disliked because it advocated atheism. Christian nationalists were deeply concerned that trade unions, led by communists like Solly Sachs,[71] would recruit Afrikaners into "godless communism" and hence divide the Afrikaans working class from the rest of the *volk*. Ardent anticommunism was a consistent feature of NP ideology. Hence, one of the first NP actions after coming to power was the 1950 Suppression of Communism Act. This was

used to hound communists out of the trade union movement, while Christian nationalists built alternative trade unions to ensure the large Afrikaner working class was brought into the fold of a unified *volk*. This accorded with the NP's *verzuiling* logic that national groups should have their own organizations, including trade unions.

Fourth, apartheid grew out of the way in which capitalist urbanization impoverished many Afrikaners.[72] Entwined into 1930s–1950s Afrikaner nationalism was a powerful resentment against (Anglo) liberal capitalism, referred to as "*Engelse geldmag*" (English money power)[73]—a resentment symbolized by the opulent Hoggenheimer[74] caricature in D.C. Boonzaaier's cartoons. During the *Eeufees* celebrations, these resentments spawned a nationalist *reddings* (salvation) movement, (geared to ending Afrikaner poverty/economic subjugation), when NGK pastor "Vader" Kastell called for action to end Afrikaner poverty, saying "we must look after each other because we are of each others blood."[75] Kastell's 1938 "a people rescues itself" speech encapsulated what Afrikaner social work academics, Calvinist church pastors, and nationalist politicians had been saying for some time, namely, charity was no solution to Afrikaner poverty. Instead, political action was required—Afrikaners needed to mobilize and rescue themselves. This mobilization call progressed in two trajectories. First, in 1939, it produced the *Reddingsdaadbond* and *Volkskapitalisme* (people's capitalism), driven by M.S. Louw.[76] A *reddingsdaadfonds* (salvation fund) was created, and Afrikaners were called upon to contribute every penny they could to build up "Afrikaner capital" to establish Afrikaner-owned businesses where they could work and trade in their own language. From this emerged an Afrikaner corporate sector. It also led to the founding of an Afrikaans Chamber of Commerce and Industry and an Economic Institute. Second, it led to the idea that Afrikaners needed to capture the state and change the rules of the game. As early as 1934, Verwoerd (as social work professor) had called for a sort of "socialist state"[77] to end Afrikaner poverty. He was consistently a key player driving the agenda of political interventionism instead of charity.[78] Verwoerd's paper, delivered at the 1934 People's Conference on the Poor White (which he organized), represents a seminal statement of the economic and anti–black migration motivations underpinning apartheid. Significantly, the paper begins with Verwoerd expressing frustration at the powerlessness of ivory-tower academe to end poverty.[79] This conference represented Verwoerd's transition from academic to politician.

The NP came to power in 1948 because it convinced enough Afrikaners that creating Afrikaner prosperity, and/or ending Afrikaner unemployment (which was rising in 1948), required an interventionist state deliberately modifying the rules of racial capitalism and stopping black migration to the cities.

Fifth, apartheid represented an explicit rejection of Afrikaner second-classness encoded into racial capitalism's system of ethnic ranking. A feature of the British Empire was a hierarchy of "backward and advanced" groups and "positional psychology."[80] One's worth as an individual was ascribed according to one's ethnic group. White Anglos saw themselves, and were seen by others, as automatically superior and "advanced." Blacks were automatically deemed "backward," while Afrikaners, coloreds, and Indians were allocated an intermediary position—not as "advanced" as Anglos, but not as "backward" as blacks. This Anglo-manufactured ranking system affected not only one's economic life chances, but also affected one's perceived self-worth. It was a social order in which non-Anglos could never feel fully "worthy." This produced a sense of inferiority, weakness, and helplessness vis-à-vis the "advanced" group, and self-stereotyping in which members of "backward" groups adopted compliant personalities characterized by unassertiveness, unambitious demeanors, and the assumption that others were more intelligent, better educated, and more worthwhile.[81] Besides being psychologically unsettling, exclusion from the "advanced" group produced envy, insecurity, and deprivation.[82] This created catch-up nationalism in the form of Afrikaner and black nationalism.[83] Catch-up nationalisms, triggered by pain, have been attempts by groups traumatized by Anglo ethnic ranking to rearrange the ranking order and so achieve the "same recognition" accorded to the "advanced" group.[84] In the 1940s–1950s, Malan's NP specifically worked to convince Afrikaners that they could challenge this imperial ranking system. The NP successfully mobilized militant Afrikaner assertiveness against Anglos by inventing a new "forward-looking" (urban-based) ethnic identity grounded in the proposition that Afrikaners had a right to replace Anglos as South Africa's rulers.

Sixth, apartheid emerged from the need to invent a political message able to overcome the six-way split within 1940s Afrikanerdom so as to produce Malan's dream of a "united people." At its heart, Malan's NP was an alliance of the emergent Afrikaner petit bourgeoisie (especially those organized within the *Broederbond*), a large Afrikaner working class, and the small Afrikaner capitalist sector. The Cape-based Sanlam group represented the heart of Afrikaner capitalism and the NP's main financial backer. Smuts's declaration of war drove Hertzog's Afrikaner constituency out of the UP. These Hertzogites fragmented into three groups—those (mostly northern farmers) who eventually switched allegiance to Malan, the Afrikaner Party (AP), and the *Ossewabrandwag*/OB. The AP represented moderate nationalists who, although they opposed Anglo imperialism and the war, felt uncomfortable with Malan's militant anti-Anglo rhetoric. During the 1950s (after merging with the NP), the AP was a moderating influence within the NP, holding it back from full-blown republicanism. The OB espoused anti-imperialism and advocated a Nazi republic. As soon as the OB moved from "cultural" to political mobilization, the NP became concerned and, from 1941, Malan's NP and the OB fought a bitter struggle over the direction Afrikaner nationalism would take.[85] Malan argued that Anglo imperialism should only be removed by constitutional parliamentary means and not by the undemocratic and violent methods advocated by the OB. Malan, Strijdom, and Verwoerd launched repeated attacks on the OB's Nazism as "unchristian," "foreign," and "unafrikaans"; sought to remove OB sympathizers from NP leadership positions;[86] and reported OB activities to the UP government. After the OB was politically broken, the NP absorbed its rank-and-file membership. By 1948, Malan's NP had successfully overcome Afrikanerdom's six-way split. Apartheid became the vehicle for uniting them, because it offered different things to each of these groups: protection of the working class from black migrant labor, improved labor conditions, plus Afrikaans schools and technical colleges for improving their children's prospects. Apartheid promised the petit bourgeoisie jobs (administering the new state) and promised to end Anglo discrimination against them and their children. The (formerly Hertzogite) northern farmers were won over by the promise that restrictions would be placed on urban Anglo capitalists recruiting their laborers. Apartheid held out to the Afrikaner business sector the prospect of a government that could challenge Anglo corporate dominance and promote new opportunities for Afrikaner capital accumulation. Finally, apartheid promised all Afrikaners their own "cultural space" (own-ness) with the promise of new Afrikaans schools, colleges, and universities.

Seventh, apartheid emerged from a growing fear that if Anglo capitalists kept importing black migrants, Afrikaners would be demographically swamped and South Africa would inevitably become a black African state. The wave of black migration to the cities during World War II meant 44.6 percent of the urban population was black by 1946. South African cities began to look "black" for the first time. The Atlantic Charter, plus the rise of black militancy across Africa, exacerbated this fear. This was deepened when, in 1943, the African National Congress (ANC) drew up its "African Claims" document based upon the Atlantic Charter. In South Africa, "most of the English-speaking community were neither impressed nor particularly interested. They continued to make their money and live their lives secure in the conviction such events could never affect their society. By contrast Afrikaners were deeply apprehensive."[87] As Eiselen, head of Verwoerd's Bantu Administration Department, said:

> It stands to reason that if all were thrown together into one social melting pot, an entirely new society, definitely not European in character and culture would emerge. White South Africa is numerically not strong enough to absorb and can

therefore only choose between being absorbed or survive by the maintenance of separate communities.[88]

In 1944, the People's Congress on racial policy placed this issue of a "black threat" firmly onto Afrikaner nationalism's agenda.[89] At this congress, Christian nationalism (*verzuiling*/own-ness) was proposed as a "just" and "Christian"[90] way to stop this "swamping threat." Apartheid was formulated on two core assumptions: First, Afrikaners regarded themselves as culturally, linguistically, religiously,[91] and racially different from black people—an attitude toward indigenous/black people no more racist than that of Anglo settlers.[92] Second, because of this "difference," Afrikaners believed they had a right to their own country. Whites were deemed to have as much right to parts of South Africa as blacks because they had simply migrated to new areas in ways no different than how black people had migrated and settled new lands.[93]

Apartheid mutated between 1948 and 1990, but the following remained consistent from Malan to Botha:

- Afrikaners (as a small ethnic group) feared cultural swamping by global Anglo culture and black majoritarianism.
- A belief in *verzuiling*/own-ness.
- A belief that "apartness/separation" was just and Christian. This need to justify apartheid as being Christian was based upon a deep Afrikaner religiosity that prevented the sorts of genocide seen in other settler societies.
- A passionate anticommunism (deemed the unchristian "other").
- Afrikaner nationalists were legalists—obsessed with constitutionalism, the rule of law, and legally codifying every detail of their ideology. So whereas racist practices simply existed *de facto* before 1948, the NP made these *de jure* (something Anglo South Africans criticized as foolish, for drawing attention to practices best kept informal).
- A search for ways to secure Afrikaner self-determination.

These themes still underpinned P.W. Botha's last speech at the Voortrekker Monument on 16 December 1988, the 150th anniversary of the Great Trek. This speech effectively became the last assertive (if plaintive) statement of Afrikaner nationalism, the theme of which was the threat posed to small peoples (*volkies*) like Afrikaners, and the way history had contrived to launch a total onslaught against them. Botha accused Americans of failing to understand the need to protect the security and rights of minority groups and small peoples. He said South Africa was a "nation of minorities" and cultural diversity, South Africans had to learn "good neighborliness" toward each other, and the solution to South Africa's "demographic problems" had to include political mechanisms for Afrikaner survival.[94]

CONSTRUCTING JUSTIFICATIONS

Afrikaners are a deeply religious people who needed to believe their apartheid/partition policies were fair,[95] so justifications were constructed and incorporated into school syllabi.

The historical justification[96] was that both blacks and whites were migrants to South Africa. The only indigenous group was the Khoisan, who had been militarily defeated (annihilated and absorbed) by black colonists (trekking from the north) and white colonists (trekking from the south). Further, it was argued that the Difaqane had depopulated those high-veld areas settled by Boer voortrekkers. Consequently, it was argued, Afrikaners had as much right to the land they occupied as blacks had to theirs.

At heart, apartheid was a radical survival plan.[97] Apartheid theorists constantly referred to a demographic problem—that is, Afrikaners are a minority group[98] within a British-created South African polity. They insisted that Afrikaners possessed a clear "separate" identity (that was Western-, Christian-, and African-rooted) that they had every right to maintain. An important feature of apartheid theorizing was the notion that Afrikaners were not colonial settlers—unlike other African whites, Afrikaners had become "Africans." When colonialism ended, English, French, and Portuguese settlers could return to overseas cultural home bases,[99] but Afrikaners had no such luxury. Hence, if the "Afrikaner nation" was to survive, it had to fight to secure an African "home-base." This was seen to require Afrikaner political sovereignty over an African territory of its own. This was apartheid's core goal. Apartheid was not about Afrikaners wanting to dominate blacks or differentiate themselves from "others" deemed inferior[100]—it was about constructing "a bulwark against the infiltration of people of another civilization."[101] Apartheid was the construction of a minority group deeply fearful about being subjugated (politically and economically) by another people, and/or being culturally swamped by black Africans. These fears were best expressed by the poet N.P. van Wyk Louw,[102] who saw Afrikaners as a separate ethno-national group whose very existence was at stake. Louw argued (in 1952) that Afrikaners faced extinction from three potential sources:[103] (1) being overwhelmed militarily or by mass immigration (e.g., the Boer War defeat, Milner's migration plans, and the mass migration of blacks to South African cities); (2) if Afrikaners began doubting their right to survive, they would be absorbed by either Anglo or black culture; and (3) if Afrikaners used unjust means to survive, this would generate a future crisis because Afrikaner intellectuals would eventually turn against such survival through injustice. Louw supported apartheid because he believed integration meant Afrikaner national suicide—because under black rule, an Afrikaner minority would be "as helpless as the Jew was in Germany."[104]

The survival plan was, of course, based upon the assumption that "otherness" and pluralism existed, and *should* exist. This otherness was defined by most Afrikaners as ethnic, but by some as racial. Furthermore, this otherness was God-ordained, meaning that Afrikaners had not merely a right but a duty (as Christians) to survive. Apartheid represented Afrikanerdom's refusal to be absorbed by other groups.

Another justification for apartheid was the argument that the existing system (the unified polity and racial capitalism) served only Anglo capitalist and British imperial interests, and was "destructive" for both Afrikaner and black culture. It was criticized for destroying Southern Africa's rich ethnic pluralism by forcing all into a homogenizing (Anglicizing) melting pot. The result was that Afrikaners and blacks were being "denationalized" and economically exploited by a rapacious imperialist-capitalist system,[105] accompanied by Afrikaner and black moral decay caused by urban poverty.[106] In terms of this logic, apartheid was a means to save blacks from moral decay and urban degradation by demolishing slums and returning them "back to their homelands." From a Christian nationalist perspective, this also saved blacks from being wooed by (ungodly) communists. Instead, blacks would be returned to wholesome lives in black homelands that were to be upgraded by "separate development" policies. Afrikaners thereby persuaded themselves that apartheid was a just system—one in which blacks were to be given what Afrikaners wanted for themselves, namely, ethnic autonomy and sovereignty over their own affairs (i.e., "own-ness"). Of course, for those who did not want such "own-ness"—for example, urban Westernized blacks—this spelled trouble, because from within the Christian-National worldview, repressing their aspirations was justified.

APARTHEID: THE MODEL

With a view to the upcoming 1948 election, the NP appointed the Sauer Commission to codify a political program out of the "apartheid idea." Sauer's committee delivered this in late 1947, advocating political partition/"vertical separation," halting black migration to the cities, and championing the repatriation of Indians to India. From the Sauer and Tomlinson Commissions grew the apartheid model,[107] consisting of seven main features.

First was a belief in cultural "own-ness," derived from Kuyper's *verzuiling* worldview of "sovereignty in one's own sphere." Afrikaners were deemed to have a God-given right to build their own political-cultural space and protect this from Anglo cultural imperialism and black majoritarianism. Hence, building separate cultural spaces became a core feature of the apartheid state. Each "national group" was supposed to have its own schools, colleges, and universities.[108] Great stress was placed on "mother-tongue education," with Transvaal Afrikaners actually being debarred from sending their children to English-language state schools.[109] Resources were poured into building an extensive Afrikaans-language education system and codifying Afrikaans as a modern industrial language. Simultaneously, apartheid expanded the black schooling system from 1953's 800,000 places to 1963's 1.8 million places, with numbers expanding even more rapidly after that.[110] Significantly, pupils were taught in indigenous black languages, which involved the apartheid state codifying and printing textbooks in nine black languages. One consequence of apartheid was thus a population literate in indigenous languages (a rare thing in Africa). The apartheid state also built separate media systems for each "national group." The South African Broadcasting Corporation operated separate radio services in Zulu, Xhosa, Pedi, Tswana, Sotho, Swazi, Tsonga, Venda, Ndebele, English, and Afrikaans, plus separate language-based television services—TV1 (English/Afrikaans), TV2 (Zulu/Xhosa), and TV3 (Sotho/Tswana/Pedi).

Second, apartheid was fundamentally designed to facilitate the dream of Afrikaner self-determination within its own independent Christian-National Republic. To achieve this—given South Africa's demographics—the NP needed to do two things:

- Resist post–Atlantic Charter pressures for one-man–one-vote. Much apartheid theorizing involved seeking justifications for restricting the franchise to whites, and devising mechanisms to give the vote to blacks, coloreds, and Indians in ways that Afrikaners did not become an electoral minority. Giving blacks a vote in homelands, and coloreds and Indians a vote within the tricameral (three-chambered) system was designed to ensure that Afrikaners retained political sovereignty over the area they designated "white South Africa." Developing a moral justification for restricting the franchise in this way was important for Afrikaners because, having experienced Anglo domination, many were uncomfortable stepping into a similar role.
- Try to unify all Afrikaners behind the NP. Because Afrikaners constituted 60 percent of the white electorate, a unified Afrikaner electorate would guarantee NP control within a one-party dominant democracy.[111]

Third, apartheid was a renunciation of racial capitalism's ethnic-ranking system, which rated Anglos superior, and justified Anglo rule over "lesser human types." Afrikaner nationalism in the 1940s–1950s was primarily about Afrikaners challenging this ranking system and the second-class status it accorded to them. Jesudason has noted that "deprived individuals and their leaders, especially if they possess strong cultural and affective ties, are prone to using the state to . . . modify the opportunity structure of society."[112] The NP's project was to win political power and use the state to implement a socioeconomic catch-up policy. Hence, in part, apartheid was an "affirmative-action" project, designed to rerank Afrikaners impoverished by Anglos after the Boer War by creating opportunities for their advancement. From this grew an ethnic patronage system, as the NP used its control of the state to dispense patronage to and upgrade its ethnic constituency by providing public service jobs and building Afrikaans schools, colleges, and universities. An interesting feature of this Afrikaner affirmative-action program was that the NP created *separate* structures alongside and parallel to the Anglo structures.[113] Initially, "standards" were not as high in the parallel Afrikaner institutions—Afrikaners were effectively "protected" from Anglo competition until the standards reached the same level. This parallel infrastructure was paid for by taxing businesses (mostly Anglo-owned). The trade-off for business was that the state facilitated the exploitation of black workers. Apartheid meant that businesses could—even after paying tax—generate substantive profits and not be "damaged" by having less-competent people forced on them by affirmative action. Hence, the Anglo business sector was left unscathed by Afrikaner affirmative action during the upgrade period.

As an affirmative-action program for Afrikaners, apartheid was successful. Whereas in the 1940s most Afrikaners were part of a struggling working class, by the 1970s Afrikaner education levels had been raised, a large Afrikaner middle class built,[114] and the working conditions of the (still large) Afrikaner working class improved. The NP's objective of ensuring that Afrikaner workers were not recruited into "godless communism" was achieved by providing these workers with an alternative (NP-run) "affirmative-action" upgrade program. The NP's petit bourgeois leadership saw themselves as having successfully "saved" Afrikaner workers from poverty, communism, Anglicization, and absorption into an ethnic hodgepodge. This had been achieved by providing them with work opportunities, teaching them to help themselves, developing a work ethic and discipline (within Afrikaans-language CNO schools), and promoting "nationalist morality" and a "decent Christian" way of living in the city.[115] In the 1950s–1960s, the NP did what Verwoerd (the social work professor) had proposed in 1934 when he called for a sort of "socialist state"[116] to create a *volksekonomie* (people's economy)[117] with opportunities for Afrikaners to raise themselves up. Under the NP, a parallel Afrikaner economy (offering employment in Afrikaans) blossomed, for example, *Federale Volksbeleggings* (Federal People's Investments), *Federale Mynbou* (Federal Mining), *Federale Nwyerhede* (Federal Industries), *Volkskas Bank* (People's Bank), Trust Bank, *Saambou* ("Building-Together") Building Society, Rembrandt-Group, and Sanlam.

Fourth, apartheid was a form of immigration control/migration policy.[118] Milner created an economy dependent upon black migration. Although migrant labor was internally recruited (from Transkei, Ciskei,

Zululand, and Northern Transvaal), South Africa—as a sparsely populated country—did not have a large enough population to supply the enormous quantities of cheap labor the mines required. Consequently, huge numbers of migrant laborers were imported from Malawi, Lesotho, Botswana, Swaziland, and Mozambique. Afrikaner nationalists became alarmed about the implications of large numbers of black migrants being urbanized in order to feed the insatiable labor needs of Anglo capitalists. The NP saw[119] these migrants as a threat to Afrikaners because they competed with Afrikaners for jobs, driving down the price of labor. Further, this mass migration looked set to turn Afrikaners into a small minority within a new, mostly black, urban world. When the 1948 Fagan Commission (appointed by Smuts's government) proposed that black migration was "unstoppable," "natural," and "advantageous" for industrial development, the NP was provided with the ammunition required to persuade Afrikaners to vote for apartheid as a form of migration control designed to halt the demographic "swamping" process that the apartheid theorists argued would necessarily lead to black political power.

In 1948, the NP promised a new migration dispensation to protect Afrikaner interests by halting the flow of blacks (and Anglos) into South Africa. Verwoerd, as minister of Bantu affairs in the 1950s, went further and proposed eventually reversing the flow of black migration using three stages:[120] (1) a continuation and even a possible increase in black migration into "white SA"; (2) a stabilization period, when the inward flow would be stopped; and (3) an exodus period, when black labor would be replaced by whites, and blacks would be returned to the homelands or other African countries from which they had come. For Verwoerd, black migrants were temporary guests in "white SA" with no permanent right to be there. With this in mind, the Bantu Administration Department under Verwoerd set about finding ways to break down bridgeheads of black integration into city life.[121] Only blacks with long-standing urban residency were granted Section 10 rights (the right to remain permanently in "white" cities). All the rest were deemed temporary and could be "endorsed out" at any time. Blacks were seen as belonging to a homeland and had no right to migrate outside of its territory without the necessary permits. Until the mid-1980s, a migration-control system was rigorously applied, and blacks found illegally in "white SA" were deported back to their homeland (or other African countries).

Fifth, apartheid wanted to replace the British segregation model with a partition model (apartness/apartheid). This translated into the notion of "separate development" (sometimes referred to as "grand apartheid"). Separate development grew from Du Plessis and Cronje's model of "vertical" (separation) based on Kuyper's *verzuiling* logic. Separation/*verzuiling* involves a logic different from segregation.[122] Segregation characterized Anglo South African thinking, having first been introduced into Southern

Africa in the British colony of Natal.[123] Anglos founded many new states/colonies around the world geared to maximizing wealth creation opportunities by building and organizing productive populations. Creating these new productive economies frequently involved mixing together people who were different religiously, culturally, linguistically, or racially. This was especially the case when building large urban-based capitalist economies. The problem was that these different groups did not always get along or enjoy being placed in close proximity to one another. The "solution" in many parts of the British Empire (and the United States) was segregation—that is, people lived in the same cities and participated in the same economy, but (formal and informal) mechanisms were developed to segregate them residentially, on public transport, in schooling, and so on. Milner's racial-capitalist society was based upon economic integration, social segregation, and an integrated/unified political system (grounded in "white supremacy"). Malan's NP rejected this Milner model of political economic integration and social segregation as "too integrated." Instead, they advocated full political and social partition (not segregation) and strove to reduce (end?) economic integration. Verwoerd opted for gradually implementing partition because Afrikaner nationalists believed blacks did not have the required skills to administer the proposed autonomous homelands; therefore, a period of tutoring and trusteeship was needed.[124] Further, the violence accompanying British India's partition suggested that a planned/gradualist approach was needed. In addition, Afrikaners realized they first needed to sell Kuyper's *verzuiling* vision to those black South Africans who would administer the new homelands.

In 1955, the Tomlinson Commission's report proposed South African partition. Tomlinson rejected a unitary South Africa since, it was claimed, this would lead to conflict because whites would never accept giving up their political power to a black majority, while blacks could not be expected to indefinitely accept white supremacy. A unified state, it was argued, precisely generated conflict over political power and resources; therefore, partition was proposed as a less-violent solution. Tomlinson advocated:

- Creating seven homelands from the existing "black reserves" (i.e., partitioning South Africa eight ways).[125]
- Creating homeland governments able to promote modern development (i.e., not tribal governments).
- Adding more land to the black reserves so they could be consolidated into seven "nations."
- Incorporating Bechuanaland/Botswana, Swaziland, and Basutoland/Lesotho into South Africa.[126] (These territories were originally supposed to have been incorporated into a unified South Africa, and their populations were ethnically related to black South Africans.) Tomlinson suggested they be built into the

homelands/partition/development scheme such that 45 percent of South Africa could be allocated to the new "black nations."

- Promoting commercial agriculture in these homelands.
- Creating a development corporation to channel funds to the homelands to promote industrial development.
- Encouraging businesses to decentralize their industrial plants to homeland border areas, thereby providing work opportunities to encourage blacks to migrate back to their homelands.

The Tomlinson Report constituted a refusal of South Africa's British-made boundaries and of the unified modern state Milner's kindergarten had worked to create. The NP believed this unitary state threw together people who did not belong together, and who would eventually fight each other over its control. They believed their partition (apartheid) model was a rational way to avoid this struggle between blacks and whites for political supremacy.[127] Ultimately, apartheid, far from preventing conflict, exacerbated it.

The NP regarded the Population Registration Act as the foundation of its partition model[128] because it defined the different groups (categories of "own-ness")[129] to be given their own "cultural spaces." The NP's *verzuiling* model then sought to peg each group to its own territory through the Group Areas Act. Verwoerd understood that, having opted for partition, the NP's credibility depended upon Verwoerd and demonstrating that this partition could be practically implemented. The 1950s saw Verwoerd, as Bantu administration minister, and Eiselen, as head of this department, attempting to design and implement a partition plan. For Eiselen, partition meant "separate development," encoding two features: (1) creating "apartness" (vertical separation), and (2) creating conditions for development. Development involved "nation building" and (parallel) socioeconomic progress for each of the identified "nations." Verwoerd and Eiselen zealously pursued:

- The ideal of black self-government in separate homelands.
- Separating out the different ethnic groups (by forced removals and population relocations) so each group would eventually live in its own area.
- Black education reform aimed at providing the necessary skills for eventual "black self-government"[130] and improving black productivity,[131] yet simultaneously anchoring children in their own cultures through mother-tongue schooling,[132] and avoiding curricula encouraging black children to identify with Western culture and/or promoting desires to live in "white" cities. Eiselen abolished 5,000 mission-run schools because they were seen to be creating a Westernized black elite who demanded a unified South Africa.[133]
- Ending the migrant labor system built during the Milner-to-Smuts era.
- Providing services for black people—hospitals, welfare, colleges, universities, and the like—in the homelands, while cutting back black service provision in

"white areas." Verwoerd's logic was that if blacks wanted services, they should return to "their own areas."

- Building housing programs to remove slums. The slums that had grown up during World War II's rapid urbanization were demolished in the 1950s–1960s, and black workers relocated to new "townships" (like Soweto). Township houses were state owned, so black people had no permanent property rights there. Verwoerd (as a former social worker) advocated spending large sums on these housing programs to remove slums, which he regarded as potential hotbeds of "communist revolution." The UP[134] actually branded Verwoerd a *kaffirboetjie* (lover of blacks) for allocating so many resources to black housing.[135]

During the 1950s–1970s, the NP set about reconfiguring South Africa in accordance with its partition plan. This involved four key phenomena:

- Transforming the black reserves into self-governing homelands and then "national states." Within the NP, differences emerged about how seriously the homeland policy should be pursued. The "dominant camp" advocated only allocating to homelands the territory that was set aside in the 1936 Land Act. A second camp—which included F.W. de Klerk[136]—argued that this was not enough land to make the homelands viable "national states." They advocated dramatically increasing the amount of land allocated to homelands. A third camp never saw complete economic partition as viable and was never committed to the full partition plan.
- Building migration-control (and policing) systems to halt migration, breaking chain-migration patterns, and deporting those defined as "surplus" to the economy's needs. This generated conflict with Anglo business, which complained about the NP's anticapitalist state interventionism and its interference with their right to recruit labor and maximize profitability.
- Promoting the relocation of industrial plants to homeland border areas. This eventually led to millions of black people being housed in cities just inside homeland borders (e.g., Mdantsane). This provided South African capitalists with labor defined as "foreign citizens" (hence denying them South African enfranchisement). Because they "migrated" short distances, these workers could live settled urban lives with their families (unlike migrant laborers within Milner's model).
- Reconfiguring the cities according to the logic of "orderly urbanization."

In the process, the apartheid state constructed a huge government infrastructure for administering black self-government, migration policing, and the "blacks-only" education and services sector. One reason apartheid survived for as long as it did was that the system delivered jobs,[137] services, and education on a scale unprecedented in Africa—in other words, apartheid involved a complex mix of repression, patronage, and service delivery. Blacks became complicit in apartheid because they staffed homeland bureaucracies, police forces, and the like, plus "separate development" eventually succeeded in constructing loyalties to homelands like Bophuthatswana and KwaZulu.

Sixth, apartheid involved redesigning South African cities[138] according to *verzuiling* logic. Each ethnic group was to have its own "group area" within which would be located its own educational and cultural facilities (see figure 2.3). Those residing in the Zulu suburbs would be citizens of, and vote for, the KwaZulu government, Tswanas for the Bophuthatswana government, and so on. The NP's insistence on "orderly urbanization" was premised upon each group having its own territorial and cultural "space." All groups interacted in shared work spaces (i.e., industrial zones and city centers). Within each "group area" there were suburbs for different classes. Although not encoded into the apartheid plan, white Anglos and Afrikaners tended to reside in different suburbs. Further, "orderly urbanization" involved deliberately restricting black migration into "white" cities in order to prevent "demographic swamping," unemployment, and the growth of slums (of the sort that emerged before and after apartheid). Verwoerd believed an oversupply of black labor created unemployment and slums, which promoted social instability and the growth of communism. Further, he saw slums as melting pots encouraging the breakdown of "own-ness." This produced Westernized black people, who then demanded a unitary state and one-person–one-vote. Not surprisingly, breaking up slums became a core feature of early apartheid (e.g., Sophiatown in 1955).

Seventh, apartheid limited contact between the different groups outside of the work environment. This involved enforcing *verzuiling* (separation) through the creation of urban "separate amenities" for each group. What Milner and his successors had thrown together was now to be pulled apart. This came to be called "petty apartheid"—that is, separate restaurants, hotels, hospitals, beaches, sports clubs, buses, trains, and so forth. It also involved outlawing interracial sex and marriage. The NP's restrictions on such social contact (and other behaviors like gambling) reflected the fears of an emergent Afrikaner petit bourgeoisie, who apparently did not trust the Afrikaner working class and lumpen proletariat. In part, this derived from church pastors and social workers witnessing the effects of rapid urbanization, which produced "moral decay" amongst a highly dislocated slum-dwelling Afrikaner underclass during the first decades of the twentieth century. For the NP, "petty apartheid" was never as important as "grand apartheid" (separate development), and during the final ("reform") years of apartheid, they were quite willing to abandon petty apartheid as long as they could retain *verzuiling*/own-ness and some form of Afrikaner self-determination.

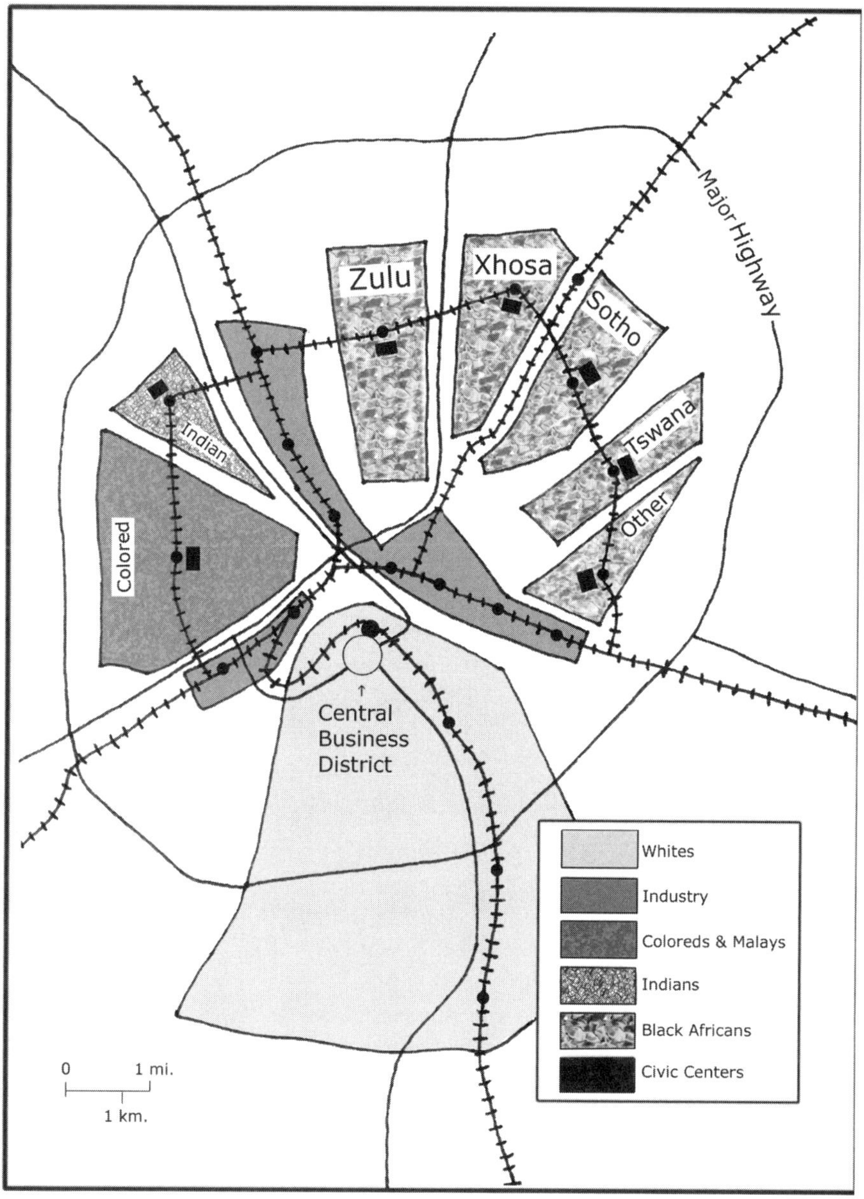

Figure 2.3:
An Ideal Apartheid City

Source: Western, J. 1981. *Outcast Cape Town* (Cape Town: Human & Rousseau), 91.

BUILDING APARTHEID: A CHRONOLOGY

1948	Malan's NP wins May election
	Smuts government's British immigrant scheme (and special migrant ships) cancelled
	Bilingualism (50 percent Afrikaans/50 percent English) was enforced in the civil service (which drove out Anglos unable to communicate in Afrikaans)
	The Smuts government's ban on employing *Broederbonders* in the civil service rescinded[139]
	Government departments instructed to fill low-grade jobs with poor whites in preference to blacks
1949	Separate government schools created for Afrikaners and Anglos. CNO "mother-language" policy enforced in the Transvaal
	South African Citizenship Act (made it more difficult for Britons to become South Africans, removed privileges of British subjects, and removed citizenship pledge to British crown)
	Native Laws Amendment Bill (designed to introduce black migration/"influx control"—defeated in Parliament; reintroduced 1952)
	Prohibition on Mixed Marriages Act
1950	Right to appeal to British Privy Council abolished
	Population Registration Act (registers all South Africans as white, colored, Indian, or black)
	Group Areas Act (pegs each group to its own area)
	Immorality Amendment Act (prohibits interracial sex)
1951	Bantu Authorities Act (created government structures for separate black homelands)
	Separate Registration of Voters Bill (attempts to remove coloreds from common voters roll, but was blocked by the courts)
	Prevention of Illegal Squatting Act
	Native Building Workers Act and Native Services Levy (facilitates slum clearance and the building of black urban housing by black builders. White employers forced to pay for this)
1952	Abolition of Passes and Documents Act (creates Reference Book as internal passport for black migration control)
	Native Laws Amendment Act (limits number of blacks with the right to live permanently in "white cities")
	Separate Amenities Act
	Urban Bantu Authorities Bill (defeated in Parliament; reintroduced 1961)
	Resettlement of Natives Act (used to forcibly move Johannesburg blacks to Soweto)

1953	Bantu Education Act (places all black schools under Bantu Education Department)
1954	Bantu Urban Areas Act (tightens migration/"influx control")
1955	Tomlinson Commission Report (proposes black homelands model)
	Negotiated closure of Simons Town naval base removes last British military forces from South Africa
1956	Right of appeal against "influx control" removed
	Industrial Conciliation Act (promoted segregated trade unions and created job reservation)
	Coloreds placed on separate voters roll
1957	British flag and national anthem ceased to have any standing in South Africa
	Eiselen line creates colored employment preference zone. Black migration to Cape Town and Port Elizabeth thereby discouraged (and "illegal" black migrants deported if caught)
1959	Promotion of Bantu Self-Government Act (created legal framework for internal decolonization. Black territorial governments created with jurisdiction over courts of law, education, welfare, and social services. The act also abolished the three Members of Parliament representing blacks in the central Parliament)
	Bantu Investment Corporation Act (to promote homeland investment to create job opportunities there)
	Extension of University Education Act (creates separate universities for blacks, coloreds, and Indians)
1960	British Sterling is replaced with a South African currency (the Rand)
1961	South Africa becomes a Republic
1962	The Urban Councils Act (created elected urban black local governments *with ties* to homelands)
1963	Departments of Indian and Colored Affairs created; Indians become South African citizens
1966	Prevention of Improper Interference Act (stops whites from participating in black politics)
1967	Physical Planning and Utilization of Resources Act (allows government to stop industrial development in "controlled areas" like Johannesburg and Port Elizabeth in order to redirect new economic development to homelands and homeland border areas)
1968	Colored Person Representative Council created (a separate government for coloreds; disbanded in 1980)
	Prohibition of Political Interference Act (stops coloreds and blacks from participating in white politics)
1970	National States Citizenship Act (makes all blacks automatically citizens of one of ten homelands)

1977	Community Councils Act (created elected urban black local authorities *autonomous* of homelands. This overturned apartheid orthodoxy by effectively recognizing black permanence in "white cities" and giving blacks a vote in "white" South Africa)
1982	Black Local Authorities Act (created full-fledged black municipalities with elected councils)
1984	Tricameral parliament reforms (granted coloreds and Indians representation in a consociational central government)

CHAPTER 3

Apartheid in Practice

The twentieth century was a messy interregnum between nineteenth-century European (especially British) domination and the eventual emergence of the Pax Americana. One element of shifting power across the Atlantic was the Atlantic Charter,[1] which reconfigured the post–World War II world by ending Europe's mercantilist empires, and replacing them with independent states. The new states, operating within the administrative boundaries drawn by European imperialists, were meshed into a world-trading system with the United States at its heart. Institutions like the International Monetary Fund (IMF), the General Agreement on Tariffs and Trade, and the United Nations (UN), facilitated postcolonial global coordination. The newly created states, led by Westernized development-oriented elites, were encouraged to adopt ideals and institutions valued by Americans (e.g., majoritarian democracy). Apartheid was the Afrikaner's response to this new global order.

Afrikaner nationalists responded by rejecting continuance of the British-made unified South African state (administrative region), and by refusing to adopt majoritarian democracy within a unified state. This response was premised on two arguments: (1) British imperialism had thrown together people who did not "belong together," and (2) majoritarianism in a unified state would render South Africa's white minority politically powerless and thus unable to maintain its distinctive Western culture in the face of Africanization pressures. Instead, apartheid advocated partition. The problem was, by 1948 racial capitalism had already economically integrated South Africa's population and disrupted the region's former ethnic geography. Hence, partition would require moving millions of people to create geographically discrete ethnic blocks. Relocating people and enforcing apartheid's migration policy necessarily involved repression and undermining existent civil liberties. It also meant dislocation and human suffering. In this sense, apartheid was like so many twentieth-century political projects[2]—the creation of modernist social engineers prepared to sacrifice others to their intellectual dreams.[3]

But in 1948, the National Party (NP) was not yet ready to implement a partition model because it had not expected to win the election. On coming to power, the NP possessed a set of intellectualized principles of apartheid, but no blueprint for implementing the partition model. Hence, early apartheid (1948–1958) became an ad hoc affair. As Posel[4] notes, when apartheid emerged during the first few years of NP rule, it reflected a number of influences, including the original intellectual model, struggles within the NP, and forces outside the NP that contested the partition plan. Importantly, the NP was in a very weak position in the early 1950s, and feared losing the next election. The party was fully aware that implementing its total partition would generate considerable opposition,[5] which could cost them the next election. Hence, holding back on implementing its radical plan until the party was in a stronger position was strategically wise. The NP's weakness was also apparent in Parliament, where the United Party (UP)—representing the interests of Anglo corporates[6] (who saw partition as undermining capitalist interests)—was able to block and modify[7] a number of NP attempts to legislatively enact the apartheid plan. The NP also used much of the first half of the 1950s simply getting its hands on the levers of power and learning how to use them. During this learning period, the Tomlinson Commission and apartheid intellectuals (now organized in the South African Bureau of Racial Affairs/SABRA) fleshed out how partition might be practically implemented. Ultimately, it was not until the late 1950s that Christian nationalism's social engineers had fully operationalized their "apartheid idea" into a practical partition model and positioned themselves into the state's administrative machinery to execute this model. However, even after 1958, practical apartheid never matched the theoretical model, because it continued to require pragmatic adjustments to contextual pressures. Ultimately, apartheid never congealed into a clear definitive plan—it was always more like a "process" as real-world apartheid mutated through three phases during its 40-year existence.

STAGE 1: AFRIKANER SOVEREIGNTY AND RERANKING MILNER'S MODEL

The NP won the 1948 election under D.F. Malan by advocating apartheid. Malan's apartheid ("apartness") model had two concerns: (1) establishing an independent state over which Afrikaners had sovereign control, and (2) ending the control Anglos had exercised over Afrikaners since the Boer War. Malan personally showed little concern with the issue of race; blacks are not even mentioned in his autobiography, which focuses on the Afrikaner struggle against Anglo domination. Under Malan, Afrikaner nationalists concentrated on:

- Creating spaces for Afrikaner "own-ness," particularly in relation to Anglos.
- Reranking Afrikaners upward within racial capitalism and ending Afrikaner poverty.
- Learning how to get their hands on the levers of power.
- Finding ways to win the next election (which was far from assured).
- Creating the legal framework for differentiating South Africans into "population groups," with a view to separating these groups.
- Dismantling those features of Anglo hegemony that most concerned Afrikaner nationalists, including: English dominance over Afrikaans, Anglo migration (regarded as a means to culturally swamp Afrikaners), the symbols of Anglo power, mission schools (seen to produce Anglicized blacks who advocated majoritarian democracy), the pressures driving Afrikaners into the poor neighborhoods of culturally mixed cities where they lost their cultural identity, and the way capitalism encouraged black migration from across Southern Africa into urban slums. The NP believed these slums were dangerous because they created recruiting grounds for communism, and threatened to swamp "white South Africa" in a flood of black migrants.

Apartheid's first phase was consequently characterized by seven features. First, under Daniel Malan and Johannes Strijdom, the NP was centrally concerned with challenging Milner's ranking system, which bestowed second-class status upon Afrikaners. Because the Transvaal NP relied heavily upon Afrikaner working-class voters, the party heavily promoted Afrikaner economic upliftment. Verwoerd—a former social work professor—was a key player in this Transvaal NP "upliftment camp." The NP effectively instituted an affirmative-action program to rerank Afrikaners upward by providing employment opportunities through "job reservation" (for poor Afrikaners), and through offering employment on the (state-owned) railways and civil service. Although generally low-paid jobs, they provided stable home environments for children entering the expanding Afrikaner education system. The building of Afrikaans-language schools, colleges, and universities, plus a national Afrikaans radio service, was another feature of the NP's reranking program. This NP-run reranking exercise, launched in the 1950s, was so successful that within 25 years, a large Afrikaner middle class inhabited the expanding suburban landscape of South Africa's cities. The children and grandchildren of an Afrikaner working class and lumpen proletariat (who had harbored strong anticapitalist feelings)[8] were thus educated, embourgeoised, and transformed into a procapitalist middle class. A third feature of the NP's challenge to Milner's ranking was the enforcement of Afrikaans-English bilingualism, with Anglo children compelled to learn Afrikaans at school.

Significantly, during phase one, the NP left the basic outlines of Milner's racial capitalism untouched: the mines continued to run on cheap black migrant labor, and the system of white supremacy and segregation (characteristic of the Milner-to-Smuts era) was left in place. Given the strong anticapitalist sentiments of the NP's poorer constituents during the 1950s, this lack of NP intervention against Anglo capitalism is noteworthy. It was partly due to Malan's goal of maintaining Afrikaner unity at all costs—"unity" required that the (small) Afrikaner business sector (which bankrolled the Cape NP) and prosperous (procapitalist) farmers should not be alienated by making moves that would have appealed to the Afrikaner lumpen proletariat and workers.[9] So instead of attacking racial capitalism, the 1950s NP opted for a different form of state interventionism—the Afrikaner underclass were upgraded in a parallel set of Afrikaner infrastructures (alongside those of Anglo South Africans) by an affirmative-action program paid for by taxing businesses (mostly owned by Anglos opposed to the NP's state-interventionism). However, except for taxation and some "job reservation," racial capitalism was left unscathed by affirmative action. And as compensation for taxation, the state facilitated the exploitation of black workers so businesses remained profitable. Hence, for the first decade of NP rule, the basic outlines of the British-built state and economy were hardly touched. However, although racial capitalism looked unaltered, significant changes were under way—Afrikaners were systematically reranked upward within the existing socioeconomic order; the NP placed its bureaucrats into position and learned to run the bureaucracy; and behind the scenes, apartheid ideologues (centered on Verwoerd) developed a plan for transforming the partition ideal into a practical program for dismembering the British-built unified state and economic order.

A second feature of early apartheid was legally defining "population groups" in order to create a legal framework for cultural separation and territorial partition. The latter involved outlawing cross-racial social interaction through what came to be called "petty apartheid" legislation (e.g., the Mixed Marriages and Separate Amenities Acts). This legislation appears to have been inspired by middle-class Afrikaners (especially Calvinist Church pastors and social workers) who were deeply concerned that many Afrikaners lost their cultural identity and "morality" in the poor neighborhoods of South Africa's culturally mixed cities. Many middle-class NP activists appeared not to trust their fellow Afrikaners to behave "correctly" in the cities. Apparently, the Afrikaner underclass needed to be "rescued," not only from the ravages of Anglo capitalism, but also from their own incapacity to police themselves. Consequently, NP middle-class activists spent much of the 1950s "rescuing" the Afrikaner underclass by building CNO (*Christelik-Nasionale Onderwys*/Christian National Education) schools to teach their children the importance of "own-ness," discipline, Christian national morality, and a puritan work ethic. Simultaneously, their parents were provided with jobs and nationalist trade unions to protect and guide them. But, in case this was not enough, legislation was enacted enforcing Calvinist (antigambling and antipromiscuity) moralities, as well as petty apartheid legislation enforcing loyalty to "own-ness."

Third, early apartheid involved the widespread demolition of slums. The NP invested considerable energy into the related policies of "orderly urbanization," slum clearance, and migration control. Apartheid town planning built cities wherein each "population group" had its own highly planned orderly neighborhood or "Group Area" (see figure 2.3). The NP's first forced removals were associated with slum clearance—blacks were forcibly moved to new townships like Soweto, Indians to Chatsworth, and coloreds to Mitchell's Plain. As Bantu Affairs minister,[10] Verwoerd (drawing upon his former social work theories) argued that it was imperative to demolish existing slums and stop new slums from growing, because such areas created the conditions for communist mobilization. Verwoerd forced a reluctant Anglo business sector to pay for building the new state-owned black housing. He also proposed stopping new slum growth by halting the free-for-all black migration to the cities (that had emerged under Smuts), and ending urban unemployment by restricting the number of blacks allowed to live in the cities.[11] Only employed blacks and their families would be allowed to stay. Unemployment resulted in deportation to the black homelands—that is, unemployment was exported to rural areas. This unleashed upheaval and suffering in both urban and rural black areas, and also created bad public relations images for the NP—especially those associated with demolishing Sophiatown.

Fourth, early apartheid saw Cape coloreds removed from the common voter roll. In 1951, the NP passed legislation removing coloreds from the voter rolls of "white" constituencies, placing them on a roll to elect five "separate" colored representatives to Parliament. Apartheid's social engineers seemed to face their greatest conceptual difficulties regarding coloreds because cultural proximity between coloreds and Afrikaners made it difficult to justify placing coloreds in a separate "population group." Of all the apartheid ideologues, only one, namely Cronje, justified colored separateness in openly racist terms. The others either fudged the issue (perhaps revealing discomfort) or deployed one of two "pragmatic" reasons to explain the NP's treatment of coloreds, that is:

- When the NP came to power, some Cape coloreds were enfranchised. Because they tended to vote for the UP, colored voters seriously threatened the NP's reelection chances (by impacting on the outcome of nine parliamentary seats).[12]

In 1948, the NP came to power by forming a coalition with the Afrikaner Party, and many doubted they could win the next election. Hence, in 1951, the NP tried to expel them from the "white" political system. The courts declared the 1951 Act unconstitutional because it was not passed by two-thirds of both Houses of Parliament. The next six years witnessed a struggle between the courts and Parliament over this issue, which also gave rise to (white) protest movements like the Civil Rights League, Torch Commando, and Black Sash. In 1956, after altering the composition of the Senate, the NP finally mustered the two-thirds vote required to move coloreds to a separate voter roll. This had the effect of driving many coloreds into a political alliance with black South Africans, despite the cultural proximity between Afrikaners and coloreds.[13]

- Coloreds were seen as the "thin edge of the wedge"[14]—mixed-race marriage/sex was quite common in the slums that emerged after the Boer War, and apartheid theorists saw this as a direct threat to the demographic survival of Afrikaners, who as a "*klein volkie*" (small people) could not afford to lose numbers to "another group."[15] If coloreds were allowed into the "white" system, it created a gap for Afrikaners to be disloyal to their "own-ness" and thereby weaken Afrikaner numbers. Coloreds became the victims of this convoluted thinking.

Fifth, during apartheid's first phase, the continuities with Milner-to-Smuts segregation were strong. In many ways, the Malan period had more in common with segregation (and white supremacy) than with what later emerged as Verwoerdian apartheid (partition).[16] At a 1953 election rally, Malan said "apartheid" simply meant "segregation,"[17] and in 1954, he reportedly complained that, under Verwoerd (as Bantu Afffairs minister), the apartheid idea had "got out of hand."[18] Malan's real passion was for replacing Anglo hegemony with Afrikaner hegemony, and he appears to have been only marginally concerned with the issue of "blacks." On one occasion, he even rejected full partition as an end goal.[19] Certainly, Malan and Strijdom wanted to stop black migration into the cities and unscramble the culturally mixed cities created by Anglo capitalism. But under Malan, this basically meant more rigorously codifying and enforcing segregation[20] policies first developed in British Natal.[21] Ultimately, Malan simply assumed whites could and would continue to rule over blacks (a widespread perception in the early 1950s). However, apartheid intellectuals looked further into the future and realized that in the wake of the Atlantic Charter this was not possible; hence, their advocacy of partition. However, even if Malan was not committed to partition, his government created the conditions wherein those intellectuals advocating partition, such as SABRA, Verwoerd, and Eiselen, could flourish and nurture their ideas to fruition. Malan also appointed the Tomlinson Commission soon after coming to power, and Frederik Tomlinson's report[22] became the blueprint for establishing black homelands and apartheid-as-partition. However, significantly, Verwoerd originally rejected three key aspects of Tomlinson's report, namely, allowing white capitalists to invest in black homelands, replacing communal land tenure with individual tenure, and a proposal that the government spend millions developing black homelands to create economically viable states.[23] Although he later recanted, Verwoerd's initial refusal[24] to implement these recommendations significantly crippled Tomlinson's partition plan.

Sixth, one of the earliest Malan government moves was appointing the Eiselen Commission to examine black education. Werner Eiselen's report led to the closure of mission schools because they were seen to produce Anglicized blacks—that is, the very Westernized black elite who were demanding the implementation of Atlantic Charter decolonization and majoritarian democracy. Eiselen advocated mother-tongue education in black primary schools to promote "own-ness" amongst Zulus, Xhosas, Tswanas, Pedi, and others. This mirrored the NP's drive for Afrikaans mother-tongue education and their general passion for winding back Anglicization. The NP moved quickly to create Bantu Education to replace mission schools and disseminate the values of "separate development" and "own-ness" among black children. The party invested enormous resources into building this Bantu Education ideological infrastructure—that is, in 1953 there were 800,000 black schools,[25] by 1963 there were 1.8 million, and thereafter black schools were expanded even more rapidly.[26] If apartheid-as-partition was to work, blacks had to be educated so they could run their separate states, but this created the danger of building a large rebellious black youth. This is precisely what happened:

- Separate black universities gave rise to Black Consciousness.
- Colored and Indian universities became hothouses of Marxist thinking.
- The huge Bantu Education schooling system ultimately became central to the 1980s township (youth-led) revolt.

Despite the NP's rapid expansion of black education, Westernized blacks and Anglo liberals were highly critical of Bantu Education because it promoted black vernacular languages and ethnic identities rather than English proficiency and Western acculturation, and was seen to be of inferior quality to white education. The central flaw with the NP's black education system was that funding levels were consistently inadequate for the size of the educational problem.

Seventh, early apartheid revealed that the NP was serious about maintaining Afrikaner sovereignty, and any political group or player seriously challenging this sovereignty would be harshly dealt with. By their very nature, certain ideologies contradicted Christian nationalism's promotion of "own-ness." In particular, the NP opposed anyone advocating socialism, majoritarian democracy within a unified South Africa, and cosmopolitanism. But, because communism was deemed the absolute antithesis to

Christian nationalism, the NP's first political repression was directed at the Communist Party, which was banned in 1950,[27] and all those classified as communists were driven out of trade unions. The result was that thousands of black communists joined the African National Congress (ANC). This ironically helped forge the black nationalist-communist alliance that dominated antiapartheid resistance for the next 40 years. One of this alliance's first actions was the 1952 "defiance campaign" against NP celebrations marking Dutch settlement at Cape Town in 1652. The 1952 mass protests, which effectively initiated the antiapartheid struggle, simply increased white support for the NP at the 1953 elections. The party responded to the defiance campaign by enacting new security laws, raiding its political opponents' homes and offices, and arresting key political organizers. Although this repression crushed the defiance campaign, it precipitated the Congress Alliance (between black, colored, and Indian activists), increased ANC membership, and reshaped the ANC around a new vision—the 1955 Freedom Charter, which "translated" the Atlantic Charter into a South African political agenda. This, in turn, precipitated more arrests and bannings, plus the (1957 to 1961) Treason Trial of 156 political activists (including Mandela) who were charged with attempting to overthrow the state and establish a communist regime. The Supreme Court's "not guilty" verdict clearly shocked the NP, generating its disillusionment with the court system, and its inclination to thereafter deploy extra legal methods to fight its opponents.

Ultimately, apartheid's first phase was a painful and negative period for nonwhites—pass laws were strengthened and more rigorously enforced, forced removals began, mission schools were closed, coloreds were taken off the common voter role, petty apartheid signage became a daily humiliation for nonwhite people, and the NP demonstrated that it was prepared to deploy repression against its opponents.

STAGE 2: SOCIAL ENGINEERING AND INTERNAL DECOLONIZATION

Phase two began when Verwoerd became prime minister in 1958. Verwoerd was a radical, intent on deconstructing the British-built unified state. He believed that applying the Atlantic Charter model to a unified South Africa would turn Afrikaners into a powerless minority in a black-ruled state. But he recognized that Atlantic Charterism and decolonization had become virtually unchallengeable within the intellectual climate of post–World War II. Consequently, he adopted the rhetoric of decolonization—arguing that British imperialists had conquered South African peoples, whom the NP would now free from colonial bondage by giving them independence in their own homelands. Verwoerdians proposed apartheid as a form of internal decolonization, and set about planning South Africa's partition (believing this was the only way Afrikaners could retain sovereignty over any state of their own).

Apartheid-as-partition necessarily also involved deconstructing the racial-capitalist economic order created by Milner's kindergarten because it was premised upon a single administrative unit and single market, plus the flow of cheap black migrant labor into the country's economic heartland. Verwoerd's dream of building a white (Afrikaner) state in Africa meant not only breaking up the existing British-built state, but also eventually replacing black labor with white labor in Milner's economic heartland. For liberals and the corporate sector, these Verwoerdian policies were anticapitalist because they involved massive state interventionism; disrupting the free market with new boundaries, barriers, regulations, and subsidies (so increasing the price of labor); and expanding bureaucracy. Verwoerd and Eiselen did indeed construct a huge state machinery staffed by apartheid intellectuals, social engineers, and bureaucrats, but it never succeeded in partitioning South Africa, partly because pressures for economic integration along with Anglo corporate resistance against partition were simply too powerful.

Verwoerdian apartheid characterized the prime ministerships of Hendrik Verwoerd and John Vorster. Apartheid's second phase was characterized by six features:

First, if Afrikaner reranking was the key feature of phase one, the issue of black enfranchisement became the key issue in phase two. By the late 1950s, it was clear that Africa was to be decolonized, and Africa's Westernized middle classes (ironically, precisely the group being disinherited by apartheid) were to inherit the new independent African states. This emboldened South Africa's urban black activists to agitate for political change, and generated a sense of siege among white Africans. In 1960, British prime minister MacMillan exacerbated white angst when, during a speech in South Africa's Parliament, he warned white South Africans that they would not be able to resist the "winds of change" blowing across Africa. Verwoerd rejected MacMillan's suggestion that South Africa should adopt majoritarian democracy, arguing this would involve political and cultural suicide for white Africans. MacMillan's speech simply strengthened Verwoerdian resolve that South Africa be partitioned so blacks could be enfranchised in ways not rendering white South Africans a powerless minority in a unified state. Consequently, apartheid's phase two was about partition (not segregation). This partition plan—often called "grand apartheid"—was set in motion by the 1959 Promotion of Bantu Self-Government Act. This precipitated Transkeian self-government (1963) and the "independence" of the TBVC states: Transkei (1976), Bophuthatswana (1977), Venda (1979), and Ciskei (1981). At great expense, these states were provided with all the paraphernalia of independence—for example, capital cities, parliaments, bureaucracies, independence stadiums, universities, armies, and embassies in Pretoria. When other countries refused to recognize their independence, the Verwoerdians mounted public relations campaigns arguing that the TBVC states were just as viable as Lesotho and Swaziland. As part of their salesmanship, the NP argued that apartheid was trying to replicate the European Economic Community model—where each nation would have its own political infrastructures tied together in an economic union facilitating economic cooperation and peaceful coexistence.[28]

Effectively, the Verwoerdians set up a neocolonial relationship to the "independent" homelands. The Verwoerdians simply operated, on a smaller scale, a system resembling how the United States exercised hegemony over Latin America through comprador ruling elites. In the process, nine million blacks (both inside and outside these homelands) lost their South African citizenship—for example, all Tswanas were now deemed citizens of Bophuthatswana (or Botswana); hence, even if they lived in Johannesburg, they were told to exercise their political ambitions in Bophuthatswana. The system gave them a vote, but gave it to them "elsewhere."

A second feature of Verwoerdian apartheid was the growth of a huge bureaucracy to manage land transfers and population resettlements. Land transfers were set in motion in 1955, when the NP opted to implement the Tomlinson Commission recommendations to buy 16,307 sq km of "white land" to be added to the homelands[29] and simultaneously remove 1,615 sq km of so-called "black spots" from "white South Africa." Further, during the "homeland consolidation" process, another 3,153 sq km of "black land" was swapped with "white land."[30] This process of swapping land plus "black spot" removals involved forcibly uprooting black communities and relocating them to homelands in order to create the conditions for apartheid's partition vision. Further, a huge migration-control policing system was developed to find and deport "illegal migrants." Because this task was allocated to the South African Police, the police became associated with one of the most painful aspects of apartheid. For black people, policemen became persecutors who stopped them from seeking jobs in the cities, forcibly resettled many, and arrested millions for contravening pass laws.

Third, under Verwoerdian apartheid, repression deepened. The one group of South Africans who could never reconcile themselves to apartheid were urban blacks who had been Westernized (and Anglicized). The NP's policies offered them nothing but pain because partition gave them only three choices: (1) move to distant black homelands, where they were allowed to aspire to becoming the ruling and/or propertied elite; (2) remain in "white cities" as (foreign) "guest workers," where they had no political rights and no right to strike to improve their conditions; or (3) fight the system. If they opted to stay in the cities, it meant enduring an environment the NP made unpleasant for black people (to encourage migration to the homelands). However, moving to the homelands meant the pain of migration and dislocation, as well as swapping exciting city environments for rural backwaters. For Westernized blacks, it also meant leaving behind Westernized areas, where they felt at home, and relocating to areas of traditional African culture, where they did not fit. Ironically, the NP came to power just as the Atlantic Charter's decolonization agenda began to be implemented, and it was precisely South Africa's Westernized blacks who stood to benefit most from it. For this reason, South Africa's Westernized blacks naturally aligned themselves with the 1950s–1960s decolonization agenda, and turned to resistance (see chapter 5). Consequently, any political organization capable of mobilizing and organizing South Africa's Westernized black population became dangerous for the NP, and any organization advocating black nationalism, black majority rule, or socialism automatically became a threat to apartheid's partition plan. Ultimately, three organizations were deemed dangerous enough to be outlawed—the African National Congress (ANC), the Pan African Congress (PAC), and the South African Communist Party (SACP). John Vorster, as police minister (1961–1966), built a security police system and enacted legislation creating an authoritarian state. Vorster's legislation empowered the police and security police to harass organizations and detain or ban their leaders. At Sharpeville in 1960 and Soweto in 1976, the police also demonstrated a preparedness to shoot demonstrators. From the perspective of Westernized urban blacks, South Africa became a police state. This only served to increase the popularity of the NP among white voters—with the NP learning to portraying itself as the only organization tough enough to defend white African interests against an "unholy alliance" of "black radicals," "communists," "terrorists," and "bleeding-heart Westerners." But, ironically, when Vorster became prime minister, he showed how, once created, an authoritarian state/security police system could also be turned against those who created it—that is, Vorster began using the security police against those opposing him inside Afrikaner nationalist ranks.[31]

Fourth, Verwoerdian apartheid represented a modernist social engineering project that drew upon the then-popular discourses of development and nation building. But whereas Africa's other development states sought to build unified economies and political systems, the Verwoerdian version of nation building involved creating a number of different (separate) nations and nation states. The very term "separate development" encoded the dual visions of "nation-building development" tied to partitioning the country. This made "separate development" a profoundly dangerous ideology for Africa's development elites trying to hold their fragile new states together because, if apartheid could be made to work, it raised the spectre of ethnic minorities all across

Africa adopting this "development-plus-partition" model to demand their own self-determination (i.e., breaking up the Afro-Asian states created by European imperialism).

Significantly, Verwoerd's own view of "development" went through a metamorphosis. He originally rejected the Tomlinson Commission's recommendations for massive state expenditure to develop the homelands, plus permitting white capitalists to invest in black homelands. He argued that black people should develop themselves and find their own capital.[32] But, eventually, Verwoerdians realized that this impeded homeland development, and blocked the likelihood of ever building viable homelands able to attract a majority of black people away from "white cities." So the Verwoerdians launched the border industry concept and established a Permanent Committee for the Location of Industries/PCLI. This PCLI attempted to decentralize South Africa's industries to homeland border areas through a mix of obstacles[33] to industrial development/expansion in Johannesburg and Port Elizabeth, plus subsidies for industries relocating to border zones. From this grew a number of black cities just inside the homelands (e.g., Mabopane) connected by highways, commuter trains, and busses to industrial zones on the South African side of the border. This facilitated the growth of permanently urbanized black communities—that is, workers commuting daily to South African factories, and returning nightly to their families, who were technically living in "another country." This facilitated large-scale urbanization and modernization of black South Africans plus the growth of trade unionism in these new homeland cites. By the late 1960s, the Verwoerdians went further, and allowed white investors to create jobs inside the homelands, for example, building tourist meccas like Sun City.[34]

Apartheid-as-partition necessarily involved rearranging the economy. This undermined the interests of many South African capitalists because it threatened to make labor more expensive and break up South Africa's single market. Under Verwoerd there was consequently tension between organized business and the government—that is, businesses viewed partition as jeopardizing the economy,[35] while Verwoerd believed partition was more important than profits. As he said: "the desire for economic gain could not be allowed to take precedence over more urgent considerations . . . [namely] the interests of preserving white civilization."[36] Ultimately, under the Verwoerdians, South Africa was modernized and developed and became a highly urbanized and industrial state. However, this development was skewed by social engineers, who left a legacy of cities and industrial development in places where this would not otherwise have occurred.

A fifth feature of Verwoerdian apartheid was the enormous energy invested into deliberately engineering into existence new (homeland-based) ethnic nationalisms. Eiselen's education policy of mother-tongue education did much to promote "own-ness," as did apartheid's codification of nine South African black languages and the explosion of a print literature in these languages (tied to schoolbook production). This encouraged the growth of ethnic identity among Zulus, Tswanas, Pedis, and others. These identities were greatly strengthened by Radio Bantu broadcasting in nine languages. The creation of the symbols of homeland "independence," plus homeland patronage networks (which delivered real material benefits to homeland middle classes) further strengthened these new identities, so that eventually homeland identities did take root.[37] These new black identities were not popular among urban blacks in the "white cities," where they were dismissed as "tribalism," and attacked for being associated with black "sellouts" to apartheid.

A sixth feature of apartheid's second phase was the gradual emergence of some "white solidarity."[38] Given how central Afrikaner assertiveness against (and even hostility toward) Anglos had featured in the 1950s, the emergence of a measure of Anglo-Afrikaner cooperation in phase two was remarkable. When Verwoerd declared South Africa a republic in 1961, Afrikaners were jubilant because it signaled both "independence" from Britain and seemingly irreversible Afrikaner control of the country. One consequence was that Afrikaners no longer felt threatened by assimilation into Anglo culture, and so became more open to regarding South African Anglos as partners in a common state. Rhodesia's 1965 declaration of independence from Britain sealed this growing cooperation because many Southern African Anglos felt "betrayed" by Britain, while many Afrikaners now saw local Anglos as potential allies rather than representatives of a foreign empire. Vorster went further than Verwoerd in gaining Anglo support for the NP, although only when P.W. Botha became leader were the last remnants of NP hostility to Hoggenheimer/Anglo business finally abandoned. By 1987, 49 percent of South African Anglos voted for the NP.[39]

During Verwoerd's era, the upward reranking of Afrikaners through affirmative action continued. But by the late 1960s, Afrikaners no longer needed affirmative action or job reservation, as they increasingly settled into suburban lifestyles indistinguishable from Anglo suburbs. Within the NP, this meant an ever-declining influence of Afrikaner workers (the group most commonly demanding "protection from blacks"), and the growing influence of professionals and businessmen. Within Vorster's NP, this generated tensions between *verkramptes* ("closed thinkers," advocating Verwoerdian apartheid) and *verligtes* ("the enlightened," open to new thinking).

Verwoerd's assassination in 1966 did not end the dream of Verwoerdian apartheid because Vorster continued implementing the "grand apartheid" partition model. But whereas Verwoerd was unbending in his ideological commitment to partition and absolute separation, Vorster initiated the first tentative shifts away from apartheid dogma. A less-zealous Vorster relaxed enforcement of the Mixed Marriages and Separate Amenities Acts, gave "Section 10" urban blacks leasehold property rights in "white" cities, and appointed the Wiehahn Commission into labor relations. Wiehahn proposed ending "job reservation" (protecting white workers) and advocated trade union rights for black workers. Vorster's tentative reforms were a response to changes within the NP plus pressures from outside. The costs of deconstructing Milner's economic order were beginning to tell, and not everyone in the NP believed Verwoerdian apartheid was practically implementable. There was also growing resistance from Afrikaner farmers to homeland consolidation[40] (as white farmers were compelled to sell their farms for incorporation into homelands), and Anglo-and-Afrikaner organized businesses were complaining about the costs of apartheid and the labor problems it generated. Whereas Verwoerd had resisted business complaints, under Vorster, the NP began to listen, hence initiating its slow ideological journey away from state interventionism toward neoliberalism.

Vorster also responded to the realization that "grand apartheid" was not working—that is, the urban black population was not "returning" to the homelands, and was deeply hostile to separate development. Further, black population growth was much faster than expected,[41] possibly due in part to illegal migration from Southern Africa.[42] This population growth undermined the demographic logic of Tomlinson's model because the homelands were designed for smaller populations and could not support the increased numbers. Vorster's early 1970s response was to intensify the border industries scheme, speed up the building of homeland towns/cities, and tighten influx controls.[43] Tightening up on apartheid-as-migration control simply intensified the black experience of apartheid as a cruel and repressive system. A more considered response to these demographic shifts flowed from the next NP leader, P.W. Botha.

The Verwoerdians/*verkramptes* lost control of the NP as a result of the "information scandal" when their leader, Connie Mulder, was discredited for the "irregular use" of state funds for covert proapartheid public relations projects in South Africa and the United States. This scandal (engineered by *verligtes* media leaks) unseated Vorster, destroyed Mulder's career, and shifted the NP leftward. The Verwoerdians finally abandoned the NP in 1982, when they left to form the Conservative Party.

STAGE 3: CONSOCIATIONALISM AND MILITARIZED REFORM

P.W. Botha became prime minister in 1978. Under Botha, the NP mutated into an organization that would have been unrecognizable to 1950s Afrikaner nationalists. Botha inherited an electorate radically transformed by 30 years of NP rule. NP rule created an educated, embourgeoised Afrikaner middle class, while the Afrikaner working class shrunk (as the black working class grew). By the 1980s, the NP's core constituency consisted of middle-class Afrikaner-and-Anglo suburbanites,[44] and there was also a small Afrikaner bourgeoisie, the emergence of which played a significant role in the NP's shifting away from state interventionism toward neoliberalism. This journey began in the late 1960s, when Anglo America Corporation (AAC) practically handed over its General Mining and Finance Corporation to Sanlam (the heart of Afrikaner capitalism).[45] For the first time, Afrikaners had a significant stake in the minerals heart of South Africa's economy. Thereafter, "slowly but surely, the Afrikaner-controlled corporations were co-opted—especially ideologically—by the English-controlled corporations."[46] This co-option was powerfully consolidated in 1976, when AAC allowed Afrikaner corporates to take control of Union Mining, placing 30 percent of gold mining in Afrikaner hands. AAC's Harry Oppenheimer had apparently decided the time had come to open the doors of the business establishment to Afrikaners in the hope that this would "help shore up a moderating tendency in Afrikaner nationalism."[47] Oppenheimer's 1976 co-option strategy worked—the consolidation of an Afrikaner bourgeoisie created an important new *verligte* voice within the NP.

A seminal moment came in 1978, when the NP abandoned its working-class constituency after Afrikaner miners went on strike to defend job reservation. The NP backed management to crush this strike, thereby losing its working-class supporters.[48] Consequently, from the 1981 elections onward, the NP was a middle-class party representing both Afrikaners and Anglos.[49] Under Botha, the NP reinvented itself by discarding Afrikaner nationalist and anti-Hoggenheimer/corporatist rhetoric, and adopting neoliberalism, "orderly reform," and "law and order" as its platforms. The 1979 Carlton and 1981 Good Hope Conferences saw Botha's NP cement an alliance with the corporate sector and adopt the rhetoric of "free enterprise," "deregulation," and "winding back the state."[50] So, while for Verwoerdians, partition took precedence over economic considerations, under Botha, capitalist economic principles reasserted themselves.

Under Botha, the NP confronted the fact that separate development was in trouble:

- The 1976 Soweto uprising revealed the depth of hostility among urban blacks.
- In response to this Soweto uprising, the corporate sector established the Urban Foundation (UF) in 1977, which aimed to stabilize capitalism by building an urban black middle class. The UF (which became a pressure group for ending apartheid's policies toward urban blacks) convinced Botha that apartheid was damaging South Africa's economy.

- The rapid rise of black trade unionism (following Wiehahn's reforms) signaled the emergence of an organized urban black power base.
- Despite "influx control," the 1960s–1970s economic boom drew a flood of black migrants, that is, apartheid failed to create any geographic base for a "white state."
- In 1976, Buthelezi created the Black Unity Front with other homeland leaders rejecting independence. When KwaZulu, Lebowa, and Gazankulu refused independence, it meant that five million Zulus, two million Pedis, and 600,000 Tsongas would remain South African citizens, thereby ending the dream of ever turning South Africa into a state where five million whites were the demographic majority.

Between 1976 and 1982 the NP was in ferment as debates raged about whether apartheid was actually implementable. There was much soul-searching, as many Afrikaners lost faith in apartheid. In 1952, Van Wyk Louw had predicted that if apartheid ever became obviously unjust, it would be abandoned by Afrikaner intellectuals, causing its disintegration.[51] In the late 1970s, this disintegrative process began, which led to a series of NP-appointed commissions of inquiry—Theron (1976) into colored affairs, Riekert (1979) into labor shortages, Wiehahn (1979) into labor relations, and De Lange (1981) into black education. In 1978, the Bantu Administration and Development Department was renamed the Plural Affairs Department, signaling a shift away from separate development (partition) toward the consociational notion of pluralism and pluralist cooperation. With this came the new NP rhetoric of "confederation"—that is, South Africa was likened to Western Europe, where national groups retained political autonomy despite integration into an economic union.[52] An outcome of the debates and soul-searching was that Afrikanerdom fractured during the 1980s into conservatives (who criticized the NP for abandoning apartheid), liberals and leftists (who believed the NP was reforming too slowly), and centrists (who continued to support the NP). This fracturing meant that the NP only remained in power because many Anglos now voted for them.

In 1982, the NP under Botha reached the seminal conclusion that apartheid-as-partition was unimplementable—they concluded that South Africa was a single country requiring a single government.[53] *Internally*, the NP abandoned Verwoerdian apartheid in 1982. This created the problem of formulating an alternative reform package and selling it to South Africans. Botha opted for top-down reform—political change would be centrally managed from his office, and order would be militarily maintained during the transition out of apartheid. This vision of political change and reform was influenced by the ideas of American academic Samuel Huntington,[54] whose work was being widely discussed by the NP's intelligentsia. In February 1983, Botha established a special cabinet committee, under Chris Heunis (constitutional affairs minister), which was given three problems to solve,[55] namely, how to:

- extend political rights to blacks in ways that would not turn whites into a powerless minority in a black-ruled state,
- protect minority rights in a majoritarian democracy, and
- maintain law and order during a reform process anticipated to unleash an explosion of expectations-driven turmoil.

Ultimately, the NP settled upon consociationalism as their preferred postapartheid model. Significantly, the consociational model developed by Dutch-born Arendt Lijphart,[56] was grounded in *verzuiling* logic. These *verzuiling* roots were to become a problem for the NP because consociationalism as a model for building pluralist democracy appeared too close to apartheid for many. The African National Congress/United Democratic Front (ANC/UDF) simply dismissed Botha's consociational reform attempts as a "continuation of apartheid."

Consociationalism proposes that in states characterized by deep ethnic cleavages, each group retains its own governmental structures, while power sharing is exercised through joint government mechanisms involving the heads of these autonomous governments. In 1984, a consociational model was institutionalized in the form of the Tricameral Constitution, which created three South African Houses of Parliament—a white House of Assembly, a colored House of Representatives, and an Indian House of Delegates. Each House legislated over its "own affairs" (laws applying only to the ethnic group in question) and "general affairs" (laws applying to all South Africans). Irresolvable conflicts that arose over "general affairs" issues were adjudicated by the president's council. The tricameral executive group was comprised of the state president (P.W. Botha) and his cabinet, which was drawn from all three Houses. Whites (demographically the largest group) remained dominant within the tricameral system.

Implementing the tricameral reforms unleashed the most serious and sustained opposition to apartheid yet seen because it led to the formation of the United Democratic Front/UDF (see chapter 6). The UDF was initially formed to mobilize pro-ANC colored and Indian opinion against the tricameral system, but mutated into the leading 1980s antiapartheid organization, not only in the Indian and colored areas, but also in the black and white areas. The UDF's successful antireform campaign meant that only 24 percent of Indians and 30 percent of coloreds voted in 1984. The NP discovered that legitimating consociationalism would be more difficult than anticipated.

However, the most serious flaw of the Tricameral Constitution was that it made no provision for black representation. In January 1985, P.W. Botha moved to address this when, during a parliamentary speech, he finally told white South Africans that blacks needed to be accommodated within a single South African political system.[57] What this meant was not spelled out, but within the NP, two ideas, both rooted in consociationalism, were being debated:

- Botha proposed developing a "constellation of states" (or "multinationalism"). He argued that South Africa's "separate nations" should have their own states (e.g., Transkei), which would then form a confederation[58] (similar to the European Union/EU). Leaders from the separate states would share power at a central (confederal) level (as proposed in Lijpart's model). Democracy would thereby be broadened by sharing power in a way that did not undermine groups retaining their "own-ness."[59]
- Others argued that urban blacks could be accommodated in the political system by adding a fourth House to the Tricameral Parliament. This was linked to the idea that in the cities/towns, "national groups" would retain their own "group areas" and schools.[60] However, "free settlement" (ethnically mixed) areas would also be allowed.[61] The NP's recognition that urban blacks were permanently part of South African society was reflected in the creation of a TV channel (TV4) and a university (Vista) to service urban blacks.

The 1980s saw Botha desperately trying to implement consociational reforms. In January 1985, he told Parliament that reform was necessary. Then, as party leader, Botha arranged to travel to each of the four 1985 NP provincial congresses to advocate that the NP formally abandon Verwoerd's partition model in favor of consociationalism. The first of these congresses was in Natal. In August 1985, a media feeding frenzy (suggesting Botha was about to announce the end of apartheid and free Mandela) caused Botha's speech to the Natal NP to be globally televised. Botha was an inept media performer; he played to an NP audience, calling for reform backed by toughness. Overseas audiences heard his toughness, but missed the reform message in the so-called "Rubicon speech." Although NP members understood the enormous significance of Botha's abandonment of Verwoerd's partition model, overseas audiences did not. When his speech failed to deliver majoritarian democracy in accordance with hyped overseas expectations, a massive outflow of foreign capital took place, the Rand collapsed against other currencies, and international pressure increased for sanctions. Nonetheless, Botha proceeded to the other three NP congresses and persuaded the party to formally abandon Verwoerdian apartheid. Hence, in 1986, Parliament abolished the core features of Verwoerd's system, that is:

- South African citizenship was restored to nine million people who had lost their South African-ness through TBVC "independence,"
- blacks were granted full property rights throughout South Africa, and
- "influx control" was abolished.

In addition, 1986–1988 saw a plethora of petty apartheid legislation (e.g., segregated facilities) abolished. The Mixed Marriages Act had already been repealed in 1985.

But the mid-1980s not only saw the NP abandon Verwoerdian apartheid; they also saw the party's hegemony disintegrate as it lost the ability to manage the process of black urbanization.[62] With this, the NP's capacity to effectively govern South Africa melted away, as millions of black people began pouring into the cities and overwhelmed the infrastructures. Because apartheid was, at heart, a system for restricting black migration and controlling black urbanization ("orderly urbanization"), once the system was no longer able to achieve this, apartheid's demise was inevitable,[63] and the system spiraled into collapse. This happened because:

- The 1982–1985 drought (especially severe during 1983–1984) caused immense dislocation across Africa. Although South Africa did not experience the famines seen in other African countries (due to government relief measures), black homeland socioeconomic infrastructures collapsed, generating massive flows of people into ever-growing "squatter" slums surrounding the cities. Apartheid's "influx-control" system simply collapsed under the pressure.
- The tricameral reforms necessitated allowing nonwhite political activity (long repressed by Verwoerdians). This opened a Pandora's box of revolt in the form of the United Democratic Front (UDF). Botha's government became so tied up managing this revolt that "influx control" and "orderly urbanization" became issues of lesser concern.
- New black migrants to the cities greatly exacerbated urban poverty, unemployment, and turmoil, as they joined an increasingly militant urban black population being politically organized (by the UDF) and unionized (by Cosatu). The state lost the ability to manage the volatile mix of political reform, mass urbanization, and unemployment.
- Ending Verwoerdian apartheid also generated a white right-wing revolt, which also distracted the NP.
- Under Botha, much political influence was handed to securocrats (military, police, and intelligence officers) in response to the above turmoil. Because these securocrats initially adopted WHAM (win hearts and minds), they abandoned "orderly urbanization" and "influx" policing. This simply accelerated the processes of hegemonic meltdown because WHAM and "reform" were interpreted as signs of "weakness" (loss of NP power), which encouraged further revolt.

Botha's attempt to reform apartheid from Verwoerd's partition model to consociationalism had been deliberately underpinned by military strength. Before becoming prime minister, Botha had been defense minister and the military were his power base. Botha was instrumental in militarizing apartheid—when he became defense minister in 1966, South Africa had an insignificant military machine. Twenty years later, Botha had created a militarized state underpinned by an armaments industry manufacturing missiles, armored vehicles, long-range artillery, aircraft, helicopters, and even an atomic bomb. By the 1980s, South Africa was not only self-sufficient in military hardware, it was also a major arms exporter. To drive his reforms, Botha centralized all power in the Office of the State President (OSP), while the defense force became his insurance policy against anarchy during the reform process. The declaration of a state of emergency in July 1985 greatly expanded the military's political influence—with the securocrat-run National Security Management System (NSMS) thereafter growing into a highly complex parallel bureaucracy operating across the country, with its command center housed in the OSP. Effectively, power shifted from apartheid social engineers, planners, and bureaucrats to securocrats. From 1982 to 1989, Botha desperately attempted to sell his consociational reforms to black South Africans and the outside world, but to no avail. Instead, political violence was triggered. This led to the NP becoming ever more reliant on securocrats, as Botha's rule became characterized as a period of unsuccessful militarized reform (see chapter 4). So ironically, Botha's attempts at ending Verwoerdian apartheid created not consociational democracy, but rather produced the most violent and brutal period of apartheid.

In 1989, Botha suffered a mild stroke. His cabinet colleagues took advantage of his hospitalization to terminate his leadership of the NP and replace him with F.W. de Klerk. Botha was forced to resign as state president in August 1989. This was done because of concerns about securocrat power within the political process, the political violence and rebellion that Botha and his securocrats seemed unable to stop, Botha's opposition to creating a fourth (urban black) House in the tricameral system, and his inability to find credible black negotiating partners in the reform process. The cabinet concluded that Botha had become an obstacle to reforming the system.

When elections were held in September 1989, the NP fought and won on the ticket of political reform. De Klerk asked for a mandate to negotiate political power sharing (i.e., introducing black political participation, while simultaneously protecting minority rights). However, for reform to succeed, De Klerk needed credible black leaders (e.g., the ANC) with whom to negotiate. The NP government had actually opened secret negotiations with Nelson Mandela in 1987, with regard to unbanning the ANC and releasing him if the ANC severed ties with the South African Communist Party (SACP) and Mandela renounced violence.[64] Mandela had refused, but fortuitously, shortly after becoming state president, De Klerk's room for maneuver was dramatically expanded with the November 1989 fall of the Berlin Wall. Because the Soviet bloc was the ANC's main source of funds, arms, and military training, the congress was weakened by the Soviet collapse. Hence, in February 1990, De Klerk unbanned the ANC, SACP, and PAC; released political prisoners (like

Mandela); and opened negotiations with the ANC (see chapter 7). The NP took its consociational vision to these negotiations. By the time it became obvious that consociationalism was a nonstarter, there was no turning back—the NP found it had locked itself into negotiations with the ANC, which were inevitably leading to majoritarian democracy rather than consociational democracy. Apartheid's 40-year resistance to majoritarian democracy came to an end in 1994, when Mandela became president.

APARTHEID'S EFFECTS

The twentieth century spawned many modernist intellectual "planners," social engineers, and grand schemes to reorder the world. Apartheid was one of these. There was always an enormous gap between the social engineers' proclaimed theory and the reality of apartheid.[65] Yet, these engineers ignored the gap and pursued their theoretical ideal with an amazing zeal, partly because apartheid's theoretical partition model had an internal consistency, rationality, morality, and plausibility, making it possible for believers to ignore its practical fictitiousness.[66] As with so many modernist projects, apartheid treated people as objects to be moved around, "developed," and reconfigured in accordance with the requirements of a "grand plan." In the process, apartheid generated social upheaval, human suffering, skewed resource distribution, and, eventually, violent political conflict. In its practical implementation, apartheid produced a number of negative outcomes.

First, apartheid-as-partition meant the mass relocation of people to create the conditions for Verwoerd's "separate nations." The scale of human suffering caused by these relocations was colossal, as has been documented.[67] The NP government acknowledged that 400,000 people were relocated,[68] while others have claimed that 3.5 million[69] were moved.[70] The 1960s to mid-1970s in particular saw forced removals executed on a massive scale. Then, from the early 1980s onward, forced removals were replaced with "persuading" people to move by relocating service delivery (e.g., pensions and schools).[71] Those receiving welfare benefits (e.g., pensioners) were especially susceptible to such pressure. The process of relocating people became highly bureaucratized because it necessarily required a complex set of arrangements, such as: obtaining information about those to be moved; dealing with the legal paperwork; numbering houses; moving graves; arranging the transport of people, goods, and cattle; organizing water, sanitation, and the like at destinations; and (often) arranging for police to enforce the removals. But precisely because apartheid social engineering became so bureaucratized, and because Afrikaners were such a legalistic people, the system was susceptible to disruption by legal activists.[72]

There were five categories of removals:[73]

- Group Areas Act removals relocated 600,000 urban people into ethnically based suburbs as apartheid town planning reconfigured the cities. These removals were often justified as slum clearance. This form of relocation especially affected coloreds and Indians.
- Unemployed ("surplus") blacks were deported from "white areas" to the homelands. Those defined as economically "surplus" included—according to the Bantu Affairs Department General Circular 25/1967—the aged, unfit, widows, and women with dependent children.[74] The homelands became dumping grounds for the unemployed.
- "Black spot" removals designed to consolidate homelands (i.e., reduce the number of "islands" of black-owned land) through land swaps.
- "Betterment programs," which consolidated scattered rural people into villages so services could be provided.
- Black labor tenants were expelled from white-owned farms (as the capitalization/mechanization of agriculture made farm laborers redundant). These people were forced to move to homelands.

The effects on population distribution were significant (as seen in table 3.1):

Table 3.1:
Results of Apartheid Social Engineering: Distribution of Black South African Population, %

Year	Urban Areas	Rural Areas	Homelands	Total
1950	25.4	34.9	39.7	100
1960	29.6	31.3	39.1	100
1970	28.1	24.5	47.4	100
1980	26.7	20.6	52.7	100

Source: Platzky, L., and C. Walker. 1983. "Review of Relocation." *South African Review* 1: 18.

An important feature of these population relocations was that "surplus" black laborers and uprooted rural communities were not free to move where they pleased. Consequently, under apartheid, South African cities did not sprout shack-land slums like Brazilian cities. Instead, "surplus" people were sent to the homelands. Most ended up not in agricultural areas, but in the new towns or shack lands that mushroomed in the homelands.[75] Only once apartheid began unraveling in the mid-1980s did South African cities experience an explosion of shack-land slum development.

One effect of apartheid's population relocations was that traditional African lifestyles were systematically undermined, as peasant "black spots" were destroyed and homelands were socially transformed by population growth, in addition to the social impact of homeland urbanization. Effectively, apartheid systematically undermined Milner's migrant labor system—a system premised upon maintaining an African peasantry in "black reserves," from which (inefficient, but cheap) migrant laborers could be drawn. Apartheid's border industry development program effectively displaced this migrant system (grounded in peasant workforces), replacing it with (more efficient) workers who lived permanently with their families in new homeland-based cities.[76] These changes—as exercises in socially engineered development—were painful, made worse by apartheid bureaucrats who implemented them and did not bother to make even a pretense at consulting the people they were "developing."

A second feature of apartheid was the rigorous enforcement of black migration control, which, Verwoerdians argued, was required to prevent the cultural "swamping" of "white South Africa." Apartheid was in many senses a migration policy. Only "Section 10" blacks had permanent residence rights in "white cities." To qualify for this, blacks had to demonstrate that they were urban-born, had worked continuously for one employer for 10 years, or had lived in town for 15 years. Spouses, unmarried daughters, and sons under the age of 18 also qualified. All others had to register as work seekers within 72 hours of arriving in town. Those unable to find work were "endorsed out," without recourse to any court of appeal. Effectively, apartheid only recognized the permanent residence rights of those who had migrated to the cities before or during World War II, while huge obstacles—for example, pass laws and limited housing availability—were put in the way of post–World War II black migrants.[77]

Verwoerdian apartheid was specifically geared to turning blacks into foreigners in "white South Africa." This criminalized large numbers of people as "illegal migrants." The Truth and Reconciliation Commission (TRC) noted how this turned people into "the other," which made ill-treating them much easier.[78] Apartheid as migration control necessitated building a large policing, processing, and deportation/transportation bureaucracy, as well as a system for prosecuting those businesses employing "illegals." This empowered a particular type of person, namely, low-level (low-status) clerks and junior policemen, who often abused their positions to extract bribes or bully those being processed. The system licensed a form of "bureaucratic terror" and corruption directed at black people. But no matter how many people were arrested and deported, more kept arriving. Under apartheid, migration control grew into a major industry. This was because (even with apartheid restrictions) people from across Africa were attracted to these South African cities, which offered lifestyles, services, and opportunities not available anywhere else. Ironically, these cities were, in part, attractive places precisely because apartheid restricted the flow of migrants (thereby reducing competition for available jobs and services) and exported the unemployed to the homelands.

A third feature of apartheid was the emergence of "human dumping grounds" in the homelands. Apartheid created rural settlements with extremely high population densities, sometimes called "displaced" urban settlements.[79] Effectively, unemployment was deliberately exported out of "white cities" in accordance with Verwoerd's plan to drive up the price of white labor, while simultaneously trying to create full employment among blacks allowed to remain in the cities (so as to limit opportunities for communist mobilization).[80] By relocating unemployment to the rural margins, the cities became safer and more pleasant places. The rural dumping grounds, on the other hand, were places of tremendous hardship and poverty—they became rural slums without electricity or piped water, characterized by malnutrition, health problems, and the daily grind of fetching water (for household needs) and finding firewood (for cooking).[81]

Beinart[82] suggests that this mass rural poverty may have fueled the rising black birthrate, which contributed to the eventual collapse of the rural socioeconomic infrastructures and thereby (ironically) contributed to the collapse of Verwoerdian apartheid. Ultimately, Verwoerdian apartheid crumbled because its key premise proved unworkable—that is, it proved impossible to locate all blacks within homelands in order to create the conditions for partition. The central problem was, Tomlinson's plan rested upon demographic calculations that proved wrong—he grossly underestimated the rate of black population growth (as can be seen in figure 3.1). A high birthrate and in-migration from across Southern Africa caused a black population explosion that simply overwhelmed apartheid's social engineers. So, although forced removals and migration policing reduced the overall *percentage* of blacks in "white areas," the *numbers* of blacks kept rising. It also meant that the numbers of blacks relocated to the homelands was far in excess of Tomlinson's plan. The resultant overpopulation placed great stress on homeland environments and social infrastructures. Hence, their socioeconomic infrastructures could not cope with the 1980s droughts, and collapsed. Faced with starvation, people simply flooded to shack-land slums mushrooming around South Africa's cities in the mid-1980s,[83] and apartheid's system of migration control and orderly urbanization crumbled. With apartheid's collapse, South African cities experienced a surge of migrants, mass unemployment, slums, overstretched and decaying urban infrastructures, and crime. By the early 1990s, an estimated seven million people lived in South Africa's shack-land slums,[84] many controlled by warlords.[85] The resultant competition over resources generated (armed) conflict between warlords, as well as between existing black urbanites (in formal townships

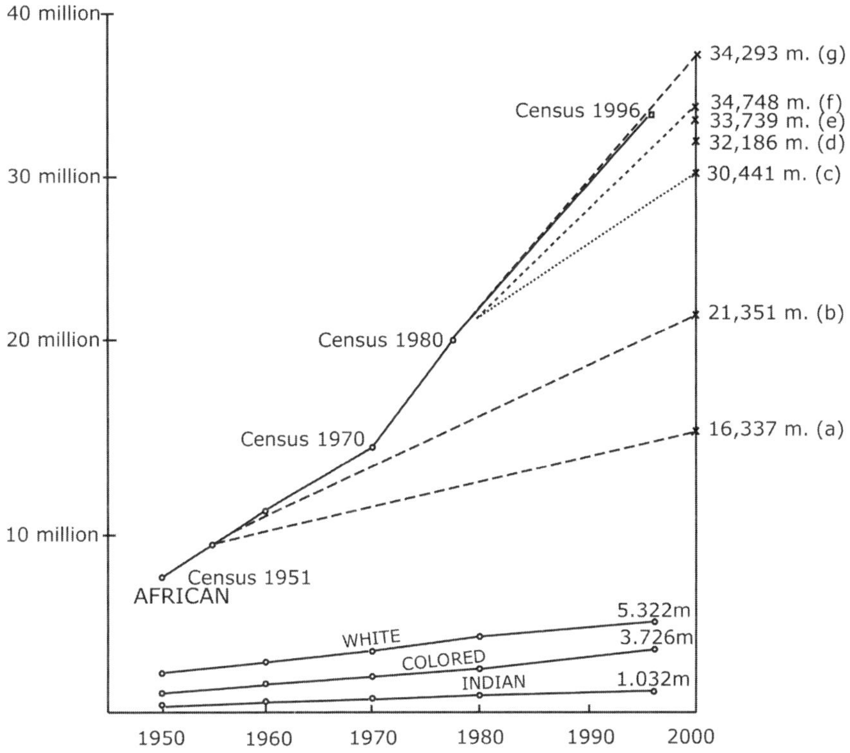

Projections: (a) Tomlinson projection A (1955); (b) Tomlinson projection B (1955); (c) Lötter and Mostert (1980); (d) Futures Institute, Stellenbosch (1996); (e) Development Bank of South Africa (1995); (f) Department of Statistics (1996); (g) J.L. Sadie (1973)

Figure 3.1:
Population Projections

Source: Davenport, T.R.H. and C. Saunders. 2000. *South Africa: A Modern History* (New York: St. Martin's Press), 427.

built by apartheid) and the new migrants moving into the shack-land slums. A massive crime wave saw middle-class people retreat into fortified houses within gated and fenced-off suburbs.

A fourth feature of apartheid was the dislocation it caused within urban black society. After 1960, the Verwoerdians deliberately curtailed the building of black housing in "white cities," and located hospitals, schools, colleges, universities, and welfare service delivery in the homelands rather than the cities, to "encourage" black migration to the homelands. Consequently, urban black life became hard and insecure.[86] The insecurity and housing shortages generated negative social consequences derived from overcrowding and alcohol abuse,[87] which, in turn, spawned domestic violence and crime.[88] It also bred, among many, resignation, apathy, and passivity due to their sense of complete hopelessness and powerlessness. However, among others—more often the youth—it bred anger, rebelliousness, hostility to all authority, and disrespect for their apathetic and passive elders. These rebellious youth featured strongly in the 1980s township uprisings and the violent crime wave of the 1990s.[89]

A fifth feature of apartheid was skewed development; hence, by 1990 there were literally two South Africas—one "Western" and developed, and the other "African" and underdeveloped. The developed parts of South Africa resembled, in many ways, the United States—comprising modern high-rise cities, sprawling suburbs, a productive agrarian capitalist sector, excellent transport and communication infrastructures, plus high-grade education and health services. This developed sector was overwhelmingly the world of whites, Indians, and coloreds, with blacks mostly filling low-grade labor needs. The "black areas" were another world—having more in common with Africa's underdeveloped regions. This led to the growth of the "two-world paradigm."[90] This paradigm (which influenced NP thinking), argued that South Africa was a microcosm of the world because the north/south split ran right through the country. The wealth gap between these two worlds was enormous,[91] although it did narrow significantly from 1970 to 1984,[92] mostly due to apartheid-induced labor shortages in "white cities."

Numerous explanations have been offered for this skewed development, the reasons being multicausal and mutually reinforcing, that is:

- A common explanation is that blacks were disenfranchised and therefore could not exercise political pressure to improve their situation.[93] The way Afrikaners used their vote to improve their situation tends to support this notion. On the other hand, Afrikaners experienced decades of poverty despite being enfranchised, Indians became economically successful without the vote, and black poverty has continued since black South Africans were enfranchised. Nonetheless, the skewing of political power was obviously a factor in promoting unequal economic opportunities, employment discrimination,[94] and black poverty.[95]
- The inequitable distribution of educational resources and lower quality of Bantu Education[96] are also cited as reasons for skewed development. Because apartheid wanted to relocate blacks out of "white areas," black schools and universities were built in the homelands,[97] and education facilities in "white areas" were poorly resourced relative to WIC (white, Indian, colored) education. This necessarily impacted upon the employability of many blacks emerging from overcrowded schools with poor facilities and low-grade teachers.

- The apartheid state put obstacles in the way of urban black enterprise until the 1970s, as part of its policy of discouraging blacks in the "white cities." This was remedied once the NP gave up on Verwoerdian apartheid in 1982 and decided that a black middle class would provide a "bulwark against communism." Thereafter, urban blacks moving into the small business sector were encouraged, but by then enormous damage had already been done.
- Once created, a black-white wealth gap translated into a poverty trap for black people. The already poor (and their children) have faced enormous difficulties escaping their deprived circumstances. A lack of capital and cultural capital has trapped black South Africans at the bottom of society.
- Cultural (and racial) prejudices militated against black advancement.
- Disjunctures between traditional African[98] and Western worldviews[99] (in a situation where Western values are hegemonically imposed) economically favor Westerners.

A sixth feature of apartheid was the waste of resources caused by the social engineers' interventions. The Verwoerdians were perfectly aware that apartheid made labor more expensive by interfering with Milner's migration system, and consequently expected howls of protest from the business sector. However, they simply ignored these protests, since their political (partition) vision took precedence over the needs of the business sector for maximizing profit. Similarly, the NP's political goals of economically upgrading Afrikaners and building an Afrikaner cultural infrastructure necessarily required an interventionist state interfering with market forces and using taxation to transfer resources from Anglos to Afrikaners. The NP simply ignored Anglo business objections.

Once the implementation of Verwoerdian apartheid got into full swing, the costs mounted:

- Homeland consolidation required buying white farms and paying for relocating large numbers of people and their property.
- Policing influx control (i.e., arresting and deporting migrants) required the ongoing staffing of a substantial infrastructure.
- Creating homelands involved building capital cities and staffing 10 new political infrastructures, bureaucracies, education departments, police forces, and so on. This produced administrative duplication[100] and a fragmentation of service delivery, for example, the building of two hospitals to service bordering areas of Lebowa and Gazankulu, where one would have sufficed.[101]
- Homeland bureaucracies, education systems, welfare services, and the like needed to be subsidized from Pretoria because homeland populations were poor and hence provided a very small tax base. Because these bureaucracies were not directly under Pretoria's control, corruption and lack of coordination became a problem.[102] Pretoria eventually created the Development Bank of Southern Africa to try and overcome this.

- The homeland policy gave birth to a large parasitic network of black bureaucrats who were part of an apartheid patronage system. In the homelands, those staffing the bureaucracies, schools, universities, hospitals, welfare agencies, police, and military constituted a privileged elite. The emergence of a class gap in the homelands was further strengthened when homeland development funds were used to purchase retail businesses from whites and transfer them to black owners (who were generally well connected to the political patronage networks of homeland leaders).[103]
- The homelands gave rise to the phenomenon of long-distance commuting by bus, rail, and taxi from towns and shack-lands just inside the homelands (especially Bophuthatswana, KwaNdebele, and KwaZulu) to jobs in "white cities" (such as Pretoria). These bus and train services were state-subsidized, therefore adding to apartheid's burden on taxpayers.[104]
- The border industry policy led to industrial parks located far away from the established cities and infrastructures. This involved major state expenditure on new rail and road links, plus the building of whole new cities in places where economic considerations would not have placed them.[105]
- To encourage businesses to relocate industrial plants to border industry zones, government subsidies and tax breaks were offered. In addition to the burden this placed on taxpayers, these subsidy schemes were sometimes abused by corrupt (often foreign) businesses.

Further, because apartheid was a system generating resistance, it required staffing a substantial police force, intelligence service, and military machine. Building up a conscript army (of 500,000 men) involved all white males spending two years in the military followed thereafter by military camps every year. This placed a significant burden on the economy, especially once the Angolan war intensified, requiring long tours of duty.[106]

A seventh feature of apartheid was that it humiliated people. This began with coloreds being placed on a separate voting roll. More obvious was the in-your-face racism of separate busses, trains, restaurants, and the like, which became a daily reminder to nonwhite people that they were considered "other" and "second-class." Although apartheid was about partition (i.e., "grand apartheid"), for outsiders, it was often "petty apartheid" (e.g., separate amenities, mixed marriages laws) that symbolized the apartheid state's highly interventionist nature, and the way it interfered in the daily lives of ordinary people. Ultimately, petty apartheid proved to be a disaster for the NP, since it generated endless bad public relations by providing images (e.g., "whites only" signs) that lent themselves to simplistic, sensationalized journalism and stereotyping. For antiapartheid activists, petty apartheid proved to be a godsend, because it made it easier to build foreign indignation at the humiliations being inflicted on ordinary people.

Influx control profoundly impacted on the lives of black people. They faced a web of red tape, developed so the state could keep track of blacks and control migration flows. They also faced daily harassment from "illegal migrant" pickup vans and policemen checking "passbooks" (internal passports). In general, the bureaucrats and police encountered daily by black people were low-level functionaries—they tended to be a mix of low-status whites (who consequently relished the power they acquired over black people) and blacks who were comfortable enforcing apartheid laws. Many of these functionaries regularly used their positions to extract bribes to supplement their low pay. During the apartheid era, millions of black people were arrested for pass offences. Many would be released if they paid bribes; others would be deported to the homelands, only to return and be rearrested and redeported.

An eighth feature of apartheid was that it lacked legitimacy among a sizeable proportion of the population. Consequently, the state turned to coercion and censorship. Censorship was especially geared to preventing blacks from gaining access to material that might promote antiapartheid political action. Throughout the apartheid era, there was a particular obsession with censoring communist material. Later, when the antiapartheid struggle turned violent in the 1980s, and pressure began to mount for sanctions, the state also (unsuccessfully) attempted to stop television images of violence reaching the outside world. Surveillance, harassment, and detention were routinely deployed against the leaders of antiapartheid organizations. South Africans (on both sides of the conflict) began to routinely deploy violence, intimidation, and terror. Interestingly, the Truth and Reconciliation Commission (TRC) noted, antiapartheid activists encountered more intense terror and violence in the homelands.[107] This occurred because the patronage networks of homeland elites were especially vulnerable and exposed; the homeland police forces showed less restraint and paid less attention to rule-of-law concerns than did the South African Police (SAP). Also, there was less media attention in the homelands than in "white cities," so the homeland authorities could act with less restraint.

Ultimately, a core outcome of apartheid was the political violence of the 1980s. This became apartheid's most brutal period because—as the TRC noted—actors on both sides developed a war mentality that generated rationalizations for killing one's opponents.[108] So, ironically, it was the NP's attempts to reform apartheid that triggered the period characterized by the most human rights abuses. The result of this 1980s struggle was a traumatized and brutalized society, where violent behavior became "normalized," and many lost respect for authority and law in general. These attitudes outlived the 1980s struggle, and fed into the crime wave beginning in the 1990s. Given that the legacies of this 1980s struggle are likely to be long lasting, it is worth spending some time examining apartheid's final years of crisis and militarization. To this we now turn.

CHAPTER 4

Apartheid in Crisis and Militarized Reform

Apartheid bred the conditions of its own demise: it was a partition model that failed to bring about partition. Measured in terms of its own criteria, apartheid failed because the National Party (NP) never allocated enough land to black homelands to make them viable. Early apartheid theorists like Eiselen said that partition required whites making economic sacrifices and handing over large tracts of land to blacks. He (correctly) anticipated resistance to this.[1] Ultimately, the NP crumbled in the face of resistance from farmers and businessmen. The NP in power was not prepared to expropriate land from its own constituents in order to create meaningful black states, nor to seriously disrupt the racial-capitalist economy by single-mindedly pursuing full partition. Even at the very end, when Botha tried to revive the idea of serious homeland consolidation, he could attract no support.[2] This meant that the NP never created a territorial base for a "white South Africa"—that is, apartheid's core notion that nonhomeland areas constituted a "white South Africa" was simply a myth, given that these areas continued to be occupied by huge numbers of black people. To make matters worse, Verwoerd's early failure to fully implement Tomlinson's report (by refusing to transfer capital to the homelands to make them economically viable) effectively scuttled Tomlinson's homeland plan. What apartheid did instead was exacerbate the skewed development and black poverty that had emerged during the Anglo racial-capitalist period.

Apartheid's Achilles' heel was that it necessarily alienated urbanized Westernized blacks, because it did not even try to politically accommodate this section of the population. When apartheid was conceptualized, only about 25 percent of blacks were urbanized, making this issue less dangerous; but as black urbanization exploded, this alienation became ever more politically salient. By the time the NP tried to reform apartheid to accommodate these people in the 1980s, their alienation and anger was such that they refused to negotiate.[3] To make matters worse, the NP had (inadvertently) created excellent conditions for fermenting urban revolt because the apartheid state:

- humiliated urban black people;
- facilitated political alliance building between black middle-class and working-class people;
- built black, colored, and Indian universities that produced the radicalized intelligentsia who led the 1980s struggle;
- built a huge black schooling infrastructure that effectively created sites where angry young people could mobilize themselves (these schools became the heart of the 1980s black uprising);
- forcibly resettled people, thereby providing political mythmakers with powerful symbols for black nationalist mobilization; and
- offended the sensibilities of many Westerners, generating valuable encouragement for antiapartheid activists (e.g., material resources and sanctions).

By the time Botha became leader, it was clear that the NP had to confront a number of issues. The most serious was the demographic issue. Apartheid-as-partition was premised upon Tomlinson's demographic projections. However, South Africa experienced a black population explosion (see figure 3.1) that literally overwhelmed the apartheid plan. In 1969, the NP had already realized that its partition idea was in danger of being rendered unworkable by the black population explosion.[4] By the late 1970s, there was no mistaking the fact that apartheid faced a demographic crisis—there was no way the existing black homelands could accommodate all these people. The more astute members of the NP realized that the model required some adjustments.

The second problem faced by Botha's NP was that three homelands (KwaZulu, Lebowa, and Gazankulu) refused independence, which effectively ended the myth that the partition model could create a "white state."

A third problem was the coming to power of FRELIMO (Front for the Liberation of Mozambique, a Marxist liberation movement) in 1975. This destroyed South Africa's military cordon sanitaire and awakened a spirit of resistance among young urban blacks (evidenced in "pro-FRELIMO" rallies).

A fourth problem was the growing disillusionment of Afrikaner intellectuals, as it became clear that the homelands were not a realistic alternative to black urbanization. By the late 1970s, many Afrikaner intellectuals were losing faith in the implementability of apartheid and in the morality of the existing system. Hence, although the 1976 Soweto uprising was quickly crushed, and never seriously challenged the apartheid state, it did raise troubling moral issues. The growing disillusionment was given impetus by the publication of *The Sins of the Fathers*.[5] By the mid-1980s, the NP had lost its intellectual base, which stripped it of its ability for renewal. By the end of the 1980s, the party had lost its way, lost its map, and not many were prepared to help it draw a new one.

Fifth, the NP had been so successful in upgrading its constituency that by the 1970s, a large Afrikaner middle class, and even a small bourgeois class, had been created. The NP had effectively changed its constituency and these "new Afrikaners" primarily wanted their government to facilitate economic growth and prosperity. These socioeconomic changes underpinned the *verligtes-verkramptes* (reformist-conservative) split that tore the NP apart between 1978 and 1982. The conservatives (mostly working class) accused middle-class and bourgeois reformists as being co-opted by "Hoggenheimer," and therefore prepared to abandon apartheid (and the "Afrikaner nation") for economic gain. Vorster had managed the early stirrings of these in-house conflicts and skillfully held the NP together (in part by "doing nothing" so as to "offend no one"). But Botha could not hold the party together, and the NP finally lost its working-class constituency in 1982,[6] thereby opening the doors for the NP to abandon Verwoerdian apartheid.

On coming to power in 1978, Botha moved quickly to explore ways of reforming apartheid out of its impasse. He set up a cabinet committee under Alwyn Schlebusch to explore constitutional change. In 1980, Schlebusch recommended abandoning the Westminster system and converting the Senate into a President's Council (comprising whites, coloreds, and Indians) as a think tank for new political ideas. A President's Council was duly established under Schlebusch, and its work generated conflict between the NP's two main reformist thinkers—Chris Heunis and Dennis Worrall. Worrall was packed off as ambassador to Australia and another cabinet committee was established under Heunis to map out a reform plan. From this emerged the Tricameral Constitution—a reform initiative that, instead of solving apartheid's problems, opened a political Pandora's box, leading to violent political struggle and South Africa's most intense period of repression.

MAPPING A REFORM AGENDA

It is important to note that NP reformers retained a commitment to Christian nationalism's original beliefs, namely:

- The rejection of majoritarian democracy because it would produce black domination and the politico-cultural swamping of minority groups (e.g., Afrikaners/whites)
- *Verzuiling*/own-ness

- Legalism, constitutionalism, and the rule of law
- Finding a political mechanism for Afrikaner self-determination

The reformers therefore *retained* the idea of political *partition*; however, they now recognized the need to widen their *verzuiling* system to politically accommodate coloreds, Indians, urban blacks, and "gray areas" (for people not identifying with existing defined groups). The reformers (influenced by developments in the European Union) began talking about federal and confederal systems as a way to:

- *retain* the original black homelands,
- create new *verzuiling* structures (for coloreds, Indians, and urban blacks), and
- integrate all of these into a complex confederal system to "unify" South Africa in ways denying black majority rule.

In devising their reform package, Botha's reformers drew extensively from the work of Arend Lijphart, Samuel Huntington, and Andre Beaufre.[7] Lijphart and Huntington (both U.S.-based political scientists) were brought to South Africa to talk to political scientists and NP reformers.

Lijphart's basic thesis was that societies deeply divided by ethnic schisms were not good candidates for functioning liberal democratic systems because in ethnically divided societies, majoritarian democracy simply translated into a winner-takes-all system for the largest ethnic group. Minority group resentments and resistance to such domination would create inherent political tension and instability. Lijphart's alternative, "consociational democracy," proposed separate government structures for each ethnic group. The elected leaders of these separate ethnic-based governments thereafter became members of a united confederal government—a "grand coalition" (the NP called this "elite bonding"). Lijphart argued that this minimized the dangers of ethnic competition/conflict because all groups felt they had a stake in the system, and political contact between different groups was restricted to the leadership level. This "depoliticized" potentially explosive issues by removing them from the realms of grassroots politics and placing them at leadership level. Lijphart assumed that leaders were more likely to put ethnic emotions aside, act reasonably, and make the necessary compromises for a joint political system to function. He further proposed that leaders of the different groups share the overall presidency within a rotation system; plus, each group should have the right to veto any policy formulated by the confederal government that it believed threatened its interests—in other words, a "mutual veto." Lijphart argued that consociationalism would force leaders of the different groups to work collaboratively and make concessions for the common good.

Lijphart's consociation democracy model was highly compatible with Christian nationalism's partition vision, and easily accommodated the existing black homeland system. Hence, to reform (rather than abandon) the apartheid idea, all the NP needed to do was build additional ethnic-based political structures (for coloreds, Indians, and urban blacks) and then build an overarching confederal system to integrate them all together.

Lijphart's ideas had an enormous impact on Botha's thinking, and the language of consociationalism became a constant feature of Botha's 1980s speeches.[8] Botha's new lexicon referred to South Africa as a "nation of minorities" who needed to live together in "good neighborliness." He called for "multiculturalism," "universal suffrage," "parallel structures," "joint responsibility," "power sharing," "codetermination," "protection of minority rights," "group security," and a system preventing the domination of any group over others. He argued that each group had a right to bring up its children inside its "own culture," which required separate schools and neighborhoods. He further argued that constitutionally each group should have "sovereignty over its own affairs," but simultaneously needed to work together with other groups within a confederal arrangement. Botha concretized this notion in two ways: (1) within the tricameral parliamentary system, it translated into "own affairs" and "general affairs," and (2) he advocated a "constellation of states" (confederation). During the 1981 election, the NP's manifesto called for "the establishment of a constellation of Southern African states, with respect for one another's culture, traditions and ideals." In 1982, this constellation (mini-European Union) idea was concretized when the independent homelands and South Africa signed an agreement establishing a council of ministers, permanent working groups, and a permanent secretariat to coordinate common matters. Botha's reformers shifted away from apartheid's "hard boundaries" between groups ("total partition") toward a "soft boundaries" approach. Homelands would become independent, but would then be reincorporated into a confederation. So Botha's reform retained apartheid's "group identities" approach and continued to reject majoritarian democracy in a unitary state. But now the boundaries between groups would be relaxed within a modified partition model.

Botha, as a Christian nationalist and in accordance with Lijphart's model of consociational democracy, stressed group rights rather than individual rights (emphasized in liberal democratic logic). Botha argued that differentiation between groups did not have to mean discrimination: "As I understand it . . . hurtful discrimination takes place when one draws a distinction in the treatment of people . . . however, when one speaks of differentiation . . . it is possible to differentiate and still accord equal treatment."[9]

Botha's reform map consequently remained solidly grounded in *verzuiling* logic—a principle those outside the Netherlands, Belgium, and

South Africa had considerable difficulty understanding. This was to become a huge problem for NP reformists because it generated an incomprehensibly convoluted political lexicon for anyone operating within the liberal democratic tradition. Western politicians and journalists (especially in the Anglo world) were simply baffled by Botha-speak, which translated into a major public relations liability in a world where five-second sound bites dominated politics. It was an NP public relations problem that the African National Congress/United Democratic Front (ANC/UDF) learned to skillfully exploit.

The second major input into Botha's reform map was made by Huntington. In a paper delivered at a South African conference, Huntington argued that reforms should be introduced from a position of strength[10] because they would unleash heightened expectations, increase political activity, and lead to political violence from nongovernment sources (i.e., organized "revolutionary" violence, popular "spontaneous" violence, and conservative "backlash" violence).[11] If reform was to be successful, law and order had to be maintained during the difficult transition period and the government would need to skillfully mix reform and repression. Huntington argued that bringing about democracy might necessitate temporarily replacing existing "white democracy" with "enlightened despotism"/authoritarianism[12] because to "manage" and "curtail" violence, the state needed to have a strong security system in place. This "security" notion became a core feature of Botha's agenda (tied to the "total strategy" concept); he therefore systematically militarized South Africa, strengthening defense force capabilities, and centralizing/coordinating defense/police/intelligence command structures within the Prime Minister's Office (later, the Office of the State President/OSP).[13] Botha clearly tried to model himself (unsuccessfully, in the end) on Huntington's model:

> The reformer . . . requires a much higher order of political skill than the revolutionary. The successful reformer is always a master politician. He will . . . retain the trust of his followers even as he enlists aid and support from new quarters. He . . . [has to] play to several quite different galleries. The reform leader must . . . engage in log-rolling and back-scratching, to shift allies and enemies from one issue to the next, to convey different messages to different audiences, to sense the eddies and tides of public opinion and time his actions accordingly.[14]

Huntington said the reformer should use a mixture of "Fabian gradualism" (to pacify conservatives) and "blitzkrieg" (to outmaneuver radicals), and argued that good timing was crucial for ensuring the government appeared to be in control (so radicals did not seem to be driving the reform agenda). Botha never got his timing right. Huntington also argued that the reform plan needed to be developed in relative secrecy, and should be revealed only to a small group of political leaders whose support was needed for its success. The aim was to deliver reform by stealth—to keep as many whites onside as possible, while bringing new constituencies into the political process (as allies) on a piecemeal basis. Within South Africa, Huntington was hailed as a guru by government reformers, as part of an American plot to destroy white rule by the Far Right,[15] and as a reactionary by the Left.[16]

A third major input into Botha's worldview came from French general Andre Beaufre. Beaufre's cold war counterrevolutionary warfare model had an enormous impact on Botha (as defense minister) and the SA Defense Force (SADF) officer corps. Beaufre's counterinsurgency strategy (developed from his Indochina and Algerian experiences) became influential in cold war U.S. military circles and was taught at Fort Leavenworth Defense College. General Magnus Malan (SADF chief under Botha, and then defense minister) was a Leavenworth graduate.[17] Defense Minister Botha formally introduced Beaufre's ideas into South Africa's political discourse when a 1977 Defense White Paper argued that South Africa faced a "total onslaught" orchestrated by the Soviet Union. It was argued that Soviet/communist imperialism used "surrogates" (like the ANC) to fight their wars. The ANC was branded as part of revolutionary communism's "total onslaught" against Western Christian civilization (of which South Africa was deemed a part). The 1977 White Paper argued that South Africa needed to construct a "total strategy" (i.e., counterrevolutionary strategy) in response to the "total onslaught," which aimed to undermine society at all levels. Under Botha, this "total strategy" discourse became intermeshed with Huntington's ideas on reform. During the 1980s, white South Africans almost universally believed the "total onslaught" idea.

Beaufre's basic argument was that insurgency wars simultaneously involved direct strategy (military confrontation) and indirect strategy (nonmilitary "social" struggles). Indirect strategy ("political struggle") involved both sides in a complex mix of "winning hearts and minds" (WHAM) and instilling fear—that is, struggling for the love and respect of citizens. Beaufre argued that, in revolutionary/insurgency warfare, indirect strategy was more important for securing victory than actual military combat. This led to Beaufre's idea that insurgency wars were fundamentally battles of will, or psychological battles—the first side to psychologically surrender lost the war. Within this model, terrorism was designed to induce psychological surrender. Beaufre's model was thus a rather idealistic[18] understanding of warfare, which placed great emphasis on winning mass support for one's political position—in other words, WHAM. Botha and his SADF officer corps therefore argued that to ensure communists did not win the war in South Africa, it was necessary to engage in an "indirect maneuver" to convince the black masses that Christian nationalism/consociationalism was preferable to communism.

Within this model, soldiers necessarily became political players/analysts because they needed to outwit the enemy politically. Under Botha, this transformed securocrats (SADF officer corps and intelligence community) into a powerful reformist lobby group—Beaufrian securocrats argued that Verwoerdian apartheid was a political disaster (and assisted communists) because it created malcontents whom ANC revolutionaries could recruit. For Beaufrian securocrats, the objective of reform was:

> To deprive the enemy of his trump cards. There are two facets to this; we must first maintain and increase our prestige, not merely by showing we have adequate force available but also by showing that the future we hold out has possibilities; secondly, by thoroughgoing reforms we must cut the ground from under the feet of the malcontents.[19]

South African securocrats commonly expressed this in the formula that the war in South Africa was 20 percent military and 80 percent political.[20] Botha and his securocrat allies were fighting for a Christian nationalism reformed by Lijphart's consociationalism, and executed in accordance with Huntington's model. The problem they faced was that by the 1980s, urban black political expectations far outstripped any reform message they could propagate.

Significantly, Beaufre's WHAM doctrine suggested that preparing for war was an important component of beating insurgents—that is, one had to prepare one's own team psychologically for war, plus put a WHAM program in place before any insurgents began to arrive. This constituted a justification for militarizing society because if one were facing a "total onslaught," every aspect of society needed to be prepared for battle. Botha's securocrats already had experience implementing a successful WHAM program in Namibia.[21] By the late 1970s, they were looking to implement WHAM in South Africa so as to build black allies for Christian nationalism and inoculate society against the arrival of ANC/South African Communist Party (SACP) insurgents (who they assumed would be arriving soon, due to the ANC's alliance with Mozambique's FRELIMO government). In 1978, the SADF created a *Burgersake* (Civic Action) Unit, charged with implementing a WHAM program. An interesting by-product of Beaufre's model was the idea that media messages were central to winning the war. In both preparing for war and during the war itself, the Beaufrian securocrats believed they had a right to expect the media to help them in their "ideological battle"—that is, the media was expected to help convey the "right message" to inoculate the NP's constituency against surrender, encourage others to become allies of Christian nationalism, demonize the ANC and its allies, and psychologically destabilize "the enemy." However, South Africa's political culture meant that Botha and his securocrats never got South Africa's liberal or left-wing press to play along.[22] As a result, Botha always had to contend with a critical media;[23] the securocrats consequently turned to media manipulation, intimidation, and finally, in 1986, to media censorship[24] (geared to halting the flow of images of political violence going overseas, stopping the publication of "subversive statements," and restricting publication of information on detainees).[25]

By mixing Huntington and Beaufre's arguments, Botha's reformists could justify to themselves using deception and censorship to keep whites committed to reform, win new allies for reformed Christian nationalism, and destabilize the ANC and its allies. Ultimately, Botha's politics of deception mainly served to keep most South Africans sufficiently misinformed so they were unable to make rational political decisions. Further, by demonizing the ANC, the NP ironically became its best recruiting agent. Ultimately, Botha failed to do what Huntington proposed, namely develop messages to keep his white constituency intact while adding new (colored, Indian, and black) allies. Botha never managed to build an urban black constituency supporting consociationalism because his reforms were seen as insufficient; but he did manage to lose large sections of the NP's constituency (to right-wing parties) because he was seen to be giving away too much.

But if Botha's reform messages were ultimately a failure, the management structures he created to execute his reform plans, maintain state security, and coordinate all state actions were impressive.

CREATING STRUCTURES FOR MILITARIZED REFORM

Botha recognized the need to reform apartheid, yet reform precisely meant opening up new opportunities for political participation and simultaneously raising expectations. He realized that reform was a dangerous game—it could easily awaken varieties of political participation he did not want, thereby unleashing a left-wing revolution or right-wing backlash. Almost certainly, as Huntington noted, reform was likely to unleash political violence. Unless the reform process was carefully managed, it could easily spiral out of control. Aware he was opening a Pandora's box with his reform initiatives, Botha decided to build a security machine that would enable him to mix reform with repression and coercively manage any situation that might arise. Because his top-down reform plan would be carried out from a position of (military) strength, he built the machinery for an exercise in managed militarized reform.

Effectively, Botha assembled a modernizing reforming elite of rationalist planners. Apartheid was always an exercise in social engineering; Botha continued this tradition. A core component to his team of professional reformers was a group of SADF officers committed to WHAM. Close bonds had grown up between these officers and Botha as defense minister; they remained part of his inner team when he became president. A central member of this team was Magnus Malan. Botha was always a leader keen to have expert input into policy formulation. As president, he assembled a team consisting of a military elite, top civil servants, academics, and business leaders.[26] He even reached beyond the NP's traditional support base of Afrikaners, and increasingly incorporated members of the Anglo business sector. The result was, in many ways, a government by technocratic professionals. This caused much unhappiness among NP politicians who were excluded from Botha's inner circle of professional reformers. Conservatives also became deeply troubled by this *verligte* technocrat team assembled in the presidency. Botha effectively created an executive state[27] by centralizing power in the Prime Minister's Office (later, the OSP). This was a team of people who had strongly imbibed of Huntington and Beaufre's ideas, while a parallel team of professional reformers in Heunis's Constitutional Development and Planning Department beavered away, trying to develop consociational schemata to reinvigorate (and save) Christian nationalism. Together, the OSP and Heunis teams set about top-down reconstruction of the apartheid state.

The core reform agenda driven by Botha's political technocrats involved the following:

- Saving Christian nationalism (and avoiding majoritarian democracy) by building a consociational democracy
- Widening political participation—that is, creating (consociational) mechanisms for colored, Indian, and urban black enfranchisement
- Removing "hurtful discrimination"
- Stabilizing labor relations through black trade unionism
- Implementing new regional development strategies
- Finding new mechanisms to manage black urbanization pressures
- Upgrading black living standards and infrastructures (i.e., transferring wealth from whites to blacks)
- Creating a (conservative) black middle class that could be co-opted into "managing" urban black townships within the envisaged consociational model

A particular danger for Botha was that reform would necessarily create spaces for left-wing political and trade union mobilization. Under Verwoerd and Vorster, security police repression had smashed left-wing and black nationalist organizations like the ANC, SACP, and Pan African Congress (PAC). Reform would now give their constituencies the opportunity to remobilize themselves. And in addition, such political mobilization would have to be allowed for democratic reform to be achieved.

But Botha's intention was to outmaneuver this left opposition through mixing reform and repression; to achieve this, he built the National Security Management System (NSMS).

The NSMS was built to manage and secure the reform process. The system was primarily designed to identify potential political problems (e.g., "grievances" revolutionary insurgents could "exploit") so these could be fixed through WHAM programs. NSMS infrastructures brought together the three intelligence services, ensuring all information gathered was shared, coordinated, and acted upon. Second, the NSMS included welfare divisions focused on eliminating "welfare grievances" (identified by the intelligence services) and upgrading black living standards generally. Because the NSMS brought together the managers of all government departments, the elimination of red tape was facilitated so "welfare delivery" and solving/fixing "grievances" could happen speedily.[28] The NSMS could also identify left- and right-wing individuals/organizations who (in terms of the Beaufre/Huntington models) were deemed a threat to the reform process, and mobilize repression against such "threats." From mid-1986, the NSMS shifted away from WHAM and toward repression.

The NSMS was the core power base of Botha's technocratic reformers, generating a phenomenon called the securocrats—that is, those people who drove South Africa's militarized reform process. In accordance with Huntington's idea that authoritarianism might be needed to bring about reform, the NSMS was precisely not accountable to elected bodies. Instead, it operated out of the Prime Minister's Office (later, the OSP). At its head was the State Security Council (SSC), one of four permanent cabinet subcommittees. In due course, the SSC became so powerful that the cabinet merely rubber-stamped its recommendations.[29] The council was chaired by Botha and had a permanent secretariat, which consisted of top-level officials on secondment from other government departments, especially the intelligence services, defense force, police, prison services, foreign service, and Justice and Constitutional Affairs. This secretariat worked alongside/with the National Joint Management Center (NJMC), which coordinated a network of Joint Management Centers (JMCs), sub-JMCs and mini-JMCs. Each center within the NSMS comprised five subcommittees[30]—joint intelligence, communications, constitutional/economic/social (coordinating "welfare"/economic upgrade functions), security (coordinating repressive functions), and joint operations. The NSMS system had a dual role—to "eliminate grievances" and to disrupt the activities of "revolutionaries." Under the NJMC were 11 JMCs, which coordinated 60 sub-JMCs and 350 mini-JMCs. Sub- and mini-JMCs were expected to be in tune with their community; they analyzed local intelligence, and implemented WHAM measures designed to fix grassroots problems. Since they were required to understand their communities, lower-level JMCs included black securocrats living in "targeted communities." Only problems that couldn't be fixed locally were passed up to higher levels.

WHAM securocrats in the NSMS channeled billions of dollars into socioeconomic upgrading projects in black areas, and also played a key role in racially integrating South Africa's security forces.[31] The NSMS also played a major role in militarizing both the police[32] and society in general. Under Botha, securocrats came to control an enormous security infrastructure. They could call upon a standing army of 75,000 soldiers, 30,000 South African Police (SAP), and 26,000 black homeland police. They also had available a citizen-force army of 500,000 (quickly mobilizable white conscripts). All white males were conscripted for two years, plus another 10 years of "military camps" which blurred the line between civilian and military life. In the mid-1980s, the securocrats recruited another 16,000 special black police called *kitskonstabels* ("instant policemen"). Further, within the wider Pax Pretoriana, they had *de facto* access to 45,000 troops in the black homeland armies. Under Botha, not only was the size of the defense force expanded,[33] but also the economy was significantly militarized. To circumvent sanctions, Botha built Armscor into the world's tenth largest arms manufacturer, and Sasol oil-from-coal plants were built to guarantee fuel supplies. These "security companies" absorbed enormous quantities of South Africa's capital and manpower. Armscor eventually had 23,000 employees, and provided work for another 100,000 people through 9 subsidiaries and 3,000 subcontractors.[34] Botha cleverly used Armscor to give the Anglo corporate sector a stake in his militarized reform process.

Botha used the securocrats as his power base, becoming an autocratic reformer unprepared to countenance opposition. The presidency and NSMS became the hub of South African politics as Parliament and even the cabinet were increasingly marginalized as Botha single-mindedly pursued his dream of building a reformed Christian nationalism. By working from Huntington's model of "reforming from a position of strength," Botha militarized South Africa and South West Africa/Namibia. He also militarized Southern African due to the doctrine that in an "insurgency war" it was necessary to destabilize the insurgent's rear bases and lines of communication. Securocrats argued that this required attacking ANC (and the South West African People's Organization/SWAPO) bases in neighboring states, and destabilizing those states allowing ANC (and SWAPO) guerillas/"terrorists" to operate from their territory. This led to SADF support for surrogate guerilla/terrorist forces—Renamo (Mozambique National Resistance Movement) and United National Army for the Total Independence of Angola (UNITA). In Angola, this escalated into a conventional war between Angolan/Cuban/Soviet forces versus the SADF/UNITA.[35]

BOTHA'S REFORMS REJECTED

Botha's technocratic reformers implemented many changes:

- Dismantling key Verwoerdian apartheid power bases (e.g., the Bantu Administration Department and the South African Bureau of Racial Affairs/SABRA)
- Allowing a large powerful black trade union movement to grow
- Creating the (consociational) Tricameral Parliament
- Recognizing urban black permanence—establishing urban black councils (i.e., urban black political participation)
- Creating rudimentary infrastructures for a future consociational "Constellation of States" (multiracial confederation)
- Dramatically increasing spending on black social services, housing, and education—representing a significant shift in wealth from whites to blacks (to create a black middle class)
- Abolishing petty apartheid—allowing mixed marriages and racially integrated facilities

Botha's reforms sparked the rebellion predicted by Huntington. Creating the Tricameral Parliament and black local authorities became the key catalysts for the 1980s revolt (see chapter 6).

The Tricameral Parliament—the centerpiece of Botha's reforms—gave rise to a major antireform organization, which became the core fulcrum for the 1980s antiapartheid struggle. That organization was the United Democratic Front (UDF). The UDF became the grave digger of Christian nationalism by successfully mobilizing a huge multiracial constituency against Botha's reforms. The tricameral system (which enfranchised coloreds and Indians) represented an enormous danger to those wanting majoritarian democracy in South Africa because if Botha's reforms succeeded, he would have won over new allies for Christian nationalism (as per Huntington's model) and created a workable prototype for a consociational democracy. One of the key dilemmas Botha's team faced was whether to implement consociationalism in one fell swoop, or to do so piecemeal.[36] The piecemeal approach involved enfranchising coloreds and Indians in stage one, and only enfranchising urban blacks at some indeterminate future date. The advantage of this tactic was that it was less likely to generate a right-wing backlash, because only four million new voters were being added, meaning whites could remain dominant during stage one. The disadvantage of the piecemeal approach was that it created legitimacy problems for consociational reforms by excluding blacks, failing to address apartheid's core political dilemma (not accommodating urban black political aspirations), and by providing anti-tricameral campaigners with ammunition to use against the reforms. Because Botha's reformers were more fearful about a right-wing backlash, they opted to build consociationalism in two stages. This turned out to be a mistake because it greatly exacerbated urban black alienation, and contributed to rejection of black local authority reforms. It therefore crippled and delegitimated the consociational model from day one.

However, the tricameral reforms necessitated allowing coloreds and Indians the right to engage in full democratic debate, including the right to reject tricameralism. Into this new political space jumped Indian and colored supporters of ANC Charterism. Because the ANC was banned, they organized themselves as the UDF and set about mobilizing opposition to Botha's reforms. In the process, they organized an ANC constituency. Significantly, since the UDF was (in the first instance) concerned with mobilizing coloreds and Indians, it deployed not the ANC's black nationalist language, but the language of nonracialism. This was juxtaposed to Botha's (consociational) terminology of ethnic-based politics. The UDF was able to capitalize on the fact that apartheid had made ethnicity and multicultural differentiation unfashionable, successfully making it even more so. The tricameral reforms were attacked as "merely apartheid" and as an attempt by the NP to "co-opt" coloreds and Indians as "junior partners." The UDF's campaign to boycott the first (1984) tricameral elections was immensely successful—only 30 percent of colored voters and 24 percent of Indians voted. This was to set the tone for the 1980s—no matter how far Botha took his reforms, the Charterists were able to mobilize the "politics of boycott." By 1989, the Charterists had simply out-politicked Botha, and he could find no credible black politician willing to accept consociationalism. His reform initiative was stalemated.

A second element to Botha's reforms was the (unsuccessful) search for a formula to accommodate urban blacks in the political system (in ways excluding majoritarian democracy). Botha's reformers seemed to have in mind a mixed system:

- Urban cantons would be constructed (modeled on the Swiss canton model). Urban blacks would be given the power to govern themselves in separate black cities/towns (alongside WIC/white, Indian, colored cities/towns).
- Some urban blacks would (at a future date) elect representatives to a black chamber within an expanded Tricameral Parliament.
- Other urban blacks would retain their links to the homelands, voting for homeland governments (the homelands and Tricameral Parliament would be integrated into an overall confederal system).

In 1982, Botha extended the powers of black urban councils as part of the above reform agenda. This reform failed for a number of reasons. First, black local councils faced a legitimacy problem—being rejected as a sop for noninclusion in the tricameral system. Second, it was difficult to attract good-quality candidates for black councils because councilors were viewed as "sellouts" (Uncle Toms). Many elected (in polls with very low turnouts) were simply interested in self-enrichment, which meant black local authorities became associated with corruption and poor service delivery. Third, there was a dearth of administrative ability to run black local government structures. Fourth, urban black communities were poor, and consequently provided a low tax base. Another of Botha's reforms exacerbated this low tax base problem—that is, the Urban Foundation had convinced Botha of the need to create a black middle class as a bulwark against communism.[37] One mechanism for building this black middle class was the privatization of black township liquor monopolies, which had previously been the main source of revenue for funding black municipal services. So just as the new black local authorities came into being, they were deprived of a key source of revenue. Consequently, during the critical early reform period, black local authorities had to increase the rents of council-owned housing and increase service charges.[38] The result was spontaneous community anger. In fact, the 1980s black uprising started with the killing of the Sharpeville black council deputy mayor seen as responsible for rent increases in September 1984.

WHAM could only work if those executing it had a saleable message. Botha's reformers believed consociationalism could be sold to enough South Africans to make it work, but, of course, this was premised on Botha's continued rejection of majoritarian democracy (because it would produce black domination). There was one group of South Africans who had a clear vested interest in majoritarian democracy, namely Westernized urban blacks—after all, demographics and majoritarianism would deliver into their hands the whole country if they could defeat Botha's consociational reforms. Ultimately, Botha's reformers failed to appreciate the levels of internal resistance they would encounter. Ironically, the securocrats (as cold war Beaufrians obsessed with "communist insurgency") greatly overestimated the ANC threat. In the early 1980s, the ANC was an external organization with hardly any capacity to operate inside South Africa.[39] Even by the late 1980s, ANC capacity was minimal.[40] What was a threat, however, was a latent internal Charterist support base. And Botha's reforms allowed the UDF to turn this latent support base into an active, mobilized, and organized political force. The threat was "internal" and "political" not "external" and "insurgent-based." Botha's securocrats focused on the wrong issue. Botha simply could never develop messages resonating with most urban blacks—he played Huntington's "Fabian gradualism" well (to pacify conservatives), but completely failed to deploy *"blitzkrieg"* methods (to outmaneuver the Left). Ultimately, WHAM/NSMS was simply not up to the challenge of demobilizing the levels of support the UDF mobilized for Charterism. Once mobilized, a reconstituted urban ANC constituency was a political reality, which removed any possibility that Botha's reformers could successfully launch stage two of consociational parliamentary reforms by creating a fourth black chamber.

By the mid-1980s, Botha's reforms were clearly in trouble—there was a populist uprising among urban black youth, only a minority of coloreds and Indians had been drawn into Botha's consociational alliance, the reforms had generated Indian and colored left-wing activism, and Botha was losing white support to Right and Left. Right-wing activism became especially threatening. Simultaneously, Botha faced a crisis not of his making, namely, the 1982–1985 drought. This generated a deluge of economic refugees to South Africa's cities—by the end of 1983, 85,000 impoverished peasants were arriving monthly.[41] This produced growing urban competition over resources and employment, encouraging militant trade unionism. In 1982, a falling gold price and drought triggered economic recession. Urban black unemployment and poverty soared just as the new urban black councils increased service charges and rent. The surge in popular unrest, coupled with socioeconomic crisis, generated a dramatic State Security Council (SSC) policy shift—in 1986, a group of "cold war warriors"—notably, Generals Charles Lloyd, Johan van der Merwe, and Bert Wandrag—persuaded Botha that it was time to abandon Beaufre's "insurgency model," and replace it with John McCuen's[42] "counterrevolutionary" model.[43]

SHIFTING TO COUNTERREVOLUTIONARY WARFARE

In 1984, a black rebellion started in the Transvaal, spreading to Free State, and eastern Cape townships. The rebellion was overwhelmingly driven by youth organizations, using schools as their key bases (and demanding that "apartheid education" be replaced with "people's education"). Although many adults were concerned with how these rebellious youths challenged generational authority, youth activists secured reluctant adult support by utilizing the issue of rent/service charge increases.[44] The youth activists deployed high levels of violence, becoming brutalized in the process[45]—they attacked (and often killed) those regarded as apartheid collaborators (e.g., town councilors, policemen, and teachers), and burned schools, local government offices, and the homes of black policemen and councilors. This produced a civil administration collapse in black urban areas, while the killing of collaborators decimated NSMS intelligence-gathering networks.[46] The police proved unable to stop the rebellion. In fact, black policemen and their families were hounded out of the townships. Hence, in July 1985, a partial state of emergency was declared and 35,000 soldiers were sent into the townships.

During the first 20 months of township rebellion, the securocrats deployed Beaufre's "soft repression" strategy. However, in mid-1986, the adoption of McCuen's counterrevolutionary model produced a shift to "hard repression." Colonel McCuen, a U.S. Army officer, developed an approach deploying Mao Tse Tung's revolutionary warfare model, but "reversing" it. Significantly, McCuen's approach focused on authority, not welfare. Shifting to McCuen's model saw the NJMC activated as a counterrevolutionary command center. Hard-line military, intelligence, and police securocrats came to the fore, while the "welfare" reformers were sidelined.[47] Heunis's "constitutional officials" within the JMCs were also sidelined. Consequently, negotiations between Heunis officials and grassroots UDF structures were stopped.[48] The shift to "hard repression" was first signaled by May 1986 South African Defense Force (SADF) attacks on ANC exiles in Mozambique, Zimbabwe, and Zambia. A June 1986 national state of emergency was declared, and the emphasis shifted to "eliminating revolutionaries," "countering subversion," and reestablishing law and order so the reform process could be reinitiated. The JMCs began ripping communities apart, removing leftist leaders and facilitating the emergence of conservative black leaders (backed by vigilante forces) willing to work within the consociational reform model.[49] The securocrats set about destroying Charterist organizational capacity—leaders were detained and interrogated (sometimes involving torture). Some leaders escaped and went underground, but this still rendered their organizations inoperable. The detention of 20,000 people smashed the youth organizations' and UDF's organizational capacities.[50] As General Wandrag said: "First we neutralize the enemy, then we win over the people so they will reject the ANC."[51] Significantly, because the NSMS ultimately wanted to "win over the people" (to consociationalism), South Africa's "hard repression" was actually "quite mild"[52] in comparison with other societies engaged in similar conflicts—as Seekings notes, the 100 UDF leaders killed during the 1980s was a small number compared with the mass killings/"disappearances" recorded during Latin American conflicts. This was because NSMS repression "always operated within political limits" and the securocrats never had the scope to conduct the kind of dirty wars seen in South America.[53] In 1986, the NJMC identified 34 "problem" urban areas where revolutionary influence was to be removed and state authority restored. Simultaneously, "grievances exploited by revolutionaries" were to be removed. Hence, areas (termed "oil spots") were earmarked for special JMC-run upgrading projects carried out by the army. The NSMS also ran 1,800 urban renewal projects. The "hard repression" and "oil spot" approach quickly restored order and created a gap for black conservatives to organize politically. The NSMS promoted such conservative mobilization.[54] Because the violence and undisciplined acts carried out by the rebellious youths had alienated many township adults, these adults took advantage of NSMS repression to organize vigilante groups.[55] The NSMS allowed and encouraged such vigilantism, plus the emergence of black warlord armies, as a means to help them suppress Charterists.

By early 1987, securocrats had crushed the black township rebellion, and the NSMS withdrew the SADF and SAP from the townships; in their place were deployed black "instant policemen" and municipal policemen.[56] These new black forces allied themselves with conservative vigilante groups.[57] These combined black forces were less disciplined and more vicious than the SADF had been—they effectively imposed a reign of terror on the townships (matching the earlier reign of terror that youth organizations had imposed). By 1988, Botha and his allies were back in control of the townships, and the extraordinarily high levels of 1985–1987 political violence subsided. But there was no return to counterinsurgency's "soft repression" approach. Hard-line McCuen-inspired securocrats remained in control—banning the UDF in 1988, consolidating their alliance with conservative black forces (e.g., vigilantes, KwaZulu police, and municipal policemen),[58] and refining their machinery for "eliminating revolutionaries"—for example, the Civil Cooperation Bureau (which used "turned" ANC guerillas to wreak havoc among ANC cadres). These NSMS strategies conformed to Huntington's notions of "necessary authoritarianism" and alliance building.

However, regaining authority did not translate into a Botha victory; restoring law and order came at a tremendous cost to his reform agenda:

- Botha's reform agenda was now completely delegitimized; no credible black leader would negotiate with him.
- Securocrat repression alienated former intellectual and business allies. The corporate sector opened negotiations with the ANC, and intellectuals abandoned the NP (including the Afrikaner Calvinist churches), making intellectual renewal of the now-shattered reform agenda unlikely.
- Emotive televisual images poured into the Western world. By simplistically framing the war in "good" (black) versus "bad" (white) terms, this television coverage greatly assisted the ANC in winning overseas (especially U.S.) support, which dramatically escalated disinvestments and diplomatic pressure on Botha to accept majoritarian democracy.
- Disinvestment, sanctions, and war costs meant the economy was stagnant. This undermined a key feature of Botha's reform agenda (i.e., building a conservative black middle class).
- Authority was restored at the price of empowering black vigilantes and private black armies. This created a future problem once the ANC was unbanned because armed conservatives and Charterists thereafter struggled for political power.[59]

MILITARIZED STALEMATE

By 1997, South Africa was trapped in a stalemate. The securocrats demonstrated that the NP possessed the military capacity to remain in power for decades to come. The rhetoric of "people's power," "armed insurrection," and "a people's revolution" just around the corner was demonstrated to be a utopian myth, encouraged in many ways by the "romantic approach to revolution"[60] of ANC exiles. The speed with which hard-line securocrats had reasserted authority exposed this romanticism—a "South African revolution" was simply not on the agenda. However, South Africans found themselves in an unstable interregnum—"in which the inability of the dissidents to overthrow the hegemony of the state is countered by the incapacity of the state to eliminate dissidence completely."[61] Effectively, South Africans were trapped:

- The securocrats demonstrated that they could hold the fort, but not deliver total victory.
- Now that reform had been initiated, there could be no going back to Verwoerdian apartheid (the conservative dream).
- "Revolution" was impossible (the left-wing dream), but the UDF had successfully mobilized a large internal Charterist constituency and no amount of NSMS repression could now dislodge this political reality.

The securocrats had always argued—dating back to the days of Beaufrian "total strategy"—that South Africa's solution was political, not military. The militarized stalemate therefore merely afforded an opportunity for finding a political solution. The problem was, Botha's reforms were stalled because he could find no serious negotiating partners. By 1987, it was clear that there were two main South African political players—the NP and the ANC. Recognizing the impasse, Botha began exploratory discussions with the ANC—in 1987, two secret discussion processes (talks about talks) were initiated. First, talks were held with Nelson Mandela in Pollsmoor Prison.[62] Second, discussions were held in Britain with an ANC team led by Thabo Mbeki. Consolidated Goldfields brokered the British talks.[63] The two parties to these exploratory talks had radically different visions of the future—the NP favored consociational democracy and capitalism, while the ANC favored majoritarian democracy and a socialist redistribution of wealth.

Then, in 1989, the political ground shifted. Botha suffered a stroke. Pressured by his cabinet colleagues (who saw him as an obstacle to further reform), Botha resigned in August 1989, and was replaced by F.W. de Klerk. In February 1990, de Klerk unbanned the ANC, SACP, and PAC; released political prisoners (like Mandela); and opened negotiations with the ANC to create a new political dispensation (see chapter 7).

Botha adhered to Huntington's conceptualization that reform should be carried out from a position of strength, and reform and repression would need to be mixed to achieve the final result. Ultimately, Botha came to rely on repression to such an extent that further reform became impossible because he alienated so many constituencies that eventually no one would openly negotiate with him. Botha's style of militarized reform proved unsuccessful. De Klerk's style of reform, on the other hand, went to the other extreme—he eschewed the securocrats because he was one of those NP politicians who had grown unhappy about how Botha had militarized politics. From the start, de Klerk refused to use the military to underpin his negotiating position. Instead, he moved quickly to disband the NSMS, sideline the SSC, cut military expenditure, and halve conscription.[64] Also, he never fought to protect securocrats from the Truth and Reconciliation Commission (TRC) in the way that the ANC protected its military wing. In 1992, he purged 23 military officers whom he believed were contravening government policy/instructions, stockpiling weapons inside South Africa and abroad, still assisting the Inkatha Freedom Party (IFP) and vigilante groups, and planning to sabotage the negotiation process.[65] Although he stopped short of a wholesale purge (because he wanted to maintain a functioning SADF as an insurance policy),[66] de Klerk significantly deconstructed military infrastructures and demilitarized the reform process.

CHAPTER 5

The Struggle Against Apartheid: Evolving Visions

In 1910, the South African state was created as an explicitly "white polity." Before World War II, the black population was a sideshow within South African politics because the majority were rural dwellers, far removed from the cities where most whites lived. In 1939, only 750,000 blacks were permanently urbanized.[1] This rendered them out of sight and out of mind (assisted by the fact many lived in mining compounds). Further, whites "commonsensically" regarded blacks as members of separate political entities—namely, tribes conquered during the nineteenth century, which now existed in a dependency relationship to the core white polity.[2] Even blacks no longer living in the tribal territories were deemed as belonging to the defeated/conquered "political entities" outside of the white political system. Consequently, within the white political system, blacks were of concern only as a migrant labor issue. World War II changed this for three reasons: (1) rapid wartime black urbanization meant that by 1946, 44.6 percent of the urban population was black; (2) politicized members of the growing urban black population saw themselves as South Africans and began agitating for incorporation into the core body politic; and (3) the international environment (modified by the Atlantic Charter) supported their incorporation. Consequently, from World War II onward, black political demands and white engagement with these demands moved center stage in South African politics.

Post–World War II black politics revolved around three visions:

- Multiracialists demanded incorporation into the existing state.
- Africanists rejected assimilation into a "white state," advocating instead a black African state.
- Socialists wanted to overthrow the existing state and racial capitalism.

Post–World War II white politics revolved around three alternate visions:

- White supremacists wanted the prewar status quo maintained.
- Partitionists wanted an India-Pakistan type division.
- Liberals wanted blacks assimilated into the existing system.

These six visions surfaced in various (shifting) configurations within the different political parties. Understanding the trajectory of the antiapartheid struggle is helped by unpacking South Africa's main political positions.

MAPPING SOUTH AFRICA'S POLITICAL POSITIONS

During the twentieth century, eight main political positions emerged in South Africa:

White supremacy was the policy of Smuts's United Party (UP), which represented Anglo corporate interests. The UP advocated Anglo-Afrikaner unity (called "South Africanism"). This unified white nation was to rule over blacks. The UP justified this on the grounds that whites were responsible for building the country/economy and had a more advanced civilization. This model was associated with the notions of *trusteeship* and *segregation*. Trusteeship accepted the theoretical possibility that nonwhites might eventually be assimilated into "white civilization."[3] However, drawing on the ideas of Cecil Rhodes and Lord Milner, white supremacists assumed that black assimilation would take a very long time (because blacks were deemed to be primitive and hence would need a long time to "grow up"). The trusteeship model allowed nonwhites to become enfranchised as long as they became Westernized, adopted middle-class values, and accumulated sufficient property. This was the basis of the Cape (and Rhodesian) franchise, which granted limited numbers of blacks and coloreds the vote (within a system nonetheless ensuring continued white domination).

The white supremacist model was premised upon a unified (capitalist) economy—that is, blacks were economically integrated, but politically excluded. In urban areas, racial segregation was practiced to facilitate using black labor, while avoiding social integration.

Partition, or apartheid, was the policy of the National Party (NP), which argued that the UP's supremacist model was patronizing and no longer sustainable. The NP argued that South Africa consisted of many different "nations" thrown together by British imperialism. These nations did not belong together, and each should therefore be given sovereignty over its own polity. A central NP concern was building a state (from a section of South Africa's territory) over which Afrikaners exercised sovereignty. The partition idea evolved into consociationalism.

Majoritarian democracy was advocated by liberals in the Progressive, Progressive Federal, Democratic, and Liberal Parties. These (mostly Anglo) white liberals envisaged a multiracial democracy within which Western liberal (white) values would be hegemonic. Majoritarian democracy was also adopted by the ANC—being especially appealing to Westernized middle-class blacks (who dominated the ANC before 1943), whose greatest desire was to be fully assimilated into the "white" South African state. ANC liberals tied the majoritarian democracy notion to the concept of a multiracial democracy in which all four "South African nations" recognized by the ANC (blacks, whites, coloreds, and Indians) would share the same polity.

Black nationalism 1: Black majoritarianism became the mainstream position within the ANC after 1943. Given South African demographics, ANC Africanists recognized that universal franchise would necessarily translate into black majority rule. Hence, in the hands of the ANC, majoritarian democracy could provide the means to radically transform (Africanize) the South African state and society.

Black nationalism 2: Africanism/black supremacy was advocated by the Pan African Congress (PAC). Africanism first emerged in the ANC in 1944, but was toned down during the 1950s to facilitate alliance politics between the ANC and white, colored, and Indian organizations. In 1959, the PAC was formed by an ANC splinter group arguing that South Africa belonged to black Africans, and white communists and Indians should be excluded from the struggle. Black domination was justified on the grounds that blacks were the original inhabitants and constituted a majority, while whites were "foreign" settlers and a minority. Africanists advocated "Africanizing" South Africa (i.e., replacing "Eurocentric culture" with "Afrocentric culture").

Black nationalism 3: Black consciousness (BC) emerged in 1969. BC upheld the Africanist view that the land belonged to black Africans, South Africa should be "Africanized," and whites should be excluded from the struggle. However, BC modified the designation "black" to also include Indians and coloreds. BC was geared to developing "black pride" and getting blacks to stop collaborating with apartheid structures.

Socialism was advocated by a range of organizations including the South African Communist Party (SACP), the Non-European Unity Movement (NEUM), and workerists, who built the 1970s–1980s trade union movement. The SACP-ANC alliance significantly influenced ANC policies. Because whites were prominent in many socialist organizations, antiapartheid politics were disrupted because of Africanist/BC objections to white involvement in the struggle.

African traditionalists were politically significant in all black tribal areas, where they were generally allied to the apartheid state. The most significant expression of this traditionalism was the Inkatha Freedom Party's

(IFP's) advocacy of Zulu self-determination, a Zulu monarchy, the promotion of traditional African culture, and black liberation from whites. The IFP adopted consociationalism.[4]

ANTIAPARTHEID POLITICS: THE ROOTS

The roots of the antiapartheid struggle were laid before apartheid was even invented because the organization that came to dominate resistance politics was born in 1912, as the South African Native National Congress (SANNC). In 1923, the name was shortened to the African National Congress (ANC).

In 1910, blacks were tribally divided and not politically organized on a countrywide basis. But labor and mines legislation passed by the new Union government so alarmed a small group of Westernized blacks that they decided to establish the congress. Congress politicians were products of a tiny number of mission schools—Lovedale, Healdtown, Adams, St. Peter's, and Kilnerton—which produced a black elite of educated, Christian liberals. This small Westernized elite was part of a community substantively isolated from mainstream black tribal society. In fact, they were alienated from traditional black society, believed in the superiority of European culture, and were unabashedly assimilationist.[5] Their rejection of black African culture is visible in the 1912 speech of John Dube (first SANNC president) to the founding congress. Dube said the path was: "Onward! Upward! Into the higher places of civilization and Christianity—not backward into the slump of darkness nor downward into the abyss of antiquated tribal systems."[6] The largest concentration of these Westernized people was in the Eastern Cape "border area"—the zone with the longest history of black-white contact, plus extensive missionary activity. These middle-class black professionals were enfranchised in the Cape Province. They were not radical and accepted white trusteeship and Anglo paternalism. Politically, they wanted the gradualist assimilation of blacks into Anglo society as "junior partners,"[7] and the extension of the Cape franchise to the whole of South Africa. As assimilationists, they strongly agitated for more education.

The fact that the SANNC was created by Anglophile assimilationists would have long-term impacts on ANC policy. The pattern was set—the ANC represented Westernized urbanized blacks whose ideal was an integrated multiracial society where blacks could aspire to middle-class success. These urbanites were substantively cut off from the black peasant majority, whose politics were generally geared to resistance against white encroachment. Ultimately, a dichotomy emerged in black politics—that is, ANC assimilationists strove to build a new Westernized African nation, while those in the PAC, BC, and IFP envisaged a future nation grounded in black African values.

The relationship between the ANC and Anglos was always strong; its foundations laid in the Anglo education of mission schools (followed by Fort Hare University), which had Anglicized the small black middle class. This was strengthened by the fact that ANC multiracialism always made this organization more acceptable to whites than those liberation groups advocating "black exclusivism." Consequently, over many years, progressive Anglos (first liberals, then socialists) collaborated with, and assisted, the ANC. This strengthened ANC commitment to an English-speaking multiracial society. Mandela noted this influence when saying that the ANC owed its origins to English missionaries, and "in the process we have become black Englishmen[8] . . . [and] it may well be the black man's hostility and contempt for the Afrikaner has also been influenced by the well-known hostility and contempt of the Englishman for this group."[9] Overall, five ideological influences can be discerned in ANC thinking:

- Anglo liberalism remained a powerful undercurrent until the late 1950s. Before 1940, ANC liberals simply advocated extending the Cape's (limited) black franchise to all South Africa as their strategy for winding back white supremacy.[10] After 1943, they advocated majoritarian liberal democracy.
- The ANC's mission roots implanted a Christian belief in "the common brotherhood of man," "color-blind equality," and "justice."[11]
- African American influences began in the 1920s[12] because a number of early ANC leaders studied at U.S. universities,[13] and ANC president Alfred Xuma married an African American.[14] Sections of the ANC were influenced by Marcus Garvey's advocacy of "Africa for the Africans."[15]
- Mohandas Gandhi pioneered militant constitutional struggle in South Africa[16] to advance the interests of his Indian merchant constituency. Like ANC middle-class leaders, Gandhi was also struggling for constitutional reform and the integration of nonwhite middle classes into a common society. Gandhi's methods came to exert an influence on the ANC.
- In 1927, James La Guma introduced Marxist ideas into the ANC after visiting Moscow (he was also the first to advocate black majority rule). A La Guma-Garveyist clash produced a Garveyist/Africanist victory, after which the ANC fell into inactivity during the 1930s. Banning the Communist Party in 1950 generated an influx of communists into the ANC, triggering renewed struggle between Africanists and communists. During the 1950s, many Africanists previously opposed to communism (e.g., Mandela and Sisulu) shifted their position, and Marxist ideas grew increasingly influential within the ANC. This led to an anticommunist group breaking away in 1959 to form the PAC.

Before World War II, the dominant group within the ANC consisted of Christian democrats.[17] However, three significant splinter groups existed: Dube's Natal Inkatha group,[18] a Johannesburg left workerist group, and a Cape Town Garveyite group.[19] The ANC passed through three prewar phases:

- The years 1912–1924 were a period of optimism when ANC liberals believed that gradual reformism would work, because the British were a reasonable people[20]—in other words, the government could be persuaded by reasonable argument and petitions to remove the color bar, extend the black franchise, and not implement unjust land policies.
- From 1924 through 1930, disillusionment set in, as the ANC confronted its impotence in the face of white supremacy.[21]
- During 1931–1936, the ANC was nonfunctional; urban black politics was, however, rekindled by the 1936 removal of blacks from the common voter roll. But because the ANC was moribund, it fell to the All African Convention (AAC), founded in 1935, to try and mobilize resistance to this black disenfranchisement. Having failed, the AAC also fell silent. However, the AAC interlude produced black activists who trickled back to a demobilized ANC during the late 1930s.
- The ANC's fourth phase started with Alfred Xuma's 1940 election as ANC president. Xuma resurrected the ANC.[22]

ANC REVIVAL AND "AFRICAN CLAIMS"

The resurrection of the ANC in the 1940s was a fundamental moment in South African politics—creating the NP's main political opponent, and laying the foundations for a form of African nationalism that still lay at the heart of South African politics 60 years later.

The ANC's rebirth was the outcome of one internal and one external factor. Internally, sociodemographic changes created a natural constituency for the ANC. Externally, the Atlantic Charter transformed the global context.

The ANC was always an urban phenomenon, with little rural support. Before World War II, this was a highly limiting factor because most blacks were rural, and there was not a large urban black constituency for the ANC to organize. World War II triggered South Africa's industrialization, thereby providing the ANC with an expanding constituency. The 1940s–1970s witnessed large-scale black urbanization. By 1980, 49 percent of South African blacks were urbanized.[23] During these 30 years, black South Africans replicated Afrikanerdom's early twentieth-century painful encounter with urbanization and modernization—that is, urbanizing Afrikaners found themselves in cities dominated economically and culturally by Anglos, where they encountered Anglo racism and poverty; from this grew Afrikaner nationalism. Black nationalism's roots were strikingly similar—urbanizing blacks found themselves in cities dominated by whites, where they encountered white racism and poverty. Hence, during the 1940s–1950s, the ANC's middle-class leadership transformed themselves—abandoning liberal reformist Christian democracy, and adopting instead radical (nationalist and socialist) discourses. The ANC learned to deploy the language of black identity politics—tapping into the pain, anger, and dislocation caused by urbanization and racial capitalism. A new radical language of "Africanism" emerged from two ANC branches—Johannesburg and Fort Hare University.

The 1941 Atlantic Charter imposed on Europe (except Russia) the abandonment of empires. Middle-class Africans were quick to realize the implications of this—if the empires were to go, there would be power vacuums to fill. The ANC (still dominated by middle-class leaders) moved quickly to claim South Africa as theirs—through the 1943 "African Claims" document.[24] Margaret Ballinger (one of three white parliamentarians elected to represent blacks) formally tabled these African Claims in Parliament in 1943.[25] Afrikaners mounted a counterclaim in the form of apartheid's partition model—demanding a large part of South Africa for a "white state." The struggle between these two competing claims (Africanist and Afrikaner) underpinned South African politics for 40 years. Throughout this struggle, the ANC had the advantage of "automatic" support from both the United Nations (UN), established to promote Atlantic Charter ideals, and an international pool of decolonization activists (exercising influence within Western media and education circles). ANC skill at mobilizing these allies played a role in the organization's ultimate success.

The African Claims emerged from a 1942 Xuma-appointed ANC committee, geared to study the implications of the Atlantic Charter. African Claims rejected the Cape's qualified black franchise, calling for "one-person–one-vote," access to full political and economic participation, and a redistribution of land.[26] The ANC never believed that the UP government would give up white supremacy and grant any of their claims. Instead, Xuma saw the African Claims as an ANC rallying document around which to organize a black liberation movement.[27] The advent of the Atlantic Charter meant that the moderate liberalism of ANC middle-class leaders could now be remolded into a radical program of change—because, in South Africa, universal franchise translated into more than "democracy"; it translated into a transfer of power from whites to blacks. African Claims had inescapable revolutionary implications.[28]

But Xuma's leadership was not radical enough for the new generation of urbanizing blacks; hence, the 1940s produced a significant generational leadership change—a process initiated by the 1944 formation of the ANC Youth League (ANCYL). Its key leaders were Anton Lembede, Nelson Mandela, Oliver Tambo, Ashby Mda, Jordan Ngubane, Walter Sisulu, Robert Sobukwe, William Nkomo, and Vivien Ncakeni. The ANCYL rejected the older leadership's "constitutional reformism," advocating instead the overthrow of white domination by mass struggles, black self-assertion, and the notion that South Africa should be ruled by the black

African majority. The ANCYL argued that blacks were oppressed as a nation, in ways different to the conditions applying to Indians and coloreds.[29] Consequently, they argued that blacks needed to be organized as a separate self-conscious political unit, and only when this was accomplished could blacks consider forming alliances with Indians and coloreds. For its first few years, the ANCYL rejected collaboration with white communists, but over time a number of its leaders—notably Sisulu, Mandela, and Tambo—shifted ground,[30] and by the mid-1950s, they had integrated Marxist class analysis into their Africanist thinking.[31] This encouraged a shift from black supremacist thinking to black majoritarianism. In 1949, ANCYL leaders ousted Xuma, took control of the ANC, and the ANCYL Program of Action became ANC policy. This program advocated:[32]

- Self-determination for black Africans in all of Africa (including South Africa)
- Asserting the black numerical majority to bring about black political power (i.e., black majoritarianism)
- Using this power to restructure society
- Rejection of white domination
- An African nationalism promoting vigorous pro-black policies
- Promotion of black self-confidence and pride, the rooting out of any sense of black inferiority, and a rejection of racism and liberal paternalism
- Mass action and strikes to assert black self-determination rights

This program (largely the outcome of Lembede's thinking) was captured in the chanting of two slogans that came to characterize ANC meetings, namely, "*Afrika Mayibuye*" (Africa come back to us) and "*Amandla*" (power). Lembede's Africanism asserted a black nationalist claim over all South Africa, and recognized the need to build black political power in order to win control of this territory.

The most significant youth leader was Lembede, head of the ANCYL from 1944 until 1947. He was the chief architect of a form of black nationalism called Africanism. Lembede rejected the old ANC leadership's assimilationist thinking, arguing that blacks needed, above all else, to develop self-reliance. This required working out a "nation-building faith"[33] that transcended tribal divisions, created unity, and built the confidence to be politically assertive. He called for detribalization and the building of a single unified black nation in Africa (i.e., Pan-Africanism). He argued that blacks needed to assert their rights to Africa because "Africa is a black man's country . . . Africa belongs to them."[34] Under Lembede, the ANCYL revived the Garveyist slogan of "Africa for the Africans," his aim being to build a love for the African's God-given blackness[35] and develop a "race pride."[36] He proposed building African nationalism as an antidote for the way blacks were being psychologically damaged by their subservience to white supremacists—that is, their "moral and spiritual degeneration . . . loss of self confidence, inferiority complex, a feeling of frustration, the worship and idolization of white men, foreign leaders and ideologies."[37] A significant feature of Lembede's race-conscious nationalism was that blacks needed to go it alone and build their own autonomous political organizations. This was tied to the idea of developing self-confidence and asserting black political rights. This Lembedian principle led to the ANCYL disallowing white, Indian, and colored (WIC) membership of the ANC. Africanists argued that there was nothing to be gained by collaborating with any whites; some cooperation with coloreds was acceptable because they were partially descended from indigenous Africans,[38] and Indians would not be regarded as "intruders" provided they "did not undermine the African struggle."[39] This Lembedian principle became a powerful theme within the antiapartheid struggle—that is, the ANC did not allow WICs to become members until 1969, and only allowed them into "decision-making roles" in 1985.[40] Further, the Lembedian principle underpinned PAC policy and resurfaced (in a modified form) in BC thinking.

Lembede's political career was short (because he died in 1947), but his (long-term) influence on South African politics was dramatic. For this reason, it is worth summarizing his Africanist (black supremacy) political manifesto:[41]

- Africa is a black man's country.
- Africans must be united (detribalized) into a single (race-conscious) nation.
- The leaders of Africa must come from their own (black) loins.
- Cooperation between blacks, coloreds, and Indians must only happen once blacks have (separately) organized themselves, and must be based on tactical alliances with other groups in ways safeguarding black decision-making autonomy.
- The divine destiny of blacks is to achieve "national freedom."
- After national freedom will come socialism.
- "Freedom in our Lifetime" was Lembede's motto.

Africanist nationalism overlapped with certain aspects of Afrikaner nationalism, and differed in other regards. Both were race-conscious nationalisms, believed in the "divine destiny" of their nations to achieve freedom, claimed they were rooted in Africa's soil (in fact, they claimed the same soil), demanded self-determination, wanted to capture the state to rearrange "opportunity structures," and advocated self-confidence and pride as a counterweight to prejudices against their group. However, there were also differences—Afrikaner nationalism was based on *protecting* an existent (minority) culture and language. ANC nationalism was based on *inventing/building* a new nation—to be actively constructed through a "nation-building" process of deconstructing/destroying existing tribes (detribalization) and merging these into a new unified black nation. This new nation would be Westernized and grounded in the use of English, and hence, (ironically) would be, to some extent, "de-Africanized" and "Anglicized." So, whereas Afrikaner nationalism explicitly rejected Anglicization and Anglo cultural imperialism, ANC nationalism effectively promoted assimilation into global Anglo culture.

The ANC old guard under Xuma struggled against Lembede's militancy and bravado, warning him it was a mistake to think blacks could "march barefoot" against whites.[42] However, Lembede's ideas, codified into the ANCYL Program of Action, became ANC policy in 1949. By then, Lembede was dead and Mda was the Africanist group's leader. Under Mda, Africanists adopted the view that political cooperation with Indians and coloreds was acceptable, as long as they accepted an "African outlook on life."[43] Mda also drew a distinction between radical and moderate African nationalism—Garveyism's advocacy of "hurling the white man into the sea" was the radical version, while ANCYL Africanism recognized that "other race groups had come to stay," and would be tolerated as long as they accommodated themselves to an "African outlook on life" and black self-determination.[44]

The 1949 Program of Action advocated civil disobedience, strikes, boycotts, and noncollaboration. This involved a break with old-guard constitutional reformism, and the shift toward activism, law breaking, and confronting the state. For the old guard, the "white state" had legitimacy; for the new guard, the "white state" was "the enemy." From this seminal shift grew the 1952 Defiance Campaign.

1950s DECOLONIZATION FEVER

During the 1950s, decolonization fever spread through Africa's middle classes, and the ANC was caught up in a sense of optimism sweeping the continent. For Africanists, South Africa was just another European colonial possession, little different to Nigeria or India. How one views South Africa's relationship to European imperialism alters how relevant the decolonization model is in the South African context. Four perspectives emerged:

- If South Africa was just another British colonial possession, then independence could be achieved relatively easily by exerting sufficient political pressure on the colonial system. Enough pressure would make "the colonials" give up.
- The South African Communist Party (SACP) argued that South Africa was "colonialism of a special sort"[45] because whites had become indigenized over 300 years. Most had no European metropolitan ties (and no European base to "return" to). Further, white South Africa included a large locally rooted

capitalist class, and possessed political power autonomous of London. The SACP argued that black South Africans lived in a special type of colonial relationship—one of "colonial dependency" to locally rooted white South Africans, who were not going to give up as easily as colonials with European bolt-holes. "Colonialism of a special sort" became ANC policy by the 1960s, which required conceptualizing a special-sort of decolonization struggle.

- Other Marxists argued that "colonialism of a special sort" was "mystification" because South Africa was simply a classic capitalist state,[46] and any "decolonization struggle" approach mistakenly deployed populist nationalist slogans and romanticist thinking.[47] Both the Marxist Workers Tendency and the workerists who built the 1970s–1980s trade union movement agreed with this position.
- Afrikaner nationalists rejected the decolonization thesis, arguing they were European-descended Africans, and pioneers of an African anti-imperialist struggle (against Britain).

But in the early 1950s, ANC's middle-class leaders were convinced that victory would come swiftly, because the global context was favorable and the rhetoric of decolonization put them on the "right side of history." The ANC seriously misread the NP, as seen in their 1948 belief that apartheid was simply a continuation of "the long established policy of segregation."[48] Instead of reading apartheid theorists, ANC leaders relied on secondhand (mis)interpretations developed by liberal and leftist Anglos[49] (who also did not read apartheid theorists). The ANC consequently made the mistake of naively thinking Afrikaner nationalists would respond to ANC pressures in the same way Anglo colonials would. By the end of the 1950s, it was clear that this was not the case.

In the early 1950s, three factions existed inside the ANC—Africanists, liberals, and communists; Africanist thinking was dominant. Then, the 1950 banning of the Communist Party generated an influx of communists into the ANC. Once Sisulu (the Africanist leader) agreed to Africanist-communist cooperation, an alliance emerged that dominated the ANC for the next half century. The 1952 Defiance Campaign—jointly mounted by the ANC, Natal Indian Congress, and Transvaal Indian Congress (TIC)—was to strengthen this alliance. Africanist-communist collaboration led to Africanist leaders Sisulu and Mandela becoming strongly influenced by communists like (TIC leader) Yusuf Dadoo and (ANC executive member) John Marks. This helped promote an ANC shift from black supremacist thinking to black majoritarianism. This eventually caused a rift in the Africanist camp, when Africanists unhappy about the growth of Marxist Africanism abandoned the ANC for the PAC. For the ANC, its shift to Marxist Africanism ultimately proved very useful because it generated rhetoric attractive to South Africa's ever-expanding black working class confronting the trauma of urbanization, racial capitalism, and apartheid's influx control.

Essentially, the 1950s saw ANC Africanists:

- consolidate their hold over the ANC (gradually sidelining old-guard liberals);
- popularize their decolonization and black majoritarian messages;
- learn the value and limitations of mass action, strikes, and boycotts;
- learn how to mobilize the growing black working class, while retaining the loyalty of the black middle class;
- reshape Africanism by incorporating Marxist class analysis, so producing Marxist Africanism;
- develop the art of multiracial alliance politics with Indian, colored, and white organizations in ways not undermining the integrity of the ANC as a black organization; and
- learn to use the opportunities provided by NP attacks on urban black interests.

The ANC was the pivotal player in 1950s antiapartheid politics—its political journey involving the Defiance Campaign, writing the Freedom Charter, the Communist Party's absorption into the Charterist alliance, and the ANC's eventual unraveling in the face of government repression.

The Africanists launched their first mass political action in 1952 (the 300th anniversary of Dutch settlement in South Africa) in the form of a Defiance Campaign against "unjust laws." This campaign was the outcome of joint ANC-South African Indian Congress (SAIC) planning, thus setting the stage for what became an ANC hallmark, namely, multiracial alliance building. The 1952 campaign (drawing on Gandhi's passive resistance model) involved mass civil disobedience by nonwhites refusing to obey apartheid laws. The aim was to get arrested to clog up the criminal justice system. However, the only areas of significant civil disobedience were Port Elizabeth, East London, and Johannesburg.[50] The main outcomes were new repressive laws and increased white support for the NP in the 1953 election. The ANC discovered that passive resistance only worked if a government allowed it to—and the NP demonstrated they were not going to respond like Britain's colonial authorities in India. The Defiance Campaign's clear failure caused the ANC to shift its position on whites[51]—that is, the ANC decided to widen its multiracial alliance to incorporate the Congress of Democrats/COD (of white leftists). This "federal" alliance of four organizations (ANC, SAIC, COD, and Colored People's Organization) organized what became the defining ANC event of the 1950s—the Congress of the People.

The Congress of the People became for the ANC what the 1938 Great Trek celebrations had been for the NP—an exercise in building nationalist sentiment and mobilizing a national political network. In 1953, Z.K. Matthews, a Fort Hare professor, proposed collecting grievances and desires, and distilling them into a People's Charter. By way of mobilizing political activity, ANC volunteers moved around the country collecting ideas, making the Congress of the People more a mobilizing process than an event. It culminated in successful political theatre when, in June 1955, 3,000 delegates proclaimed the Freedom Charter at Kliptown. Henceforth, the ANC and its multiracial alliance partners were called Charterists. The charter cleverly combined both liberal and socialist appeals, calling for majoritarian democracy plus a redistribution of wealth. It began: "We the people of South Africa, declare for all our country and the world to know—That South Africa belongs to all who live in it, black and white." These words were an explicit rejection of white supremacy, partition (apartheid), and black supremacy, while they served to rally majoritarian democrats, black majoritarians, and social democrats. The charter grew out of a realization that the earlier "decolonization optimism" and Lembede radicalism had been misplaced. South Africa was not like other colonial possessions because the ANC's opposition was a locally-rooted powerful white polity that was going to fight back. Hence, the charter deliberately sought to allay minority group (WICs) fears and created the basis for a multiracial alliance against apartheid (although the ANC itself remained a blacks-only organization). The charter's liberal moderation helped secure Western sympathy, although its overall tone conformed to Marxist Africanism, then emerging as the ANC's mainstream position. Mandela argued that the charter was a revolutionary document,[52] but Lembedian Africanists saw it as a "sellout" of the black man's exclusive right to the land. They blamed this on the moderating influence of Indians and white communists, who naturally enough wanted "shared nationhood."[53]

The growing influence of Marxist thinking within the ANC was indeed a noteworthy 1950s development. The Communist Party had emerged in 1921 as a white organization. In 1922, a communist-Afrikaner nationalist alliance mobilized white workers and seized control of the Witwatersrand. Smuts's government militarily crushed this Rand Revolt. Thereafter, a new government improved white working-class conditions, and Afrikaner nationalists abandoned working with communists. The Communist Party thereupon turned away from organizing white workers and shifted its focus to black workers; in 1928, the party (following Moscow's instructions) adopted a policy of working for "an independent native republic" in South Africa.[54] This led to the Communist Party's adopting the two-stage revolution strategy: stage one involved communists working with black nationalists to create a majoritarian democracy (i.e., a capitalist state ruled by a black middle class), and stage two involved working for a socialist revolution (i.e., replacing black middle-class with black working-class rulers). The "native republic" policy saw dissident whites leave the Communist Party, which was reduced to a small Stalinist vanguard trying to build contacts with, and ideologically influence, the ANC. However, ANC liberals, Garveyites, and Africanists spurned their advances, and during the 1930s and 1940s, communists remained a marginalized faction within the ANC. This changed when the banning of the Communist Party generated an influx of communists into the ANC. Hence, although the SACP retained an autonomous existence from the ANC, one consequence of the two-stage strategy was that, from 1950 to 1994, the SACP virtually subsumed itself into the ANC—Marxism and Africanism melded into the joint "national liberation struggle" discourse. The resultant Africanist-communist alliance had the effect of driving the Lembedians out of the ANC in 1959. It also meant that the ANC gradually adopted a pro-Soviet/anti-American position.[55] During the 1960s–1980s, this proved valuable to the ANC because the Soviet bloc became the main source of funds and arms for the ANC's armed wing, MK (*Umkonto we Sizwe*).

However, by the late 1950s, the ANC was in trouble for two reasons. First, state repression was working. The state had used the Congress of the People campaign to infiltrate many informers into the Charterist camp. Further, following the Congress of the People, the state charged 156 ANC activists with treason. All were eventually acquitted, but the treason trial (1957–1961) crippled the ANC by tying up its entire leadership in court proceedings. Second, factionalism became rampant and the Transvaal ANC virtually collapsed.[56] The Lembedian/PAC breakaway in 1959 was both symptomatic of ANC problems and exacerbated its organizational crisis. Earlier ANC optimism associated with decolonization fever was being seriously strained.

The ANC's weakness at this time is revealed by its organizational inability to respond to the wave of 1950s rural revolts that broke out as the Verwoerdians moved to co-opt chieftains into the apartheid machinery, improve homeland economies by ending erosion (reducing cattle/goat numbers and initiating land rehabilitation), impose taxes, and move people to concentrated settlements (lowering service-delivery costs).[57] This sparked rural unrest in the Transvaal, Natal, and Eastern Cape, as peasants resisted government-imposed changes.[58] The ANC played no role in these uprisings due to their urban bias and general organizational weakness.

PAC FORMED

In 1959, a Lembedian faction, led by Robert Sobukwe, Potlako Leballo, and Ashby Mda, left the ANC to form the Pan African Congress (PAC). They regarded the Freedom Charter as a "reformist" sellout of black nationalist interests, and objected to the ANC appeasing white opinion and/or working with (left-wing) whites. As Sobukwe wrote:

> Africans are asked, through their spineless leaders, not to "embarrass" their "friends" and "allies" . . . [and] to "water-down" their demands in order to accommodate all the Anti-Nat elements in the country; in short we are asked to

"grin and bear it" so that our friends can continue "to plead for us." And we are told that in that way we shall achieve freedom. What rubbish.[59]

Some PAC supporters went as far as alleging that the charter was "imposed" on the Congress alliance by the "communist-dominated" COD.[60] Collaboration with whites was seen to reduce militancy and hence cripple the struggle; and collaboration with communists and "the Indian merchant class" within a multiracial Charterist alliance was seen as responsible for having watered down the original 1949 Program of Action.[61] Collaborating with whites and Indians blunted the struggle because, Sobukwe argued, ordinary blacks do not hate abstract concepts like "oppression or capitalism. They concretize these and hate the oppressor . . . the white man . . . If you remove the association, you remove the hatred."[62] Having white allies blunted hatred. Further, Sobukwe argued, "the privileged (whites/Indians) only offered assistance for the purpose of 'directing and controlling' the struggle, so as to make sure it 'does not become dangerous.'"[63] For Sobukwe, only blacks had a truly revolutionary interest in changing South Africa because of their material position.[64]

A fundamental feature of PAC policy was a return to original Lembedian principle that Africa belonged to blacks; whites had conquered the land, and all land needed to be returned to blacks. The PAC rejected white claims of a right to some land because they had settled in the "empty parts" of South Africa. The PAC asserted that blacks had "an inalienable claim on every inch of African soil."[65] Sobukwe rejected the "doctrine of South African exceptionalism," arguing, "South Africa is an integral part of the indivisible whole that is Afrika"[66]—that is, South Africa needed to be included in a continent-wide process of decolonization. For this reason, he rejected apartheid's partition model, saying, "nobody has the right to Balkanize our land."[67]

An important feature of PAC thinking was that blacks were conditioned to be psychologically subservient to whites, and suffered from dependency and inferiority complexes. The solution was to inspire black self-reliance, self-confidence, and "psychological liberation" by getting blacks to "walk tall" and refuse any collaboration with the white system.[68] The PAC thus favored boycott politics. The congress's first mass action consequently involved a boycott of passes, with Sobukwe realizing that apartheid-as-partition required a migration-control/pass system. If blacks boycotted using passes, the system could not work. Hence, the PAC called on black men to leave their passes at home on 21 March 1960, and to present themselves for arrest at police stations. Sobukwe presented himself and was arrested. The PAC called for nonviolent action, and its members behaved accordingly; in most places, so did the police. The PAC's call only drew a large response in Vereeniging and Cape Town, and it looked as if the anti-pass campaign was destined to be another uneventful failure. However, some Vereeniging police panicked and killed 69 people at Sharpeville. This triggered a series of events transforming South African politics.

CRUSHING BLACK RESISTANCE

Following the Sharpeville shootings, a PAC crowd marched in Langa, near Cape Town, and three more people were killed. That night, riots exploded in Langa and municipal offices and black policemen's houses were burned. The government banned public gatherings across the country, but also suspended the need for blacks to show passes. With the danger that this would translate into a major PAC victory, the ANC moved to grab some credit. ANC president, Albert Luthuli, burned his pass, called on all blacks to burn theirs, and requested a national stay-away. The government's response was to ban the ANC and PAC, detain 18,000 people (mostly, for brief periods), and outlaw acts of "defiance." When banning the ANC and PAC, the justice minister excused the repression on the grounds they were intent on "generating revolution . . . [They] do not want peace and order . . . what they want is our country."[69] Despite repression, the national stay-away grew in momentum, and mass marches in Durban and Cape Town created a crisis atmosphere. Investors lost confidence and there was a major outflow of capital. The government declared a state of emergency (to facilitate crushing the resistance) and imposed exchange controls (to halt the capital outflows). These measures stabilized the situation surprisingly quickly; by August 1960, the state of emergency could be lifted. By the end of 1961, most ANC/PAC leaders had been arrested, banned, or were in exile, the economy had recovered, and white migrants began flowing in.

March–August 1961 transformed South African politics. Because of a naïve faith in the inevitability of decolonization, ANC/PAC Africanists seriously misjudged the NP's willingness to fight back. In 1960, the NP demonstrated that it had no intention of acquiescing to the Africanist decolonization agenda—if necessary, the white state would secure its continued existence through ruthless repression, and would violently crush any attempts to mobilize mass black action against it. Hence, if the ANC/PAC wanted to pursue their Africanist decolonization agenda, they would now have to do so underground or in exile. Consequently, in June 1961, Mandela proposed that the ANC adopt violence.[70] He had first advocated armed struggle in 1952,[71] at which time he was considered too radical. Now he was given the go-ahead to establish a military wing, MK, which operated semiautonomously of the ANC's political wing. Unlike the ANC itself, MK allowed whites, coloreds, and Indians to be members.

The 1961 repression quickly decimated the PAC, because as a new political party, it had shallow organizational roots.[72] Sobukwe spent the next nine years imprisoned on Robben Island. Some PAC leaders fled into exile in Lesotho. In 1962, a PAC armed wing, *POQO*, was established. By the end of the 1960s, *POQO* was smashed, having carried out only sporadic, poorly organized terror acts.

The ANC was not as easy to destroy because it was an older organization with deep roots. Further, in the mid-1950s, the ANC had implemented Mandela's M-Plan[73]—creating a hierarchal network of small cells for underground operations.[74] It took the state longer to destroy this network. Mandela's appointment as MK commander in chief kick-started his political career. MK's high command consisted of Mandela, Sisulu, and Joe Slovo. Slovo recruited white communists into MK. The SACP played a central part in building MK[75]—buying a Rivonia farm for MK's headquarters; securing Soviet bloc resources; and training MK recruits on using bombs, grenades, and mines.[76] Mandela geared up MK to carry out its first armed attacks on the Battle of Blood River anniversary, 16 December 1961. With its first attacks, MK issued the following statement: "The time comes in the life of any nation when there remains only two choices: submit or fight."[77] This revealed Mandela's Africanist perception of a black South African nation fighting a decolonization struggle for its independence from white rule. Over the next 18 months, MK carried out 194 sabotage attacks, and assassinated suspected police informers, state witnesses in "terrorism trials," and blacks perceived to be apartheid collaborators.[78]

In 1962, Mandela spent six months traveling overseas. Many African leaders promised the ANC financial and military support. Mandela received fleeting military instruction from Algerian National Liberation Front (FLN) guerillas, which initiated his interest in revolutionary guerilla warfare. He became convinced that MK should gear up for guerilla warfare along the lines of the Algerian and Vietnam struggles.[79] A plan for rural-based revolutionary guerilla warfare—called Operation Mayibuye—was drawn up. During 1962, MK succeeded in sending 360 recruits to Tanganyika for military training,[80] with almost as many arrested en route. Mandela was arrested in 1962; MK's key Rivonia personnel were arrested in 1963. Mandela and eight others were found guilty of terrorism, and sentenced to life imprisonment.

By the end of 1963, the ANC's leadership was jailed or banned. The only senior ANC leader still operative was Oliver Tambo (who left South Africa in 1960 to establish an external office). Tambo found himself heading a demoralized ANC that was heavily infiltrated by police informers, its strategy discredited, its leaders captured, and its goals unmet.[81] The government, on the other hand, had white public opinion firmly supportive of crushing "terrorism" and "communism."[82] The state constructed an extensive intelligence network to seek out those promoting decolonization, Africanism, the national liberation struggle, and Marxism. Informers were everywhere in the black townships—for blacks opposed to apartheid, it became safer to be silent. For blacks interested in politics and governance, the only career paths now open were in the homelands or in exile.

The 1960s–1970s saw the ANC and PAC reduced to a small rump of exiled revolutionaries struggling to come to terms with the unpleasantness and isolation of exile. Exile politics became trivial and frustrating. The PAC fared much worse than the ANC in exile, abandoning its anticommunist position, then disintegrating into factionalism after some of its members sought to align themselves with Communist China in 1964.[83] The PAC became nonfunctional, and by 1967, the Organization of African Unity/OAU demanded that the PAC demonstrate a capacity to conduct insurgency operations or OAU aid would cease. PAC attempts at insurgency were farcical; by the 1970s, it was weak, divided, and operating in the realms of total fantasy and Maoist catch phrases.[84] Despite this, the PAC always exerted an influence on the ANC, because its radical Africanism resonated deeply with ordinary black South Africans, meaning that too strong an ANC commitment to nonracialism would be dangerous.[85]

This was a difficult period for the ANC. By 1965, all ANC/SACP internal political and military structures were destroyed—they simply no longer operated inside South Africa.[86] ANC exiles were based mainly in Tanzania, Zambia, the Soviet Union, and Britain. Finding themselves with little room for political maneuver, the ANC-in-exile turned to the romantic notion of a "conquest of power."[87] From 1963 to 1978, the ANC-in-exile's discourses stressed the following:

- Armed struggle was seen as the only method left open.[88] The ANC/SACP were strongly influenced by Marxist revolutionary struggles in Algeria, China, Greece, Vietnam, Yugoslavia, and Cuba.[89] The Cuban Revolution and Che Guevara's ideas were especially influential inside the ANC/SACP. Between 1961 and 1978, Guevara's "detonator approach" underlay MK's approach[90]—in terms of this romantic notion, it was assumed that "armed propaganda" (spectacular acts of violence/terrorism) could trigger the masses into action. The ANC allied itself to other Soviet-aligned guerilla groups—for example, ZAPU, MPLA, and the Front for the Liberation of Mozambique (FRELIMO)—and in 1967–1968, MK sent guerillas into Rhodesia to fight alongside ZAPU. The defeat of this Rhodesian insurgency triggered an MK mutiny,[91] which catalyzed the ANC's 1969 Morogoro Conference (in Tanzania).
- Leninist vanguardism underpinned ANC/SACP thinking.[92] Leninism entered the ANC via MK when whites were allowed to become MK members. Ultimately, the SACP's central role within MK gave the ANC an edge over the PAC because it delivered Soviet resources and a wealth of skilled cadres. However, it also brought with it vanguardist romanticism, which effectively turned the ANC away from organizing its political constituency.
- The notion of decolonization/"national liberation struggle," which was internationally popular in the 1950s–1960s, became reified and frozen within the ANC as the SACP's "two-stage revolution" theory.[93]

- A deep-seated anger and frustration in exile circles manifested itself in the need to retaliate; there was a strong desire to violently hit back at the apartheid state.[94] Hence, political work was simply not as appealing as joining MK to conquer power militarily.

By 1969, the ANC was in trouble. With no networks inside the country, the congress was cut off from developments in South Africa, making it difficult to formulate realistic strategies. The apartheid state had an effective *cordon sanitaire* around itself—the ANC simply could not get access to South Africa. With no possibility of military or political actions inside South Africa, ANC leaders were left focusing on UN and OAU diplomatic struggles, building Western sympathy (by learning to use discourses resonating with social democrats), and making propaganda against PAC exiles. For ANC (and PAC) rank-and-file exiles, boredom and frustration set in—conditions often producing mutiny, factionalism, escapist delusions, or apathy in exile groups.[95] Further, by the late 1960s, the ANC faced two political challenges inside South Africa. First, Verwoerdian homelands were beginning to work, as both Mandela and Sisulu noted from their Robben Island prison—rural blacks began to "regard the NP as benefactors and Bantustan leaders as messiahs who've liberated them."[96] Mandela recognized that the ANC's constituency was exclusively urban, having "hardly any significant following in the countryside."[97] The ANC now confronted the danger that separate development could gain middle-class black support given that homelands needed "qualified men to fill new positions."[98] Sisulu also recognized the problem, saying: "we must face the fact the enemy has made inroads."[99] Second, in 1969, Black Consciousness (BC) emerged as a growing force among urban black South Africans. The ANC-in-exile faced the prospect of losing its constituency and becoming politically irrelevant. The Morogoro Conference was called to discuss solutions, during which the ANC leadership faced a hostile assembly of those who had lost faith in them. The ANC appeared on the verge of collapse;[100] its seminal discovery was that MK could not fight an armed struggle if there was no political support network inside the country,[101] and the "detonator approach" had not generated this support base. By romantically overemphasizing armed struggle/"conquering power," the ANC had failed to maintain an internal political constituency, and this rendered armed insurgencies suicidal. At Morogoro, the ANC confronted its growing irrelevance, and adopted new policies:[102]

- Internal political mobilization was deemed crucial to building a support base for guerilla warfare.
- Armed "conquest of power" remained ANC policy and a Revolutionary Council was established to prosecute a guerilla war. The Morogoro delegates astonishingly failed to recognize that most of South Africa was geographically

ill-suited to rural guerilla warfare, plus the ANC's support was in any case urban based.

- New organizational structures were to be established in Africa—military/education training bases in Tanzania (all ANC personnel were to receive guerilla training); headquarters moved from London to Zambia; and "transit facilities" established in Botswana, Swaziland, and Lesotho.
- Whites, coloreds, and Indians were, for the first time, allowed to become ANC members,[103] but it was reaffirmed that the ANC advocated a black nationalist struggle and WICs would not be allowed to dominate.[104]

After Morogoro, the ANC failed to make any headway in internal political mobilization, or in executing its guerilla plans, but the congress did create an infrastructure in frontline African states that would serve it well in the late 1970s. In the absence of an internal ANC presence, an alternative grew, namely BC.

BLACK CONSCIOUSNESS

BC emerged from a small group of intellectuals, including Steve Biko, Barney Pityana, Charles Sibisi, Mamphela Ramphele, Mandla Langa, Strini Moodley, and Saths Cooper. It was triggered by Steve Biko's angry response to the 1968 National Union of South African Students (NUSAS) Conference—which represented the (mostly white) students at four Anglo liberal universities. Biko was a medical student at one of these—the University of Natal—which had a nonwhite medical faculty. Biko, who came from a PAC-supportive family, was angered by how antiapartheid white Anglo students were patronizing toward blacks, yet simultaneously claimed to speak on their behalf.[105] Biko's anger led to the 1969 formation of the blacks-only South African Students' Organization (SASO).

SASO was the direct outgrowth of one of apartheid's key contradictions—the black middle classes were denied a place in "white cities." However, for separate development to work, a skilled black middle class had to be created to run the homelands. Consequently, the NP dramatically expanded black educational facilities (schools, colleges, and universities). In the process, a deeply frustrated group of black university students was created. SASO literature constantly refers to feelings of social isolation, frustration, and alienation[106]—in other words, because they were educated, university students could not relate to black communities around them,[107] especially at homeland-based universities like University of the North, Turfloop (where SASO was founded). On the other hand, ordinary whites shunned them for being too educated ("cheeky kaffirs-in-the-making"),[108] while antiapartheid Anglo students treated them as inferior (for attending apartheid "bush colleges"). They could not find vacation jobs because university blacks were seen as radicals and treated with suspicion; and upon graduation, the only career paths available were in the homelands. They were expected to join the "Bantustan bourgeoisie."[109] It was a recipe for radicalization. Biko tapped into this mood and articulated the visceral anger of these students.

SASO proposed that black students were wrong to align themselves with white Anglo students. Biko argued that well-meaning white liberals, living in comfortable suburbs, could never understand the black man's perspective, and it was a huge mistake to assume that antiapartheid whites were automatic allies.[110] Biko launched a scathing attack on Anglo liberals,[111] rejecting their assimilation model because it effectively meant integration on Anglo terms[112] or one-sided acculturation.[113] For Biko, blacks needed to free themselves from Anglo liberal influence; "reject Western values"[114] in favor of "African values";[115] and refuse to join the "Anglo tea-party set," where guilt-stricken, yet condescending Anglos spoke about "changing South Africa."[116] Biko suggested that whites who were serious about changing South Africa should focus on white politics ("white consciousness") and leave blacks to sort out their own political options.[117]

The NP's initial response to BC was positive. Afrikaner nationalists were delighted with SASO's formation because, at last, it appeared the link between educated blacks and Anglo liberal "mission education" was being broken. This was taken as vindication of the enormous resources the NP had invested into Bantu Education, the aim of which had been to stop the Anglicization of blacks and the influence Anglo liberals had over middle-class black people. Thus, in 1971, the pro-NP *Die Burger* (newspaper) stated that BC was:

> The product of disillusionment over the nice sounding phrases and ideas and programmes preached in the postwar years by the . . . liberal school of thought . . . The [BC] people with whom this new thinking has taken root reject the condescension with which they have often been regarded by whites who represent themselves as their only friends . . . they do not want to be objects of white politics any longer, but desire to determine their futures themselves as people in their own right . . . [hence BC] fits in well with the objectives of our relations policy.[118]

The NP was even more delighted that SASO/BC had grown out of the University Christian Movement (and had strong relationships to the church[119]) because this seemed to suggest that Christian national thinking had been inculcated through Bantu Education.

However, in reality, Biko was reactivating neo-PAC consciousness among SASO students. He agreed with Lembede that "the land belonged to Africans" and the descendants of European settlers had no right to any land, but he departed from the PAC by including Indians and coloreds within the designation "black" because they shared a common oppression.[120] In this sense, Biko synthesized PAC Africanism with ANC multiracialism, but he excluded whites from the multiracial alliance. He also synthesized into BC Non-European Unity Movement's (NEUM's)[121] ideas that nonwhites should not collaborate with the white system.[122] Active noncollaboration became a core feature of BC thinking from whence it spread to become a central feature of all antiapartheid politics.

Biko correctly identified the three core problems facing those fighting apartheid. First, separate development had become a real threat because it was starting to work—that is, an expanding constituency of rural blacks was beginning to support the homelands and a growing black homeland middle class was developing a vested interest in Verwoerdian apartheid.[123] Biko feared that if separate development persisted too long, blacks would come to accept it.[124] He correctly recognized that apartheid could not function without millions of black people working for the system, and he was scathing of blacks who collaborated with apartheid—homeland leaders, homeland bureaucrats, policemen, informers, and the like (interestingly, Biko's own father had been a policeman). The basic BC strategy for overturning apartheid was to get blacks to stop collaborating, and for black liberation movements to make the lives of black collaborators as unpleasant as possible. BC advocated the boycott of separate development structures precisely because they were beginning to work.[125] Both the ANC and United Democratic Front (UDF) came to adopt Biko's position.

Second, Biko noted how white participation changed the struggle in two ways: (1) having white comrades broke down the notion that all whites were part of the same enemy camp (this reduced black radicalism); and (2) whites had a vested interest in "moderating" the struggle, overturning the Africanist principle of "Africa belongs to Africans," and Westernizing/acculturating blacks. In this regard, Biko regarded Charterists as the progeny of "missionaries"[126] who had produced *amagqobhoka* (converts who rejected their African heritage).[127]

Third, a key problem confronting the ANC/PAC/SASO was that most blacks were unprepared to get involved in the struggle because they were afraid.[128] Blacks lived in awe of whites and their power, believing the system was unchallengeable. Biko argued that the key was to make blacks believe in themselves and believe they could challenge the system—in other words, liberation began by creating "black pride."[129]

In formulating this vision, Biko drew on a wide array of sources and experiences:

- BC represented an explicit rejection of second-classness encoded into racial capitalism's ethnic ranking system. In this regard, BC shared similar roots to Afrikaner nationalism. The British Empire generated a hierarchy of "backward and advanced" groups and "positional psychology."[130] Apartheid inherited and continued this hierarchy, where individual worth derived from one's ethnic group. This ranking system affected not only one's economic life chances, but also one's perceived self-worth. As Biko noted, for blacks, this produced a sense of inferiority, weakness, and helplessness vis-à-vis whites, and negative self-stereotyping. Besides being psychologically unsettling, second-classness produced envy and insecurity. This gave rise to BC as a catch-up nationalism, triggered by the "pain" of being ranked badly.

- BC drew upon the U.S. black power movement, the Black Panthers, and West African negritude for inspiration. Biko synthesized into BC the ideas of African Americans, James Cone, and Malcolm X.[131] The SASO group listened repeatedly to recordings of Malcolm X's speeches.
- Frantz Fanon made an enormous impact on BC. From Fanon, BC drew the notion that black people needed to psychologically liberate themselves by standing up to whites.[132] By developing confidence in themselves, and hitting back, blacks would concretely overcome self-loathing and their fear of whites.[133] Blacks were seen to psychologically oppress themselves by internalizing a sense of inferiority and dependence on whites.[134] Biko said: "the type of black man we have today has lost his manhood. Reduced to an obliging shell, he looks with awe at the white power structure and accepts what he regards as the inevitable position."[135] At heart, BC proposed that people could choose either freedom or enslavement. The latter required confronting one's oppressors and one's fears and doubts.[136] Biko's solution was: "to make the black man come to himself; to pump life back into his empty shell; to infuse him with pride and dignity; to remind him of his complicity in the crime of allowing himself to be misused."[137]
- BC emerged just as New Left thought influenced white South African students. Biko was also influenced—hence, BC, like the New Left, criticizes capitalism without being Marxist, advocates democracy while criticizing liberal democracy,[138] and criticizes the old Left socialism of communist parties. Biko realized that aspects of liberalism, Marxism, and even African nationalism could be used to defend the status quo.[139]
- Paulo Freire's ideas on popular culture also influenced Biko and SASO's leadership.[140] Consequently, all BC self-help projects were grounded in Freirean thinking, which represented a rejection of the ANC's top-down Leninist vanguardist approach to politics. Ultimately, Biko's populism achieved what ANC vanguardism was incapable of—SASO reactivated a grassroots (youth-based) popular revolt against apartheid which, when it occurred (in 1976), terrified the ANC (because they neither created it, nor controlled it).
- Biko and BC were products of separate development. Biko was a member of the first generation to have grown up under apartheid as a Bantu Education product. Not surprisingly his nationalism has many echoes of Christian nationalism's "own-ness," racially conscious nationalism, and *Volkskapitalisme*'s self-help agendas.

Fundamentally, Biko reinvigorated the PAC's view that blacks must end their psychological subservience to, and dependency on whites, and assert their right to rule all Africa. After Biko, Lembede's Africanism was once more center stage in black politics. However, significantly, Biko simultaneously opened the door to co-opting coloreds and Indians into the black struggle. This was to pay handsome dividends during the 1980s.

Biko's vision contained five main themes:

- White South Africans were deemed "foreigners"[141]—a "settler minority"[142] with no right to rule any part of Africa. The NP's partition model was rejected because as "settlers," they had no right to rule any African land.
- A South African nation was to be built on black terms. Whites would be tolerated within this nation only on condition they accepted black rule. As Biko said, "We wish explicitly to state that this country belongs to black people and to them alone. Whites who live in our—who live in this country on terms laid down by blacks and on condition that they respect black people."[143] From this grew SASO's proposal for a radical transformation of society from white rule to black rule: "We are aware that the white man is sitting at our table. We know he has no right to be there; we want to remove him . . . strip the table of all the trappings put on it by him, decorate it in true African style, settle down and then ask him to join us on our terms if he wishes."[144] Biko proposed racially reranking South Africa—white domination was to be replaced by black domination. He justified this on the grounds of black majoritarianism (the ANC's policy). In 1976, he said: "At the present moment we have a culture here which is a European culture. This country looks, My Lord, like a province of Europe."[145] Biko proposed to radically alter this—"A country in Africa, in which the majority of people are African, must inevitably exhibit African values, and be truly African in style."[146] The white South African polity was to be obliterated and white South African culture effaced. Under white rule, acculturation had taken place on white terms; under black rule, it would take place on black terms. An African renaissance was called for,[147] in part grounded in a romanticized nostalgia for a past African communalistic culture.
- Blacks should be put in charge of every sector of society.
- History should be rewritten from a black perspective to reconstruct how South Africans see themselves, and to build a new "imagined community."[148]
- White power would not be destroyed by protests (which was viewed as "beggar tactics").[149] Rather, blacks had to simply stop collaborating and boycott every aspect of the system; this would render the state unworkable and ungovernable.

Biko's vision began with a few intellectuals in SASO. During 1970–1971, SASO dramatically expanded its adherents among black university students. From there, BC spread to the South African Student's Movement (SASM), which was organizing students in the rapidly expanding black school system. The Soweto Student's Representative Council (SSRC) was created by SASM. It was this SSRC that planned the fateful 16 June 1976 Soweto demonstration against using Afrikaans in black schools.[150] Biko's ideas on black "pride" and "assertiveness," coupled with the sense of excitement created by FRELIMO's takeover of Mozambique, triggered a mass populist uprising amongst urban black youth.

In October 1977, the Black Consciousness Movement was banned. But, in 1978, the Azanian People's Organization (AZAPO) was founded to promote BC ideals. Biko himself was killed while being interrogated by security police in 1977.

CHARTERISM RECONSTRUCTED

By the beginning of 1978, the Soweto revolt was crushed, in part because adults never joined the youth in their populist uprising. This produced an exodus of several thousand young militants who left South Africa looking for a political home. By this stage, the ANC had a Lusaka headquarters and a "reception network" in Swaziland, Botswana, Lesotho, and Mozambique. The ANC fortuitously had in place a mechanism to inherit the results of Biko's populism. The ANC consequently absorbed the bulk of these angry young exiles. For the first time since the mid-1960s, the ANC could build a force of fit young guerillas.[151] However, these new recruits brought with them BC thinking—that is, a worldview deeply influenced by PAC Africanism. For the ANC's leadership of Africanist Marxists, this posed a real challenge, and the political commissars were put to work. But ultimately they could not expunge Biko's BC ideas. Instead, the "class of '76" infused new thinking into the ANC—Lembede's Africanism had come home, and Charterism was about to be reconstructed.

The Soweto uprising changed the ANC. In 1976, it had been a weak organization with no capacity to mobilize people inside South Africa, and very little military capacity[152]—having only 100–200 MK members[153] and less than 200 political cadres[154] left inside the country. Soweto'76 changed this.

First, Soweto'76 was a rude awakening for the ANC's romantic vanguardist leadership because it revealed how they had allowed themselves to become politically irrelevant. A major populist uprising had occurred which the ANC did not create, could not control, and which had its roots in a PAC-centric ideology. Further, it highlighted the fact that a successful South African struggle would need to be urban-centric, not rural guerilla based.

Second, Soweto'76 infused new blood into the ANC, reviving the organization. An armed struggle actually became possible with MK gaining some 2,000–3,000 personnel.[155] Although limited in number and scope, the launching of ANC military operations (sabotage, attacking police stations and black township government buildings, terror attacks, and assassinating blacks working with the state) helped build political profile.[156] ANC "armed propaganda"[157] paid dividends in generating new legitimacy and hence recruiting new supporters. By 1986, the exiled ANC community was about 14,000[158] (in 1975, it had been 1,000). Many were involved in running the Lusaka administrative operations, but the ANC also ran farms, light factories, and a Tanzanian-based education/training center,[159] plus a number of military training centers in Angola (where East Germans and Soviets trained MK).[160]

Third, Soweto'76 brought about ideological changes within the ANC. From 1961, an alliance of Africanist Marxists and SACP communists set the tone for the ANC's ideological position. However, the influx of thousands of BC-inclined youth was to shift the ideological balance within the congress such that Africanism was put back on the agenda. However, while the ANC relied on the Soviets for military support (until 1989), Marxist Africanism remained mainstream,[161] and BC Africanism was less visible. But, after 1990, BC Africanism became ever more evident within the ANC, and by the time Thabo Mbeki became president, BC Africanism was setting the tone for the ANC's African renaissance vision.

Fourth, Soweto'76 triggered the ANC's 1978–1979 strategic review, which included an ANC delegation visiting Vietnam to ascertain why Vietnam's guerilla struggle had succeeded.[162] The Vietnamese told the ANC that political activity was more important than military action. The review recognized that the ANC had been too militaristic and worse, had fostered the "militaristic illusion"[163] that it could actually liberate South Africa by armed struggle.

Growing out of Soweto'76, the strategic review, and the lobbying of Mac Maharaj, the ANC recognized that military vanguardism had failed. Consequently, the primacy of armed struggle was abandoned, and the ANC turned to political mass mobilization.[164] It was decided that a broad national front should be built—a popular front to mobilize all classes and ethnic groups into a revolutionary struggle.[165] This front would operate legally and semi-legally, autonomously of the ANC's revolutionary vanguard,[166] and focus on mobilizing different urban sectors.[167] Political work was not going to replace armed struggle, but would supplement it—in other words, mobilizing a large Charterist constituency would create an internal support base for MK, thus facilitating armed struggle. This shift in ANC policy was one of the impetuses for the formation of the United Democratic Front (UDF)—an organization that lay at the heart of the 1980s struggle.

CHAPTER 6

The Struggle Against Apartheid: The 1980s Uprising

The 1980s were tumultuous—a period when unprecedented numbers of South Africans (on the Left and the Right) set themselves against the state, and all parties to the conflict turned to political violence. On the Left, huge numbers took to the streets to demonstrate. Many organizations could have captured this discontent, but ultimately the UDF emerged as the preeminent vehicle for mobilizing and organizing the 1980s antiapartheid struggle, which irrevocably transformed South Africa's political landscape.

The 1980s uprising had multiple causes, but at heart, the political turmoil grew out of P.W. Botha's reforms. As Huntington correctly predicted, dismantling Verwoerdian apartheid opened a Pandora's box of political activity. Botha's attempts to create consociational democracy (and a conservative alliance to rule this new system) posed a real threat to the Left because, if Botha had succeeded, he would have demobilized the antiapartheid cause. The Left had to fight back, stop the reforms working, and prevent Botha from successfully building a multiracial conservative alliance. The reforms created "issues" that the National Party's (NP's) opponents could use to mobilize their constituencies. Furthermore, building consociational democracy meant that the NP had to allow open debate. The logic of political reform and WHAM (Win Hearts and Minds) meant encouraging "nonwhite" political participation, and ending the 1960s–1970s repression of "nonwhite" political opposition. This led to the emergence of two left-wing opposition nodes in 1983—the United Democratic Front (UDF) and National Forum (NF); the UDF thrived, the NF did not.

Ultimately, 1980s South African politics revolved around the building of two political alliances—a right-wing bloc constructed by Botha reformists and a left-wing bloc constructed by the UDF. Botha's alliance came to include most homeland leaders (like Buthelezi, Mangope, and Sebe), tricameral parliamentarians, a range of black conservative community and vigilante groups, and sections of the black Ethiopian churches. The UDF/Mass Democratic Movement (MDM) alliance came to include Cosatu (the Congress of South African Trade Unions), and many Christian and Muslim clergymen. By the late 1980s, some homeland leaders began shifting their allegiances from Botha to the African National Congress (ANC), for example, General Holomisa. Both groupings used a mixture of emotional rhetoric and violence in their attempts to build constituencies, destabilize their opposition, and build hegemonic control (authority) over territory. Both worked to win new recruits from "the middle ground" between the left- and right-wing camps. By the late 1980s, the UDF was skilled at middle-ground politics, while the consociational reformists floundered.

Another factor in the turmoil was the way Botha's reforms destabilized and confused those running the apartheid state. Apartheid bureaucrats became increasingly unsure of what was expected of them as the 1980s proceeded, which served to undermine their former zeal and effectiveness in implementing NP policy. This increased the gaps available for left-wing mobilization.

Besides the reforms, there were five other reasons for the 1980s turmoil:

- The emergence of a large, restless school population. High birthrates meant that by the early 1980s, youth constituted 55 percent of South Africa's population. From 1972, the NP had dramatically expanded the urban black secondary school system, so by the 1980s, black secondary education was transformed from an "elite" into a "mass phenomenon."[1] This created the most highly educated generation of black South Africans. Most urban black youths were more educated than their parents, and came to oppose many of their parents' values, as well as their lack of resistance to apartheid. The new schools not only built new identities, but also drew together, on a large scale, literate youths with similar experiences and grievances.[2] The NP also expanded the black education system too quickly—for example, between 1980 and 1984, black secondary school enrolments doubled from 577,000 to over one million, and black university enrollments tripled from 10,000 to 36,000. The school system could not cope with the massive influx of pupils, and the labor market could not absorb graduates and dropouts from the understaffed and overcrowded high schools;[3] this generated frustration. Into this volatile mix came the Black Consciousness (BC) "black pride," resulting in a radicalized youth. Following the 1977 banning of BC organizations, a new student grouping—Congress of South African Students (COSAS)—emerged in 1979. COSAS mobilized black student militancy—building a network of student organizations in urban schools. The first organization since the ANC's banning to adopt the Freedom Charter, COSAS was the largest UDF affiliate in 1983.[4] It was led by fairly well-educated youths and skilled workers (i.e., the products of the expanded education system) whose constituency consisted of urban students and frustrated young people (unemployed due to the recession, but unable to attend school because of age restrictions).[5] During the 1980s, COSAS "comrades" became the shock troops of township uprisings—organizing school boycotts (against "gutter education"), organizing demonstrations, mobilizing attacks on collaborators (black councilors and policemen), manning barricades, enforcing boycotts, and running street committees and "people's courts."

- During the 1970s–1980s, the state expanded black training and education; increased black, Indian, and colored university facilities; and encouraged black trade unions. This generated a socioeconomic revolution, expanded black skills, and created an embryonic black middle class. The growth of an educated, upwardly mobile black, Indian, and colored population (radicalized by limitations placed on them by apartheid) created a pool of skilled people to build UDF structures.[6] Many UDF leaders precisely came from radical members of this middle class.[7] Significantly, from the 1970s, Marxism was taught in a number of South African universities.[8] In particular, the (Indian) University of Durban-Westville and (colored) University of the Western Cape produced many radicals who went on to establish and lead the UDF.[9] From these universities, Marxist ideas spilled into the trade unions and youth organizations.[10] The growth of trade unions also served to build black organizational skills, which became a valuable resource for 1980s left-wing mobilization.
- The 1981–1984 drought triggered massive black urbanization and socioeconomic stress. A falling gold price and drought produced a recession starting in 1982. The state consequently lacked resources to finance facilities/services for the new arrivals. Further, state food subsidies were frozen, while food prices rose. Urban black unemployment and poverty soared, especially on the East Rand, Vereeniging, and Port Elizabeth. Consequently, when the new urban black councils raised rent and service charges in 1984, these areas exploded in revolt. Consequently, whereas in 1976 most adults did not support the youth uprising, in 1984, many economically stressed adults (initially) fell in behind the youth-led rebellion.
- The UDF blossomed into a significant political force because a number of beneficial circumstances gave it access to resources. First, the ANC's strategic review channeled skilled ANC cadres into the UDF. Second, because the UDF was seen as untainted by South African Communist Party (SACP)/Soviet connections (like the ANC), it could raise Western funds. Significant West European funding meant that the UDF could employ numerous full-time staffers and pay for ongoing publicity.[11] Third, the UDF's initial focus on Indian and colored (tricameral) politics meant that it gained immediate access to the considerable wealth and skills of those communities.
- Botha proved unskilled at building a conservative consociational alliance, while simultaneously adept at alienating a wide range of opinion. The NP effectively mobilized a coalition of (internal and external) interests against itself. During the 1980s, Charterists managed to capture much of this alienated opinion, successfully coordinating it into a coherent antiapartheid force. Those alienated included: (1) South Africa's Westernized urban blacks, plus those aspiring to Westernization; (2) upwardly mobile, blacks, Indians, and coloreds frustrated by limitations placed on them by apartheid; (3) African states fearful that

apartheid-Balkanization might encourage their own ethnic minorities to demand independence; (4) South Africa's corporate sector, who saw apartheid as "bad for business" (corporate hostility became internationally significant because they owned South Africa's Anglo press, which distributed antiapartheid stories to the international media via Reuters news agency); (5) many Western intellectuals, journalists, and teachers—who found apartheid "morally unacceptable"—were mobilized into action by skillful ANC publicity and sensationalized media images (this intelligentsia helped mobilize significant antiapartheid pressure on Western governments); and (6) African Americans became an important antiapartheid lobby group. Once apartheid was enmeshed into African American identity politics, it effectively became part of U.S. domestic politics.

PLAYERS IN THE 1980s STRUGGLE

The 1980s became an era of intense organization building in South African politics, as all political players tried to mobilize South Africans into their "camp." During the most intense period of struggle (1983–1988) the key players were the NP, UDF, and Cosatu. Ironically, it was not these players, but the ANC that eventually inherited power in the 1990s.

The key driver of 1980s South African politics was Botha's NP. Botha's reformers initiated the 1980s struggle, and along with his securocrats, they set the parameters within which it unfolded (see chapter 4).

A number of right-wing organizations emerged to challenge the NP's reform agenda, including the Conservative Party (CP) and *Afrikaner Weerstandbeweging* (AWB), plus an array of smaller organizations.[12] The CP was the largest, functioning as a parliamentary party advocating a return to Verwoerdian apartheid. The extreme-Right AWB operated as an extraparliamentary paramilitary group. Although right-wingers were never able to mobilize large constituencies, they distracted Botha and imposed limits to his reforms by creating organizational fulcrums for a potential white backlash.

Until 1988, the ANC was an "external" player, but it had a "presence" in the minds of all the other players. When Botha initiated his reforms, the ANC had limited political or military capacity inside South Africa, and focused its energies largely on external diplomatic maneuvers. These maneuvers were important for mobilizing external pressures (especially sanctions) against the NP, and for limiting international acceptance of Buthelezi's Inkatha Freedom Party (IFP). The 1984 township uprising caught the ANC (once again) unprepared to take advantage of a roused black constituency because its internal underground was too small to mobilize or organize this potential constituency. The ANC, in fact, became concerned about this 1980s youth-driven populist uprising, realizing that, if it failed to keep up with this youth radicalism, it ran the risk that the youth would look elsewhere for a political home.[13] Consequently, the ANC ran to keep up with unfolding events—at its 1985 Kabwe Conference (in Zambia), the organization made two significant shifts:

- Allowing whites into ANC leadership positions.
- Adopting a "people's war" policy—that is, MK (*Umkonto we Sizwe*/ANC armed wing) violence was to be stepped up, and the ANC's earlier policy of avoiding "soft targets" and civilian casualties was abandoned.[14] MK chief, Chris Hani, proposed that terror attacks on white civilians might prove useful.[15]

Therefore, the ANC stepped up its attacks (see table 6.1).

But the ANC/MK remained weak—in 1987, MK had 12,000 trained guerillas and claimed to have deployed 6,000. However, "in late 1987 there was no evidence that 5,000 or more MK cadres were active inside the country . . . [and it was] clear . . . as many as 30% had, in effect, abandoned their missions."[16] Further, it was evident that "the majority of blacks while sympathetic, felt little compulsion to serve other than as a cheering section. Umkonto was failing to convert public approval into active military support."[17] So, despite its romantic vanguardist rhetoric of "conquering power," the ANC had no hope of ever seriously militarily challenging Botha's securocrats. Nonetheless, its "people's war" strategy paid handsome "publicity dividends" because increased ANC/MK activity—a mix of sabotage and terrorist attacks—served as effective "armed propaganda," and did repopularize the ANC in black townships. In addition, the ANC placed underground political cadres into organizations like the

Table 6.1:
ANC Guerilla Activity, 1977–1989

Year	Number of Attacks	Year	Number of Attacks
1977	23	1984	44
1978	30	1985	136
1979	13	1986	228
1980	19	1987	247
1981	55	1988	245
1982	39	1989	281
1983	56		

Source: Lodge, T., and B. Nasson. 1991. *All, Here, and Now: Black Politics in South Africa in the 1980s* (Cape Town: David Philip), 178.

UDF and Cosatu to influence them; this paid high political dividends because the ANC became the chief beneficiary of their successes.

The Congress of South African Trade Unions (Cosatu) became a central 1980s political player. Cosatu was formed in 1985, from the merger of two trade union groupings—the Federation of South African Trade Unions (FOSATU) and the "community unions." The emergence of a powerful union federation like Cosatu was the by-product of one of Botha's reforms, namely, the 1979 Wiehahn Report, which advocated deracializing the workplace and allowing the growth of black trade unionism. A group of white Marxists moved quickly to utilize this Wiehahn-created space, and began unionizing South Africa's expanding black proletariat. In 1979, they launched FOSATU as an organization focused exclusively on workplace issues. They deliberately avoided politics, to give the state no excuse for attacking them while they built the foundations of worker power. FOSATU stressed the building of professionalized unions based on factory-to-factory recruitment, democratic shop-floor organization and well-trained union organizers. A commitment to workerism, professionalism, and organizational training characterized FOSATU. Its training program created a large pool of skilled organizers, who became an organizational backbone of the 1980s antiapartheid struggle (a core trainer, Alec Irwin, became a 1990s ANC cabinet minister).

In addition to FOSATU, there were two other union groups in the early 1980s—the Council of Unions of South Africa (CUSA) and the "community unions." CUSA was aligned to BC, the "community unions" aligned to the ANC, and FOSATU advocated an "independent," nonaligned approach. The ANC-aligned community unions adopted a highly political approach—encouraging product boycotts and recruiting members in township mass meetings. Following Wiehahn, black trade union membership soared, reaching 670,000 by 1983, when the three union groups began talking about unity.[18] But unity proved difficult because of conflicts over the issue of "workerism" versus "populism." FOSATU, built by workerists, argued that workers needed an autonomous power base—that is, in any alliance, care was needed to ensure that black middle-class (ANC) populists did not subordinate working-class interests within a broader "black struggle."[19] The (populist) "community unions" saw no such danger. Cyril Ramaphosa of the National Union of Mineworkers helped bridge the workerist-populist divide, leading to Cosatu's formation in 1985. BC-aligned CUSA unions did not join because of Cosatu's commitment to nonracial membership. Initially, Cosatu did not formally align itself politically (affiliated with neither the UDF nor the National Forum/NF). However, Cosatu rapidly found itself caught up in the mid-1980s political turmoil—and (despite UDF-Cosatu tensions) became enmeshed into Charterist politics, particularly once the 1986 state of emergency crippled the UDF and left Cosatu as the main functioning left-wing organizational base.[20] Thereafter, Cosatu became an assertive political voice for socialism, wealth redistribution, and sanctions and disinvestment. A Cosatu-UDF alliance was ultimately formalized as the Mass Democratic Movement (MDM). During the 1980s, the union movement became a key player in destabilizing Botha's reform agendas by (1) building a pool of skilled and disciplined black activists; and (2) by developing the capacity to organize mass stay-aways that could cripple the economy.

The United Democratic Front (UDF) was the other major 1980s political player—it was formed in 1983, as a broad popular front of student/youth groups, and civics, women's and religious organizations. It was a highly decentralized umbrella body of antiapartheid organizations, consisting of a loose coalition of hundreds of affiliates representing a diverse array of classes, ethnicities, and beliefs. The only unifying features in 1983 were rejection of apartheid, plus willingness to participate in street demonstrations.[21] As a broad all-encompassing front, the UDF could take advantage of all political spaces opened up by Botha's reforms and all political opportunities created by 1980s socioeconomic conditions. The initial impetus for its launch was the tricameral constitutional reforms—the UDF was founded to promote a colored and Indian boycott of Tricameral Parliament elections. Later, it also tapped into the turmoil triggered by urban black reforms. The outcome was the mobilization of a massive multiracial constituency of diverse people, stirred into action by the UDF's "culture of protest," "culture of boycotting apartheid institutions," and the UDF/ANC call to make South Africa "ungovernable" (by getting people to refuse to collaborate with all government agencies). The UDF had no members; people belonged to affiliates that belonged to the UDF coalition. Most UDF followers were organized by one of three types of organization—youth, women's, or civics.[22] By the mid-1980s, affiliation to the UDF broadly meant recognizing the ANC's claim to leadership, admiration for armed struggle, messianic socialism, and millennial expectations of revolutionary change.[23] Youth/student organizations were central to the UDF's ungovernability strategy.

Although MK attacks did much to repopularize the ANC, the UDF's success was really central to reactivating a Charterist constituency, and hence putting the ANC at the center of South African politics by the end of the 1980s.

The National Forum (NF)—launched in 1983—was an organization to the Left of the UDF. Like the UDF, the NF was created to mobilize opposition to Botha's reforms, but it focused its opposition on the Koornhof bills[24] (Botha's reform of urban black rights and governance). The key drivers behind launching the NF were the Azanian People's Organization (AZAPO, the successor organization to BC) and Neville Alexander of the Unity Movement (UM). The launch drew participants from a range of BC, Africanist, independent socialist, and (even a few) Charterist organizations. The NF endorsed the Manifesto of the Azanian People: antiracism, anti-imperialism, noncollaboration with the oppressor, independent working-class organizations, and opposition to all alliances with ruling-class parties. It advocated establishing a "democratic, antiracist,[25] worker republic in Azania."[26] (The NF and the Pan African Congress/PAC called South Africa "Azania.") AZAPO, the main organization within the NF, advocated BC workerism—as with other BC groups, AZAPO had shifted leftward during the early 1980s, mixing socialism with the original BC position.[27] Alexander's "independent socialists" brought to the NF the UM's long-standing advocacy of noncollaboration,[28] a Trotskyist vision of socialist revolution, and opposition to the "pro-capitalist, anti-working class nature of the ANC bourgeois social democracy . . . [and the] unprincipled Stalinism of the [South African] Communist Party."[29]

The NF rejected the Freedom Charter, the ANC's multiracialism, and the SACP's two-stage revolution model. The NF believed that Charterism would ultimately lead to a "negotiated betrayal," producing a capitalist state and "bourgeois democracy" ruled by a black middle class. During the 1980s, sporadic violent clashes occurred between AZAPO and UDF activists. Although the NF never managed to mobilize a huge constituency like the UDF, it nonetheless played an important role in awakening the 1980s antiapartheid struggle.

Another group of 1980s players were homeland-based leaders/organizations and their conservative black constituencies. Separate development created homeland-based black middle classes (who Biko called the "Bantustan bourgeoisie"). There were 400,000 black homeland functionaries[30] staffing the bureaucracies, schools, media, hospitals, police forces, armies, and the like. They had a vested interest in apartheid, and their access to resources and institutions gave them political power. Apartheid's promotion of ethnicity also found support among those who relished identification with being Zulu, Xhosa, Tswana, Sotho, and so on. These identities were actively promoted by the NP and took hold in some areas—especially rural tribal areas. Apartheid had a natural constituency of conservative black support in rural areas because it served the interests of conservatives identifying with traditional African culture, traditional African governance (chiefs, etc.), and tribal customs. The leaders who most successfully organized these homeland constituencies into significant power bases were KwaZulu's chief, Mangosuthu Buthelezi, and Bophuthatswana's chief, Lucas Mangope. Buthelezi, in particular, built a significant political organization, the Inkatha Freedom Party (IFP), solidly grounded in South Africa's largest ethnic group, Zulus.

Inkatha's origins lay in the 1920's Zulu national movement, *Inkatha Ya Ka Zulu*, launched to generate support for Zulu traditionalism/monarchy in the face of Westernization/detribalization pressures. Under Dube, the ANC's Natal branch was enmeshed with this Inkatha movement. In 1975, Buthelezi revived Inkatha as a national cultural liberation movement with the objectives of: liberating blacks from white cultural domination, abolishing racial discrimination, promoting Zulu self-determination, and bringing about power sharing and progression toward black majority rule.[31] By the mid-1980s, Buthelezi built Inkatha into a huge organization of 1.5 million members, drawing support from the "Bantustan bourgeoisie," traditional Zulu tribalists, and Zulu migrant workers in the cities. Support for Inkatha was especially strong in rural tribal areas. During the 1980s, Inkatha promoted a form of Zulu nationalism and Zulu monarchism associated with a conservative pride in Zulu tradition and ethnicity. This was tied to advocacy of capitalism and consociationalism. Buthelezi used both the (homeland controlled) KwaZulu school system and Radio Zulu (with South Africa's highest radio listenership) to promote Inkatha, as well as Inkatha's rural branches as development agents.[32] Within Natal, Inkatha's reach was ubiquitous. Inkatha also constructed a significant coercive machinery in the form of *Impis* (armed warriors) and the KwaZulu police. From 1983 to the mid-1990s, serious violent conflict characterized Inkatha's relationships with the UDF/ANC, as both sides fought for hegemonic control over Natal and Witwatersrand urban and peri-urban areas. Buthelezi opposed the ANC's armed struggle and sanctions as being economically destructive. Botha saw Buthelezi as a crucial partner in implementing his consociational reforms, but ultimately Buthelezi was too cunning to fully commit himself to Botha, especially once he realized Botha was unable to construct a viable conservative alliance.

In general, Botha's securocrats could rely upon homeland government supporters as allies, and the homeland police, soldiers, and security police were generally more ruthless than white security personnel in suppressing antiapartheid activists. During the 1980s, the Bophuthatswana and Venda defense forces hunted down and killed ANC guerillas, the Ciskei security forces systematically crushed UDF structures in their jurisdiction, and Inkatha supporters engaged in a civil war with UDF/ANC supporters.

Another group of 1980s players were a range of black conservatives who established vigilante groups, plus some Ethiopian churches that allied themselves to Botha's government.[33] From 1986, vigilante groups sprang up in many black townships in response to a changed balance of power created by the National Security Management System's (NSMS's) adoption of McCuen's counterrevolutionary methods. From 1984 to mid-1986, youth and student organizations—calling themselves "the comrades"—rendered the townships ungovernable. Having violently driven black policemen and councilors out the townships, the comrades established UDF "street committees" and "people's courts." In many areas, they imposed a reign of terror, attacking people suspected of not supporting "the struggle."[34] Authority figures (e.g., teachers, and sometimes their own parents) were often treated harshly. A generational cleavage opened up and many adults became alarmed at the harshness of people's courts and extortions by comrades.[35]

When, in mid-1986, securocrats shifted to "hard" repression and smashed UDF youth structures/street committees/people's courts, they created a gap for black conservatives to organize themselves. Vigilante groups, often led by warlords, were the result—many vigilantes evidenced a strong antipathy toward "youngsters who called themselves comrades but are really *ntseras* [criminals]."[36] Some vigilante groups were actually the parents of the comrades, for example, Uitenhage's "African Parents Concerned Committee."[37] Although many vigilantes were conservatives, some were disaffected former UDF supporters concerned the youth were out of control, and alienated by the violence (e.g., "necklacing"/burning people alive) and the wanton destruction of property wrought in the name of the struggle. In Cape Town's shack lands, for example, a vigilante army of elders, called *witdoeke*, grew from disaffected UDF supporters changing sides.[38] The NSMS encouraged such conservative mobilization, and vigilantes became valuable allies of Botha's government. Because vigilantes were grassroots organizations, they were more effective than the police in rooting out radical activists.[39] The vigilantes imposed a reign of terror on the townships.

In the 1980s, millions of South Africans were members of some 2,000 Ethiopian churches, which mixed traditional African beliefs with Christianity. The largest was the Zion Christian Church (ZCC) with 1.5 million members. During the 1980s, a number of Ethiopian church leaders allied themselves with Botha's conservative alliance, including ZCC bishop Lekhanyane, who even invited Botha to address the annual Easter gathering of hundreds of thousands of ZCC worshipers. This was a major public relations coup for Botha's conservative alliance. The support of the Ethiopian churches did not translate into their active engagement in politics, but it was undoubtedly a psychological comfort for millions of black people who sided with apartheid during the 1980s struggle.

THE UNITED DEMOCRATIC FRONT

Of all the players, it was the United Democratic Front (UDF) that most came to define the trajectory of South Africa's 1980s political conflict, becoming unquestionably the key antiapartheid force.

The UDF was formed for seven reasons. Most fundamental, Botha's reforms threatened to undercut the basis for Charterist mobilization and therefore had to be disrupted.[40] Second, in 1981, ANC Africanists (connected to Winnie Mandela) sought to create a new organization—to be called Maluti—that would unify ANC and PAC Africanists.[41] This unnerved "nonracial" white, Indian, and colored (WIC) Charterists, partly inspiring the UDF's launch. Third, the formation of the NF (ahead of the UDF) by an alliance of BC workerists and independent socialists also unnerved nonracial WIC Charterists, inspiring the formation of the UDF as an NF rival.[42] Fourth, the ANC (especially Maharaj) encouraged the formation of a popular front after its strategic review. Fifth, following early 1980s security police successes against MK, Charterists recognized the need to develop functionally differentiated specialist organizations.[43] The UDF would specialize in internal politics, autonomously of the ANC diplomatic and military wings. Sixth, during the 1960s–1970s, South Africa underwent a socioeconomic revolution involving industrialization, urbanization, rapid economic growth, and the dramatic expansion of educational opportunities. Many Indians, coloreds, and blacks experienced tremendous upward mobility. This created many new black, colored, and Indian constituencies to be recruited into Charterism if an organizational base existed to mobilize them.[44] Seventh, it was realized that mobilizing internal Charterist constituencies required more than "armed propaganda." The UDF effectively turned to "unarmed propaganda"[45] to supplement MK activities.

The key movers behind the formation of the UDF were the Transvaal and Natal Indian Congresses (TIC/NIC), especially Cas Saloojee (TIC) and Pravin Gordhan (NIC), who advocated forming a broad popular front to fight tricameral reforms.[46] But they cleverly invited a colored Dutch Reform Church pastor, Allan Boesak, to call for the front; Boesak was an ideal choice because convincing coloreds to boycott the tricameral elections would be more difficult than convincing Indians. In January 1983, Boesak made his call for the "united front" to promote the "politics of refusal"[47] in front of a large contingent of foreign and local press (arranged by Saloojee). Boesak also launched the UDF in August 1983, using Martin Luther King–type (biblical and human rights) language.[48] This played well in the Western media, and the biblical language was well suited to the colored community. Once formed, the UDF passed through six stages:[49]

Stage 1: Opposing Botha's Reforms (1983–1984)

The UDF was primarily formed to coordinate countrywide Charterist resistance to tricameralism.[50] Botha's reforms aimed to create a multiracial conservative alliance of WICs, which would have created a solid foundation for his consociational plans. For Charterists, this was a highly threatening development necessitating an engagement with the NP government for the loyalty of colored and Indian South Africans. Before 1985, the UDF was primarily geared to this competition.[51] Not surprisingly, the UDF was born as an organization led by Indians and coloreds, and in many ways, it was always dominated by highly educated, upwardly mobile members of the Indian and colored middle classes,[52] plus members of the white radical intelligentsia—that is, WIC radicals called Yummies (young upwardly mobile Marxists). However, this leadership profile generated problems for the UDF because WIC middle-class radicals were "disconnected" from the black townships.[53] The UDF's organizational base was strongest in Indian and colored areas and hardly existed in black areas[54] (where radical organization was, in any case, weak[55]). And although they considered themselves Marxists, and had some connections to colored workers,[56] UDF leaders were disconnected from black workers.[57] This was one reason the Front was so slow to catch up with the 1984 township revolt.[58] It also led to UDF mistakes, for example, encouraging the township reign of terror (by advocating ungovernability), which then generated the vigilante backlash. It also meant that the Front needed to spend much energy trying to "identify" black leaders and then foreground them, so it wouldn't be seen as a WIC organization. Despite successfully promoting many black leaders, the UDF constantly faced an undercurrent of black resentment about WIC (especially Indian) domination. This induced many black activists to abandon UDF activism in favor of MK.[59]

Because the UDF wished to mobilize a wide cross-section of opposition to the tricameral reforms, the Front initially opted for caution—in other words, in order not to appear too radical, the UDF did not officially adopt the ANC's Charter, presenting itself instead as a broad-based antiapartheid coalition where different kinds of people could find a political home. Boesak became the UDF's key speaker in stage one. Having launched the Front, UDF activists turned to their one area of great strength—as a group of highly educated people, they understood how to use the media. The UDF avoided insurrectionism and rash confrontationism (associated with ANC romantics and township militants) in favor of generating media issues to embarrass the state (especially with overseas audiences) plus publicizing issues attracting new constituencies into the Charterist alliance.[60] The UDF launched three inaugural campaigns to embarrass and/or undermine the state—against the tricameral reforms, black urban government reforms, and the Ciskei homeland government.

The UDF's anti-tricameral campaign, advocating a boycott of the new system, was brilliantly executed—deploying a mix of quality print media, house-to-house campaigning in Indian and colored areas, and large public meetings. Although the million-signatures campaign (against apartheid reform) failed to reach its goal, it helped cement nonracial teamwork. The UDF also learned to work with South Africa's mainstream media, developing good relationships with many journalists. Consequently, throughout the 1980s, the UDF received generous (and mostly positive) coverage from South Africa's Anglo press. The UDF's anti-tricameral campaign succeeded in its objective—it delegitimized Botha's reform package and placed an alternative UDF model on the national agenda. The UDF's founding slogan—"UDF Unites. Apartheid Divides"—created the dichotomy between the NP's partition (and/or consociational) model and the Front's nonracial/"national unity" model. The 1980s struggle was about whether "partition" or "national unity" would triumph.

During the tricameral elections, seven UDF leaders were detained. When the Supreme Court ordered their release, they feared redetention and went into hiding. In September 1984, six of these leaders went to Durban's British consulate and refused to leave. The consulate occupation became a protest against state detentions—creating international bad publicity for Botha's government. This taught the UDF much about the propaganda value of systematically provoking state repression to generate negative international media coverage.

Stage 2: 1984 Township Revolt

On 3 September 1984—the day the Tricameral Parliament met for the first time—the most sustained black township revolt in South African history began with the killing of Sharpeville's deputy mayor. It spread quickly to Transvaal, Free State, and eastern Cape townships. Johannesburg/Pretoria/Vereeniging and Eastern Cape townships constituted the revolt's epicenter. The revolt took the form of marches on council offices, burning of municipal and school buildings, attacking the homes of black councilors and black policemen, killing black "collaborators" (councilors, policemen, and alleged government "spies"), and erecting barricades to enforce stay-aways and consumer boycotts. Enforcement was often violent and cruel; COSAS "comrades" (students and unemployed youths) overwhelmingly drove this political violence. The 1984 revolt repeated the pattern of earlier revolts—that is, the townships periodically erupted into populist outbursts of anger, driven by romantic insurrectionists who failed to develop good organizations or long-term plans.[61] On their own, populist uprisings did not threaten the NP government because they were easily crushed.

COSAS youth were mobilized into an almost anarchistic force. The rhetoric of "people's education" (with roots in Biko-inspired SASO) held these insurrectionists together—that is, COSAS argued that Bantu Education deliberately gave them "gutter education" in order to oppress blacks. This was blamed for their parents' poverty and youth unemployment. The apartheid state was deemed irredeemably illegitimate and violence against the state, its agents (police), and collaborators legitimate.[62] "Eliminating [killing] the enemy" was legitimate comrades' business.[63] The 1980s youth revolt lashed out at (black) authority figures, including police, teachers (especially headmasters), town councilors, businessmen, and even parents.[64] COSAS comrades abrogated to themselves the right to "discipline" anyone engaging in activities deemed detrimental to "the struggle." Discipline could mean anything from being expelled from a "people's organization" to being beaten or killed.[65] Decisions about discipline or "elimination" were taken in youth-run street committees.[66] Those deemed liable for elimination or discipline included anyone working for the state, anyone indirectly serving the state (e.g., capitalists and black conservatives), "misdirected" Charterists, and ordinary people who offended the "people's conscience."[67] Many COSAS leaders were the school system's successes, and had a coherent political vision and were controlled. However, the same cannot be said for many followers;[68] unemployed youths (often school dropouts) and weaker students were generally ill-disciplined.[69] They often turned the notion of ungovernability to their own advantage—burning schools (so as not to write exams), extorting money/goods from shops, and settling scores from past disputes. Criminals also joined up, and used the struggle for their own material gain;[70] this led to a phenomenon called *comtsotis* (comrade criminals).[71]

In the face of this populist violence, the UDF initially floundered,[72] not knowing how to capture or control this uprising for long-term Charterist organizational gain. In fact, the Front was in a degree of disarray,[73] and initially found itself on the margins of the township revolt—it could neither direct not stop the violence, although occasional statements by some UDF leaders encouraged more violence.[74]

Stage 3: People's Power (1985 to Mid-1986)

When the revolt erupted, the UDF and ANC were unprepared for directing and harnessing it. The UDF leadership saw black townships as underorganized, and believed without organization and planning there could be no victory.[75] The UDF wanted to give direction to the revolt,[76] recognizing that a directed and sustained township revolt could provide a stream of negative television images to discredit Botha's government overseas and locally, undermine the reform process, and act as a potential recruitment mechanism to inspire other areas to join the uprising. But township militants were indifferent and even hostile to UDF leadership.[77]

The November 1984 stay-away was a turning point for the UDF. The Front was opposed to this stay-away (called by COSAS), arguing what was really needed was the building of organizational structures and door-to-door conscientizing[78] visits.[79] UDF leaders like Chikane were stoned on their way to work (breaking the boycott). But when 800,000 workers and 400,000 students stayed at home, the UDF reassessed its strategy.[80] This resulted in the UDF restructuring itself toward a more centralized vanguardist organization (i.e., away from affiliates making decisions, and toward centralized leadership-driven insurrectionist activities).[81] UDF leaders began working partly underground.[82] The Front also developed a sophisticated organization and public relations machinery (with full-time employees), made possible by European (especially Scandinavian) money.[83] Crucially, the UDF abandoned its earlier concern with winning over the "middle ground," gearing itself instead to organizing and harnessing black township militancy.[84] This was partly driven by UDF (WIC) leaders' concerns that if they did not manage the township revolt, Africanists would gain control.[85] Therefore, the UDF shifted:

- The years 1983–1984 focused on building colored and Indian support by being "cautious" and deploying gradualist multiracialism (due to perceived colored conservatism[86] and the de facto racial nature of existing South African society).[87]
- From 1985, the Front shifted from "caution" to "radicalism" in order to enmesh itself with township militancy.

In January 1985, the ANC (also from the sidelines) used its externally based Radio Freedom to encourage township insurrectionism and violence with the slogan "Render South Africa Ungovernable."[88] Thereafter, the theme of creating "ungovernability" (refusing to collaborate with government bodies and boycotting payments of rents and service charges) also appeared in UDF speeches. From 1985, the revolt was given direction by the notion of building "people's power" and planned boycotts. Consumer boycotts of white shops also began. The results were dramatic.

- Botha's reformers planned to have 103 elected urban black councils operating by December 1984. In December 1985, only three councils were functioning,[89] and township administration was destroyed.
- Black policemen (and their families) were driven out of townships. The burning down of houses occupied by policemen often triggered brutal police retaliation prompting youth counter-anger/retaliation[90]—a spiral of viciousness was initiated.
- Youth-run street committees/people's courts exercised some "authority" over many townships. These structures helped develop leadership and organizational skills, and in some areas engaged in street cleaning and "crime-prevention,"[91] but other people's courts degenerated into thuggery—violence was deployed against anti-Charterists, alleged state collaborators, and activists not towing the majority's "line."[92] The most extreme punishment was "necklacing" (being burned alive).
- Destroying government authority over some townships gave the ANC internal safe havens, and MK survival rates consequently improved. In 1986, civic militia units (*amabutho*) emerged, giving the UDF some coercive power to enforce stay-aways and consumer boycotts, and punish township residents who defied "the people's will."[93]

The UDF learned to effectively harness and organize the previously "uncontrolled insurrectionism" of the township youths by building structures of "people power."[94]

The intervention of Charterist parents to end school boycotts was part of this process—that is, the National Educational Crisis Committee (NECC) was formed to get the youth back to school[95]—partly because, with schools closed and children dispersed, Charterists lost organizing sites for rallying their young township shock troops. The NECC deployed "people's education" rhetoric to steer these youths. Shifting to township mobilization meant that the UDF got caught up in waves of populist militancy. In the process, it became less of a Front and more of a political organization,[96] and came to occupy "the leading role in political developments inside the country"[97]—the UDF came to be perceived as being at the helm; and in politics, "perception" becomes "reality."[98]

The UDF became skilled at deploying the utopian symbolism of "people's power"[99] through its own media and via the commercial Anglo press. It created the perception of a revolutionary insurrection powerful enough to overthrow the state, while in reality no area was fully liberated[100]—at most, some townships were in a state of anarchy where neither the state nor UDF exercised full authority. But, reality aside, the UDF's media machine successfully turned it into the "ideological center" of a revolution.[101] Funerals became crucial symbolic moments, where the struggle could be advertised (by banners acclaiming the UDF, Mandela, the ANC, and the Communist Party), leaders were given "profile," mass mobilization could take place, and crowds were whipped into a frenzy.[102] Funerals-as-resistance were repeatedly used to provoke the police (who were foolish enough to allow themselves to be provoked), which led to more deaths, and hence more funerals. The cycle continued, and the UDF kept growing as it mobilized ever-larger numbers of people into mass protests against Botha's government. The UDF's publicity machine used funerals as carefully crafted media events. A never-ending stream of media images of funerals and the accompanying political violence served the UDF well by mobilizing new recruits (for future crowds) and generating overseas hostility to "apartheid." Chester Crocker, then the U.S. assistant secretary of state for African affairs, noted how the U.S. media, American antiapartheid activists, and Bishop Tutu "simplified South Africa's trauma into a series of emotive civil rights soundbites."[103] Television viewers were treated to a riveting spectacle of emotive images accompanied by sensationalized story lines and simplified commentary that served to whip up a frenzy of antiapartheid indignation in the United States (and the West).[104] The resultant international pressure (e.g., sanctions) dramatically curtailed the NP's room for maneuver.

Stage 4: Repression (Mid-1986 to Early 1988)

By early 1986, cold war securocrats concluded that South Africa had reached stage two of Mao Tse Tung's revolutionary formula. Hawkish securocrats (deploying McCuen's[105] logic) convinced Botha that if drastic action were not taken to crush the UDF, South Africa would soon enter stage three, and a "communist victory" (stage four) would become inevitable. The result was a shift to "hard repression" in May 1986 (see chapter 4). A national state of emergency was declared in June 1986. On the first day, 1,200 activists were detained. By the end of 1986, an estimated 16,000 to 20,000 activists had been detained. Many were interviewed and quickly released; however, for the remainder of 1986, on average 5,000 people were in detention at any one time.[106] COSAS youth structures were targeted, in particular, and layer upon layer of youth leadership removed. One consequence of decimating COSAS structures was the creation of a replacement youth organization—in March 1987, the South African Youth Congress (SAYCO) was launched under the slogan "Freedom or Death: Victory Is Certain." SAYCO had more than 500,000 members,[107] and became the Left's troops within a conservative-leftist struggle for township hegemony—fighting conservative vigilantes and Inkatha (1987–1989), and Inkatha (after 1990) in what the media came to call "black-on-black" violence.

Securocrat repression quickly smashed the UDF's organizational capacity. By early 1987, the township insurrection was over, and the state withdrew white troops and policemen. In their place were deployed black "instant policemen" and municipal policemen (employed by urban black councils). These black policemen worked closely with conservative vigilante groups. From 1987, these conservative black groups coercively imposed their control over the townships. (Conservative vigilantes were naturally encouraged by the securocrats as part of their McCuen strategy to reassert authority and drive the revolution back to stage one.)

The UDF's response to this changed situation was a "tactical retreat."[108] UDF leaders realized that township militancy and defending what had been built in 1985 was no longer a possibility. They understood that if they did not quickly build a new constituency, they would become a small isolated vanguard, highly vulnerable to being targeted by the state.[109] The UDF responded as follows:

- It stopped challenging and provoking the state.[110]
- It produced upbeat media and public relations with the message, "we are still here; we are not beaten; and the struggle continues."[111] This was geared to bolster the flagging morale of UDF activists. During 1987, the UDF organized whole-page advertisements in South African newspapers calling for the ANC's unbanning. This not only boosted the morale of UDF activists, but also had a profound political impact internally and internationally.[112] Charterist morale was also bolstered by increased ANC guerrilla attacks.
- It negotiated alliances with the South African Council of Churches and Cosatu. As UDF capacity for action declined, Cosatu and left-wing clergy were relied upon to carry on the struggle.[113]
- It returned to its earlier cautious approach.[114] Township insurrectionism was abandoned in favor of recruiting the "middle ground" into the Charterist camp.

> During the 1983–1984 cautious period, the UDF had competed with the NP for the loyalty of coloreds and Indians. Now, it shifted to encouraging whites to opt for negotiation rather than war. By the mid-1980s, the white community was clearly politically fragmenting, and it was hoped that some "middle-ground" whites could be recruited into the Charterist camp. In 1987, the Five Freedoms Forum was launched to facilitate an engagement with liberal whites[115]—geared to drawing them out of "Botha's alliance" and into the Charterist alliance. That same year, white activists were asked to implement the "Call to Whites" and build UDF white affiliates.[116] It was argued that, if organized, white affiliates could become a powerful force for change within the white community and serve to weaken Botha's alliance.[117] In 1987, the UDF also realized that its flirtation with township insurrectionism had alienated coloreds and Indians, and it now needed to reengage with "middle-ground" coloreds/Indians.[118] Cosatu workerists were not impressed with the UDF "broadening the struggle" to include middle-class whites and even liberal businessmen. The UDF acknowledged that this would slow the struggle to the pace of the most conservative whites attracted,[119] but with the securocrats ascendant, there was little option but to engage with the white community, and even white business leaders were now welcomed and mobilized through the Consultative Business Movement[120] (although they were strategically kept as arms-length allies[121]). UDF "white sector" work did weaken Botha's camp, contributing to a growing sense that Botha's reform agenda was less viable than negotiating with the ANC. Further, the visible presence of white UDF supporters served to make the ANC less threatening to ordinary white South Africans, and helped promote the ANC/UDF's positive multiracial image overseas.

By 1987, the limits of repression and rebellion were clear to both sides. It was obvious to all that a stalemate existed—the NP was powerful enough to block an ANC "conquest of power" and crush any township insurrection. However, the NP had insufficient power to neutralize the large multiracial Charterist constituency mobilized by the UDF. Neither the NP nor the ANC/UDF was powerful enough to dislodge the other. Hence, both sides faced the prospect of ongoing conflict, with no likelihood of victory for either side. Not surprisingly, in 1987, secret ANC-NP "talks about talks" began.

Stage 5: Sidelined (1988–1989)

In February 1988, the UDF was banned, but continued to operate in practice if not in name, forging links with Cosatu to create the Mass Democratic Movement (MDM). However, the UDF had been considerably weakened by the repression; consequently, Cosatu became the more significant internal player in 1988–1989.

But the defining feature of this period was the shift toward NP-ANC negotiation politics.[122] The UDF (and MDM) was effectively being sidelined. Whereas from 1983 to 1987 the UDF was politically more significant than the largely ineffectual ANC-in-exile,[123] in 1988 that changed—for the first time, the initiative moved to the ANC.[124] With the shift to negotiations, the ANC and NP faced a problem—both had spent years demonizing their opponents. Now they had to go back to their constituencies and prepare them for negotiations, and the prospect of compromises with the opposition "devil." The ANC slowly and carefully shifted its discourse from "military conquest" to "negotiations," and in 1988 released its Constitutional Guidelines (which fell far short of its earlier demands). From 1988, the ANC unambiguously took command of the Charterist camp as negotiation became more important than mobilization. The ANC kept the UDF informed of the negotiations, but the Front was never consulted; it was simply told what role to play, namely (1) building internal Charterist support for "negotiations," (2) maintaining internal pressure on the NP, and (3) generating negative publicity for the NP to help the ANC intensify international pressure.[125]

Ironically, it was the internal mobilization of a huge Charterist constituency—largely steered by the UDF—that built the ANC's stature and importance.[126] During the 1980s, both the UDF and ANC had been weak in comparison with what the NP could muster. Yet the UDF brilliantly generated a symbolic struggle that created the perception of revolutionary momentum[127]—in consequence, the ANC was given a media "presence" internationally and locally well in excess of its actual organizational capacities. Perception became reality, and the ANC was put onto the agenda as a crucial player for negotiating South Africa's future. The UDF meanwhile, slid down the agenda.

The UDF's weakness was revealed by the 1988 municipal elections when, for the first time, all South Africans voted in a simultaneous election. The UDF was so weak that some activists argued it should abandon boycott politics and participate in these consociational elections as a means to gain publicity.[128] Further, the results worried Charterists because colored and Indian participation rates went up (to 280,000 voters). More alarming, despite MDM boycott calls, 370,000 urban blacks voted for Botha's consociational councils.[129]

However, in 1989, the UDF revealed that it still had the capacity to use the media to generate problems for the NP (and weaken its negotiating position). Two campaigns were launched that year, geared at securing negative international publicity—a detainee hunger strike was used to focus overseas attention on South African political prisoners. Then a defiance campaign was launched to refute the idea that the NP was reformist. The MDM campaign mobilized crowds to defy beach and hospital apartheid, and organized protests against the Tricameral Parliament plus a two-day work stay-away. During the 1989 campaigns, civil rights language was deliberately used with an eye to the international media.[130] The defiance campaigns were geared to generating critical coverage in the Western media by highlighting racial segregation and provoking police brutality. These campaigns did much to revive the UDF by reinspiring its activists.

Stage 6: Dissolution

In February 1990, the ANC was unbanned. That year, the ANC was an exile organization with very limited internal political capacity, facing the daunting task of rebuilding itself as an internal aboveground organization. Consequently, many of the most experienced and talented UDF leaders shifted over to the ANC to help reconstitute the organization; the Front was severely damaged by this transfer of skills.[131]

In January 1990, the UDF declared itself unbanned. During that time, many UDF activists firmly believed the Front should continue operating despite the ANC's unbanning, both as an "insurance policy" (in case the NP changed its mind about negotiations), and as a vehicle to keep civil society mobilized (as an internal Charterist/nonracial pressure group that ANC leaders could not ignore). But many Charterists were opposed to the UDF, and the ANC's unbanning activated long-standing conflicts within Charterism. Many Cosatu workerists viewed UDF leaders as too bourgeois/reformist, while black township insurrectionists (often with Africanist leanings) distrusted UDF leaders for being too nonracial, moderate/reformist.[132] Resentments about too many "nonblack" UDF leaders surfaced,[133] and objections were raised that UDF funding was controlled by WICs who were not accountable to the "black majority." Pressures grew for the disbandment of the UDF. Most significantly, old claims about the Front being run by an "Indian cabal" resurfaced in 1990, bringing enormous pressures to bear on many UDF leaders. SAYCO's township youth structures, in particular, drove this agenda. In 1990, all persons in Durban (containing South Africa's largest Indian population) with alleged links to "the cabal" were purged from ANC structures.[134]

From mid-1990, attendance at UDF meetings dropped dramatically, and many affiliates effectively ceased functioning as activists and increasingly joined the ANC. In March 1991, the UDF disbanded itself.

UDF CHARACTERISTICS

The UDF was an extraordinary phenomenon that transformed South Africa's political landscape by creatively using the spaces Botha's reforms made available. Born of a particular context, the UDF was characterized by eight main features.

First, because it was a "popular front," the UDF was deliberately constructed so it could be different things to different people. This lay at the heart of its success—by fudging its discourse, the UDF mobilized an extraordinarily diverse constituency ranging from upper-middle-class professionals, through workers, to a lumpen proletariat. It mobilized communists, social democrats, nationalists, and liberals and got them to work together. Lodge[135] argues that there were three core constituencies—on the Right were middle-class Charterists (older generation activists), in the center were those advocating a national democratic struggle (the ANC/SACP position), and on the Left were socialists.

An important feature of the UDF was its call for nonracialism. This precisely appealed to South Africa's minority groups (WICs) and was initially geared to enable the UDF to recruit coloreds and Indians into the Charterist camp and stop them from joining Botha's tricameral alliance. The UDF's nonracialism also reflected a desire among WIC Charterists to contain grassroots Africanism in the townships.[136] Interestingly, despite its nonracialism, many key UDF/MDM leaders had BC/SASO roots—for example, Chikane, Lekota, Ramaphosa, Molefe, Morobe, Nkondo, Mokoena, and Jack. By foregrounding nonracialism, the UDF was strikingly successful in building a 1980s constituency incorporating all ethnic and racial groups—a political phenomenon that significantly declined in the 1990s.

Second, the UDF's vision was geared as an antithesis to Botha's reform plans, which involved devising power-sharing mechanisms between whites, coloreds, Indians, and blacks. The UDF rejected the power-sharing model,[137] advocating instead a single undivided political system and single "undivided nation"[138]—that is, a rejection of apartheid partition and/or consociationalism. The UDF also rejected representative democracy[139] and liberal democracy,[140] advocating instead popular participatory democracy.[141] Essentially, the Front rejected Botha's procedural consociational democracy, but neither was it advocating simply replacing white faces in Parliament with black faces.[142] Rather, the UDF wanted grassroots participatory democracy that empowered people to take control of their own lives.[143] In this sense, it was advocating something quite different from the ANC, which preferred a centralized state, procedural democracy,[144] and filling Parliament with black faces—all of which guaranteed the ANC/SACP's vanguard leadership maximum political control. The UDF also advocated anticapitalist[145] socioeconomic transformation involving a utopian egalitarian "socialism."[146] UDF white activists were inclined to be the most socialist.[147]

The UDF's vision entailed establishing a *nonracial* Charterist hegemony,[148] which involved struggling against two South African *race-based* political visions, namely:

- The NP's ethnic partition model
- Africanism

Although the UDF was Charterist from the beginning, it only officially adopted the Freedom Charter in June 1987. UDF activists did much to popularize this charter during the second half of the 1980s.[149]

Third, the UDF deployed a wide range of tactics, including: (1) persuasion, (2) noncollaboration/boycotts, and (3) challenging and provoking the state.[150] Broadly, the UDF was skeptical about both ANC romantic notions of seizing power by military means, and notions the state could be overthrown by populist insurrection (advocated by township youth). Instead, the UDF challenged the state politically, in other words: (1) sought out and focused on the state's political vulnerabilities, (2) used the media to embarrass and weaken the government, and (3) painstakingly mobilized a large Charterist constituency in order to deny these people to Botha's reformers (which rendered the consociational reforms unworkable)—that is, Biko's noncollaborationism came of age.

The UDF became highly skilled at creating a symbolic presence. This facilitated Charterists (UDF/ANC) moving center stage in 1980s South African politics. The other major political contenders (Africanists, BC, Unity Movement, and consociationalists) were made to seem inconsequential by the UDF's capacity to keep the spotlight focused on nonracial Charterism. In particular, the Front learned to use media campaigns, protest marches, political funerals, and staged public events to simultaneously recruit supporters; raise the ANC's profile; and weaken the government. The UDF became skilled at strategically provoking the government, then using the state's overreaction to both build local anger (as a mobilizing tool) and generate overseas media images damaging to the NP. Botha's reform message was drowned out so that eventually no one would take the NP's consociational reform agenda seriously.

Fourth, members of the UDF became masters at using the media—communicatively outmaneuvering Botha at every turn. They ran a very media-centric operation, "a conscious decision . . . [being] made to spend a major portion of UDF resources on media in order to create a media presence."[151] The Front's "symbolic dimension" was impressive—they developed a capacity "to inspire, mobilize and educate politically large numbers of people."[152] An ongoing UDF media presence generated and maintained a revolt against Botha's reforms by making resistance and change seem possible—instilling hope and defiance.[153] The UDF's "presence" gave people the confidence to stand up and say "no" to the state. This created a sense of power (even if it was illusory), the UDF was seen to be at the helm—and perception soon became reality.[154] The Front's high visibility gave it a presence outweighing its actual strength. As key UDF strategist Mohammed Valli said: "most of the time, the UDF was barking louder than it could bite."[155] Due to its "symbolic activism," the Front became the ideological center of antiapartheid activism—it was seen as such in the townships, by the state, and overseas. As an "ideological center," the UDF served to integrate those who would otherwise have acted in a disparate way—now activists in every small township saw themselves as belonging to a national movement.[156] Hence, even if the UDF did not always instigate protests, it politically harnessed all activism. The sum total became greater than its constituent parts. The UDF grabbed the lead, giving direction to the struggle, rallying activists, and maintaining momentum throughout the 1980s.

UDF-produced media shaped 1980s political discussions and created an antiapartheid "we" among activists.[157] Huge volumes of UDF media were generated—newsletters, education/discussion booklets, pamphlets, political T-shirts, banners, graffiti, and an alternative press.[158] The NP government took to calling those responsible "media terrorists"; the activists concerned were delighted, and began wearing "media terrorist" T-shirts.

The UDF was also highly adept at manipulating journalists—using press releases, creating media events, and using high-profile people to attract publicity. Bishop Tutu was an especially useful speaker because his clerical robes and biblical civil rights sound bites imparted "morality" and "respectability" to the UDF's struggle that played especially well in the West. The UDF's capacity to project a positive image in the West was not only valuable to the broader Charterist struggle, but more specifically, delivered direct benefits to the UDF in the form of significant West European funding. This funding made it possible for the Front to run a publicity machine, plus media-training programs.

The UDF invested heavily in media activist training (i.e., media production and public relations skills).[159] A large cadre of media-literate activists was built up, enabling media activism to become integrated with organizing political events. Some media activists went on to run their own UDF-funded publications.[160]

Fifth, although, the UDF could safely be called the most representative political movement in South African history,[161] it was not as representative as it liked to project itself when claiming to stand for "the people." Certainly, the UDF represented "nonracialism" and attracted support from all race/ethnic groups. However, the Front remained dominated by an Indian/colored leadership (because of its tricameral-resistance origins),[162] concentrated in only three metropolitan areas—Johannesburg, Durban, and Cape Town.[163] The dominance of urban middle-class radicals necessarily influenced the UDF's ability to mobilize in different areas.[164] In Cape Town, UDF structures were always strongest in colored areas; and after township activists were incorporated, tensions between coloreds and blacks characterized Cape UDF politics.[165] In Durban, Charterism was never strong in the black townships, and Natal UDF politics was an overwhelmingly Indian affair.[166] To make matters worse, Durban's UDF black leadership was generally not Zulu.[167] In Johannesburg, UDF penetration of black townships was uneven, and Indian/colored areas were more solidly organized;[168] the domination of Indian/colored activism was demonstrated by the way the UDF initially struggled to build resistance structures in the border region, which lacked an Indian/colored population.[169]

In 1985–1986, the UDF did move to broaden its township base to overcome township activist perceptions that the Front was disconnected from their goals.[170] The UDF also sought to find and develop black leadership; however, it consistently ignored many large constituencies, for example, black farm workers, domestic workers, and new urban migrants. Further, except for Ciskei and a Turfloop University affiliate (in Lebowa), the UDF failed to mobilize homeland populations—like the ANC, the UDF remained an overwhelmingly urban phenomenon.[171] So, although the UDF had widened its base and incorporated black workers from the mid-1980s, it retained a disproportionately strong WIC influence and remained Johannesburg/Cape Town/Durban–centric.

Sixth, the UDF was characterized by racial tensions because it operated as a multiracial alliance, and spent much of its time trying to mobilize WICs into the Charterist camp, the UDF necessarily adopted gradualist/reformist strategies. Black activists argued that this meant "the goals of the African masses were subverted . . . their militancy was diluted, and African leadership was compromised."[172] There was a constant tension between militant township insurrectionists and WICs concerned with recruiting the "middle ground" into Charterism. Many township activists resented the large numbers of nonblacks in leadership positions.[173] The complaint that black leadership was being marginalized, especially by Indians, kept resurfacing. This caused particular tensions in Natal with its large Indian population.[174] These tensions led to charges that an unrepresentative, undemocratic, and nonmilitant cabal dominated the UDF. The notion of a "cabal"—first raised in 1985—became a code for "race." As Van Kessel notes, because of its nonracialism, race tensions were a taboo subject inside the Front.[175] Consequently, these tensions emerged in a cloaked form, for example, "cabal" effectively meant "Indian domination." Further, resentments were often reformulated in class terms; in other words, Indians were "bourgeois" and blacks were "working class."[176] Opposition to "petit bourgeois influences" in reality referred to strained relationships between blacks and coloreds and black suspicion of Indians.[177] It also referred to black resentments about the education levels, status, and wealth of many WIC activists, and to the fact that Indian activists tended to dominate UDF finances (partly because it was possible to raise funding for UDF activities in South Africa's affluent Indian community). These tensions resulted in many black activists disengaging from the UDF.[178] When the Front revived in 1990, the cabal issue resurfaced; the ANC appointed a commission under Govan Mbeki to investigate the cabal issue, and 1990 saw considerable pressure placed on many UDF leaders with alleged cabal links. Many withdrew from active politics; others were purged from ANC structures. The UDF's dissolution took place in the midst of this acrimony.

Seventh, relationships between the UDF and ANC were complex. The NP government wanted to prove that the UDF and the ANC were the same. The Front constantly had to deny this, given the ANC's banned status. The result has been obfuscation of the UDF-ANC relationship. The ANC's strategic review undoubtedly played a role in the formation of the UDF, and ANC cadres were always active inside the Front. However, the UDF took on a life of its own, and grew into a form of Charterism not quite the same as the ANC's because the UDF:

- pursued "middle-ground politics" and recruited many WICs for whom Africanism was not attractive;
- advocated policies like participatory democracy, utopian socialism, and non-racialism, which were different from the ANC's Marxist Africanism and vanguardist democratic centralism; and
- saw the ANC's "conquest of power" model and township insurrectionism as dangerously romantic and reckless (many UDF leaders were concerned about the romantic and unrealistic demands the ANC made of them).[179]

Still, there were ongoing contacts between the UDF and ANC, and a 1986 (Stockholm) meeting significantly shifted UDF strategy.[180] Essentially, the UDF and ANC were part of the same Charterist camp, sought each other out, and coordinated their activities. Effectively, the ANC functioned as an armed wing, while the UDF operated as an internal political wing.

Eighth, the UDF's relationship to non-Charterists says much about the nature of the 1980s struggle. Essentially, the world was divided into two camps—the "people's camp"[181] and the "enemy camp."[182] Non-Charterists were irredeemably "other"—the enemy who needed to be fought and destroyed. The people's camp was "good"; the enemy camp was "evil."[183] Politics became a zero-sum game—a gain for one side was a loss for the other.[184] As with the NP, the UDF slipped into a "civil war" mentality, which made killing/ill-treating "the enemy/other" much easier.[185] This bred intolerance and violent clashes. UDF comrades (especially the youth) placed the following into the enemy camp, and declared war upon them: the NP, anyone deemed to be collaborating with the NP, boycott breakers, Inkatha, and AZAPO. The political violence this generated was intense.

UDF'S IMPACT ON SOUTH AFRICAN POLITICS

In the early 1980s, Botha started a reform initiative geared at transforming apartheid into consociationalism. The NP seemed well positioned to remain in power for decades to come, while the ANC was a weak exile organization with only limited political and military capacity inside South Africa. Within a decade, the political landscape was transfigured, and the NP was negotiating with the ANC, which now had to be treated as a player of equal stature. This change was largely brought about by the UDF's creative use of the gaps generated by Botha's reforms. The UDF achieved the following:

- Seized the initiative, becoming the organizational heart of Charterism, outmaneuvered its antiapartheid rivals (e.g., the National Forum/NF), and placed Charterism center stage of South African politics alongside the NP. Decades of ANC activism had not even come close to making Charterism so significant.
- Secured Western help, something the ANC (because of its Soviet links) had failed to do. Most significantly, the UDF made apartheid into a U.S. domestic issue by skillfully engineering emotional media images that turned Botha's NP into global pariahs.
- Destroyed Botha's reform initiative. On his release from jail in 1990, Mandela correctly praised the UDF for ensuring that "none of the reformists strategies of the government have succeeded."[186]
- Destroyed Botha's plans to construct a multiracial alliance (which would have governed his planned consociational state). By 1989, no credible black leaders were prepared to join Botha's consociational alliance. In the NP-UDF battle to recruit the "middle ground" into their camps, the UDF was more successful—Botha had failed to increase his alliance; the UDF expanded theirs dramatically.
- Found a mechanism for giving black anger direction and coherence. Previously, eruptions of township anger had not threatened the state, but the UDF organized and channeled this anger into a political force undermining the NP both domestically and internationally.
- Built a Charterist constituency that the ANC ultimately inherited. Whereas in 1980 most blacks were politically passive and wary of politics, by 1990, they were politically conscious and confident, and the majority had been mobilized into the Charterist camp.
- Shifted South Africa's balance of power. In 1980, the NP was absolutely hegemonic; by 1990, it was no longer in unilateral control of the political agenda.
- Created a politically unstable situation that the NP could not unilaterally stabilize. If South Africa was not to descend into permanent instability/political violence, the NP needed to negotiate with Charterist leaders to end the conflict.
- Seriously weakened the NP's bargaining position during the 1990s Kempton Park negotiations because when the NP began negotiating, they could find no urban black allies. Almost all urban blacks were in the Charterist camp.

By 1991, the ANC had a functioning internal structure that simply absorbed the UDF. This created three main ideological tendencies among ANC activists: Africanists, socialists, and "nonracials":

- The nonracials were those the UDF had mobilized; they were overwhelmingly, but not exclusively, WICs.
- Some socialists were SACP members returning from exile, others were workerists in Cosatu, and a few were UDF leftists.

- Many Africanists had been exiles within the ANC's African infrastructures, others were released Robben Island prisoners, and some had been township insurrectionists.

The socialists found their position seriously weakened by the Soviet collapse. Before 1989, socialism had been a powerful force inside the Charterist camp (partly due to Soviet funding for MK). The Soviet collapse saw ANC Marxist Africanism gradually reconfigured, as Africanists became more assertive and Marxists less aggressive. This process was encouraged by U.S. hostility to Marxism (following the Soviet collapse, the ANC could afford to ignore U.S. attitudes). UDF nonracials also found themselves increasingly marginalized as exiles, and Robben Islanders returned and filled up internal ANC structures. Anticabalism served to weaken the position of nonracials within the ANC; consequently, many of them withdrew. This could be seen in the changing character of Charterist meetings—whereas in 1990 UDF meetings were ethnically diverse, by 1994, ANC meetings were almost exclusively black. This was accompanied by an increasingly assertive Africanism within the ANC, much of it driven by those whose political careers were born in SASO and/or the 1976 Soweto revolt.

However, a number of UDF leaders did survive the ANC's absorption of the Front, and built successful ANC careers. And although the UDF's death, amid the acrimony of the cabal issue, may have been somewhat whimpering, the Front's legacy is enormous. Today's ANC leaders who govern South Africa have the UDF to thank.

CHAPTER 7

Negotiating a Settlement to End Apartheid

By 1987, South Africans were trapped in a stalemate. Securocrats had crushed the township revolt and demonstrated that the National Party (NP) possessed the military capacity to remain in power for decades to come. However, the United Democratic Front (UDF) had mobilized a large internal Charterist constituency and no amount of National Security Management System (NSMS) repression could now dislodge this political reality. South Africans were trapped—"neither side could defeat the other, but each side could prevent the other from ruling alone."[1] An unstable militarized stalemate existed. Without a negotiated settlement, South Africans faced the prospect of long-term low-intensity conflict and economic decline from which neither side would benefit. Senior members of the intelligence community concluded that although the existing state could survive, it would steadily weaken without a negotiated settlement. Mike Louw, National Intelligence Service second in command, recalled the late 1980s situation thus: "Nowhere was the situation out of hand, but it was clear that politically and morally we were losing our grip. Everywhere in the townships we encountered intimidation and a strong political consciousness. The political system had become obsolete, and a long bloody struggle lay ahead. It became clear the sooner we negotiated a new system the better."[2]

If the NP realized they could not militarily beat their opponent, so too did the African National Congress (ANC). The ANC's late 1970s strategic review had already concluded that military vanguardism had failed. This review abandoned the primacy of armed struggle in favor of political mass mobilization. By 1987, UDF mass mobilization had significantly strengthened the ANC's hand, but this too could not deliver unambiguous victory to the Charterists. The NP, its white constituency, and its tricamerial and homeland partners remained solidly entrenched. Realizing it could not win militarily, nor through popular insurrection, the ANC rethought its position, and in 1986 opted to engage the NP in negotiations.[3] For the ANC, this was dangerous, because romantic notions of "armed struggle" and "decolonization" permeated their constituency. Abandoning such notions for negotiations held real risks that ANC leaders would be accused of betraying the revolution, and their radicalized constituency would abandon them. Mandela was aware that this was being said about him—previously admired within the ANC as a radical advocate of violence, there were now whispers Mandela had been broken, and was a sellout.[4] When Mbeki became the main external advocate of negotiations, he also faced a whispering campaign suggesting he was a security police agent.[5] But, with no other realistic option, the ANC's executive formally announced in October 1987 that it was ready to negotiate with the NP.[6] In 1988, the ANC tabled its "negotiating platform" in its "constitutional guidelines."

From 1987 to 1989, two secret ANC-NP "negotiation" processes existed—one with Mandela in Cape Town, another in Britain with an ANC team led by Thabo Mbeki.[7] Then, in 1989, de Klerk (regarded as a conservative within the NP) became president. He unbanned the ANC/South African Communist Party (SACP) and the Pan African Congress (PAC), and opened formal negotiations. The following motivated de Klerk:

- The alternative was ongoing conflict and economic decline.
- The NP faced mounting pressure from South Africa's corporate sector because of economic isolation and decline.
- The Soviet collapse was seen to weaken SACP influence within the ANC, creating the opportunity for a coalition of the NP, business leaders, and the United States to "assist" ANC nationalist "moderates" to take control of the ANC by sidelining "communist radicals."
- The Soviet collapse weakened the ANC by removing its main source of funds and arms.
- Foreign pressure was mounting. After the 1986 Reykjavik summit, the United States and the Soviets began coordinating their Southern African policies—while the United States pressured the NP, the Soviets pressured the ANC to find a political solution. After 1989, the United States seriously pressured both sides to sit down and talk. And with the cold war over, the NP realized they could no longer rely on surreptitious U.S. support. Foreign pressure was also coordinated between the United States, European Union (EU), Commonwealth, United Nations (UN), Organization of African Unity (OAU), and the "Constantia group" of "progressive" heads (who worked on the ANC).[8] The pressure was unrelenting.
- Sanctions and a lack of foreign capital made economic recovery impossible, and without economic growth, social unrest would increase. Only a settlement, acceptable to the United States, would restore foreign investment.

- South Africa's intelligence heads advised de Klerk to negotiate while the NP was still in a strong position.
- De Klerk believed an "elite pact" was possible between ANC nationalist "moderates" (like Mandela and Mbeki) and the NP. This was simply an extension of Lijphart's consociational "grand coalition" idea of "elite bonding" that Botha had been trying to apply (see chapter 4). The trick was to lock the ANC into negotiations so they became enmeshed into the NP's reform process. De Klerk believed ANC moderates could be cajoled into a compromise where they accepted consociationalism/group rights.

Therefore, de Klerk's agenda was not a radical break from Botha's (Huntington/Lijphart) reform agenda—he simply believed the moment was ripe to co-opt ANC "moderates" into the NP's consociational agenda. The next few years would prove de Klerk wrong because the ANC proved to be better negotiators than the NP.

THE KEY NEGOTIATING POSITIONS

During the 1990s, there were five main negotiating positions—ANC, NP, Inkatha Freedom Party (IFP), white Right, and the Left). But essentially the negotiations revolved around the ANC and NP, and their need to find a formula to end their 40-year conflict. When formal negotiations began in 1991, the ANC and NP had two radically different visions for the future, as shown in table 7.1.

The most important of the "minor" players was Inkatha. By 1990, Buthelezi had built the IFP into a formidable political force grounded in the KwaZulu homeland. Inkatha advocated a form of Zulu nationalism and Zulu monarchism associated with a conservative pride in Zulu tradition and ethnicity. This was tied to advocacy of capitalism and consociationalism.

Like the NP, the IFP was hostile to the notion of simple majoritarian democracy. Buthelezi opposed majoritarianism[34] because, like the NP, he believed this encouraged cultural homogenization and the political dominance of Westernized urban blacks at the expense of traditional culture and cultural minorities. Zulu traditionalists believed majoritarianism threatened them with subjugation, while consociationalism promised to provide them with a space where they could survive politically. The IFP therefore found itself entering the 1990s negotiations with similar concerns and interests to Afrikaner nationalists, who also feared subjugation.

The IFP strongly advocated federalism and regional powers[35] because its objective was to secure KwaZulu-Natal as an IFP power base. Inkatha's advocacy of federalism and strong rejection of majoritarianism brought the IFP into serious conflict with the ANC, which saw federalism, confederalism, and consociationalism as (unacceptable) mechanisms to entrench apartheid—that is, entrench homelands and ethnic differentiation. When

Table 7.1:
NP and ANC Negotiation Positions

NP Position	ANC Position
• Power sharing via consociationalism[9] • Reject majority rule ("winner-takes-all") system	• Majority rule[10] • Reject power sharing and consociationalism[11]
Consociationalism as constitutionally enforced coalition government: • Multi-party cabinet with decisions based on consensus (to ensure minority parties have some power)[12] • Rotating presidency[13] • Minority vetoes[14] • Mechanisms to prevent unconstrained majority rule[15]	Majoritarian democracy in which winning party forms government: • Winning party forms cabinet • Winning party appoints president • No minority vetoes[16] • Majority rule to be unconstrained
• Minority group rights protected[17] • Constitutionally protected ethnic pluralism[18] • Meaningful participation of minorities in government[19]	• Protect individual rights[20] • Reject political system based on ethnic group rights[21] • Reject minority rights as a break on majority rule ("winner-takes-all")
Strong second chamber in Parliament representing minorities[22] Minority parties have veto power over legislation[23]	"Minority" second chamber rejected as a "loser-takes-all" system[24]
Confederal or federal state and devolution of power to provinces and municipalities (to weaken powers of majoritarian government)[25]	Unitary state (abolishing homelands)[26] with strong centralized powers (to facilitate a strongly interventionist state)[27]
Retain (and strengthen) existing municipal governments. Apartheid-created municipalities would then serve as de facto ethnically based local governments.	Reconfigure municipalities to forcibly integrate local governments.
Draw up new constitution before elections and make constitutional alterations difficult—i.e., draw up constitution before ANC comes to power to prevent ANC from setting the terms.[28]	Draw up constitution after the elections so "the majority" (ANC supporters) decides the terms.[29]
Slow transfer of power with a lengthy period of transitional shared rule[30]	Rapid transfer of power to black majority rule[31]
Create conditions for capitalism and reject state interventionism[32]	Advocate wealth-transfer mechanisms (initially via socialism, then via a mixed economy)[33]

Inkatha stuck to its federal position more doggedly than the NP, it triggered a serious ANC-IFP conflict causing over 14,800 deaths during the negotiation period.

Inkatha proposed that a new constitution be finalized before any "one-person–one-vote" election[36] so that it would reflect Inkatha's consociational position and entrench strong federalism. If the constitution were drawn up by a nonelected constitutional forum, then the ANC would be only one of many players, and the IFP, NP, white Right, and other homeland governments could produce a constitution conforming to Inkatha's preferred model. If, however, it were drawn up after an election, the ANC-as-government would be in a position to impose its majoritarian democracy model on everyone. Inkatha fought tooth and nail to prevent any process whereby the new constitution could be redrawn after an election.

The white Right advocated Verwoerdian apartheid. They were a disparate collection of players with major disagreements among themselves—ranging from extreme Right paramilitaries (*Afrikaner Weerstandbeweging*/AWB) to those believing in parliamentary democracy (Conservative Party/CP). Like the IFP, the white Right strongly advocated regional powers as a way to secure control over at least some part of South Africa.[37] In this regard, they mobilized the logic of Verwoerdian "own-ness," calling for a *Volkstaat* (Afrikaner homeland);[38] they were, however, unable to define the boundaries for such a homeland.

The CP advocated a consociational confederation between ethnic homelands. As the 1990s talks proceeded, the white Right became exasperated by the emerging NP-ANC deal, which they regarded as a sellout of minority group rights in general and Afrikaner rights in particular.

The Left consisted of a range of players including the Azanian People's Organization (AZAPO), Unity Movement (UM), Pan African Congress (PAC), SACP, and workerists. The largest collection of workerists was in the Congress of South African Trade Unions (Cosatu). Although Cosatu and SACP aligned themselves with the emerging ANC-NP centrist deal, most leftists were worried the ANC was being co-opted into a settlement stabilizing racial capitalism. The Left believed that ANC middle-class black nationalists were effectively aligning themselves with the interests of South Africa's (mostly white Anglo) business sector. The concern was that this would create an ANC-led black middle class with a vested interest in defending racial capitalism, leaving most black people trapped in poverty.

The PAC stressed the notion of *black* poverty continuing if the settlement allowed whites to retain wealth and property. AZAPO and the UM saw the whole negotiation process as an elaborate exercise to "tame" the revolution and co-opt the ANC bourgeoisie into an alliance with the white corporate sector. Workerists within the ANC alliance (i.e., UDF leftists and Cosatu members) found themselves torn between a pragmatic view (that there was no realistic alternative to negotiating a compromise/deal) and unease about being co-opted. Struggles within the Charterist camp over what concessions were acceptable saw black nationalist "moderates" emerge victorious over socialist "radicals" (as de Klerk had hoped).

THE NEGOTIATIONS SAGA

Stage 1: Preliminary Talks

Between 1975 and 1985, the NP made six conditional offers to release Mandela from jail and open negotiations with him;[39] Mandela refused. Then, in 1985, Mandela concluded that neither the NP nor ANC could win on the battlefield,[40] so he wrote to the NP government proposing talks, saying the ANC and NP should work together to deal with white fears of black domination and the idea of "group rights."[41] The NP agreed to talks on the condition that Mandela renounce guerilla warfare/terrorism and cease working with communists; Mandela refused.[42] In mid-1986, when the securocrats imposed "hard" repression, Mandela again proposed negotiations.[43] This generated preliminary talks with Minister of Justice Kobie Coetzee.

From 1986, the Soviets pressured the ANC to negotiate; in 1987, the ANC-in-exile announced it was prepared to talk. The NP rewarded this by releasing Govan Mbeki from jail. In the 1987 elections, the NP proposed to its constituency negotiations to achieve a "power-sharing" deal (which protected group rights). After winning the election, the (still secret) Mandela talks-about-talks were formalized, and the government team widened to include Coetzee (NP politician), Neil Barnard and Mike Louw (National Intelligence Service chiefs), Fanie van der Merwe (civil service), and General Johannes Willemse (South African Defense Force/SADF). From late 1988, Mandela was allowed to establish regularized communication with the ANC-in-exile and internal UDF leaders to facilitate negotiations. Govan Mbeki opposed these Mandela talks, recommending that Charterist leaders not collaborate with Mandela.

In 1987, a parallel set of secret talks-about-talks (promoted by Consolidated Goldfields) began in Britain between the ANC and Afrikaner academics aligned to the NP. The ANC team was eventually led by Thabo Mbeki (son of Govan), Willie Esterhuyse led the NP team, and Wimpie de Klerk (brother of F.W.) also joined. Many NP leaders (including de Klerk) were not happy about the 12 British meetings, which they regarded as amateurs muddying the waters.[44]

In September 1989, de Klerk became president. In October, he released Walter Sisulu (the most senior ANC prisoner). In February 1990, he unbanned the ANC, released Mandela from jail, and set about explaining to a startled white electorate why he had done so—saying it was better to negotiate from a position of strength, rather than wait until whites had their backs to the wall.[45] The ANC, completely surprised by De Klerk's actions, found itself unbanned without an internal organizational structure. It took the ANC all of 1990 to rebuild itself internally (with the assistance of UDF activists who transferred to the ANC to help reconstitute the organization).

The 1990 unbanning initiated some preliminary "positioning":

- The Groote Schuur Minute (May 1990) facilitated the release of political prisoners and the return of exiles, plus changes to security laws.
- The Pretoria Minute (August 1990) saw the ANC formally suspend armed struggle and instead commit itself to negotiations.
- In January 1991, Mandela called for multiparty talks; in February, the NP agreed.
- A (secret) D.F. Malan Airport Accord (February 1991) exempted the ANC's armed wing (MK) from restrictions on private armies, with the condition that the ANC agreed to end all violence and intimidation.
- The National Peace Accord (September 1991) was signed by 29 parties who agreed to end political violence.

During 1990–1991, the NP began reconstructing itself. In January 1991, at a Robben Island cabinet meeting, the NP decided to turn itself into a nonracial Christian Democrat party.[46] The aim was to build a party appealing to conservative blacks, coloreds, and Indians to enable the NP to become a serious political player in a "one-person–one-vote" Parliament. De Klerk hoped such a Christian Democrat party, in alliance with other conservative groups (IFP, CP, etc.), could win enough parliamentary seats to make it impossible for the ANC to alter the constitution into a simple majoritarian model (after the elections). But in order to project itself as a nonracial Christian Democrat party (rather than a white party), the NP had to move away from the language of "group rights." This was to alter the NP's negotiation stance[47] in ways that ultimately benefited the ANC, because the NP then slid into the logic of majoritarian democracy instead of being concerned with finding mechanisms to protect minority groups from black majoritarianism.

Stage 2: Codesa

In December 1991, the Convention for a Democratic South Africa (Codesa) convened in Kempton Park with 20 delegations and 300 delegates—the South African government; five tricameral parties; six self-governing homeland parties; the governments of Transkei, Bophuthatswana, Ciskei, and Venda; and four Charterist delegations (ANC, SACP, Natal Indian Congress and Transvaal Indian Congress). The white Right, PAC, and AZAPO boycotted Codesa.

The key positions to emerge at Codesa were the NP's power sharing and consociationalism, and ANC's majoritarian democracy. Codesa negotiations did not go well for the ANC, because ANC negotiators were slow to find their feet.[48] The NP also held firmly to its power-sharing position, one reason being the CP's early 1992 defeat of the NP in a Potchefstroom by-election. The white Right argued that this meant de Klerk had no mandate to negotiate. In response, de Klerk called a March 1992 whites-only referendum, receiving 69 percent support for continuing reforms/negotiations. These events saw the NP toughen its negotiation stance.

Codesa negotiations broke down in May 1992, when the NP insisted on constitutionally entrenching meaningful political participation for minorities. The NP also proposed that post-election constitutional amendments needed 75 percent of parliamentarians agreeing (so blocking ANC unilateral changes). This triggered an ANC walkout of Codesa. Mandela accused the NP of seeking to entrench "minority vetoes," and refusing to submit to the will of "the majority."[49] There were acrimonious exchanges between Mandela and de Klerk.

Stage 3: Rolling Mass Action (May–September 1992)

The NP's hard line on power sharing and its successes extracting concessions from ANC negotiators annoyed ANC supporters.[50] Workerists inside the Charterist camp became temporarily ascendant and pressed for radical action. Ronnie Kasrils and Chris Hani advocated the "Leipzig option"—that is, the sort of sustained mass action that toppled East Germany's Erich Honecker.[51] Cosatu advocated "rolling mass action" as a strategy to impose Charterist direction on negotiations, and a means to reconnect Charterist leaders with their (now restless) constituency. A June campaign began with Cosatu-organized mass stay-aways geared to showing that Charterists could paralyze the economy. The first response to this Charterist hard line came from Inkatha supporters (and their 1980s securocrat partners)—in June, Zulu migrant workers from a hostel south of Johannesburg formed an *impi* (a group of armed warriors) and attacked Charterist supporters in Boipatong, killing 48 people during a nighttime raid. In a poisonous atmosphere, the ANC and NP accused each other of using violence and intimidation to undermine opponents. The ANC demanded that the NP stop securocrat covert operations, fence migrant hostels and immediately form an interim transitional Government of National Unity (GNU). Mandela renounced negotiations and refused any more meetings with de Klerk. In the meantime, continued Charterist mass action, strikes, demonstrations, rallies, and occupations of government buildings created an atmosphere of crisis. Sixty thousand ANC demonstrators marched on de Klerk's Pretoria office. Charterists also targeted homeland governments—in September, the ANC organized a 70,000-strong march on Ciskei's capital, Bisho. Kasrils, leading a breakaway group, charged Ciskei capitol buildings. Brigadier

Gqozo's homeland soldiers responded by opening fire, killing 28 people and wounding 200.

The ANC leadership was sobered by these Bisho killings, and Bisho triggered an ANC "moderate" backlash against militants. The ANC abandoned the Leipzig option. Bisho was a turning point for the ANC and NP—it was as if both sides looked into "an abyss"[52] and realized the country was in real danger of collapsing into anarchy, which would produce no winners. The Bisho crisis gave birth to "the channel" between ANC and NP chief negotiators, Cyril Ramaphosa and Roelf Meyer. For some time during the crisis, "the channel" was the only ANC-NP link. From this time forth, "the channel" (as a bilateral mechanism) became the central negotiation site. Meyer,[53] in particular, became very eager for the negotiations to succeed,[54] and to restart the talks, the NP made a number of key concessions, encapsulated in the Record of Understanding.

Essentially, Bisho empowered ANC moderates and NP "nonracials," and these two camps "found each other." Together they staked out the "middle ground" and set about developing a joint NP-ANC position. The remainder of the negotiation process saw them grow "mutually dependant" upon each other as they jointly confronted attacks from right and left; instead of derailing the negotiations, they pushed the center together.[55]

Stage 4: Record of Understanding

The September 1992 Record of Understanding (ROU) agreed to:

- an elected constituent assembly drafting the final constitution,
- an interim Government of National Unity (GNU) governed by an interim constitution and Bill of Rights,
- an independent body to review police actions, and
- de Klerk undertook to address hostel-related violence and the carrying of "traditional weapons" by Zulu *impis*.

The ANC saw ROU as a significant victory, believing Charterists would now be able to determine the contents of the final constitution. This assessment turned out to be correct. If de Klerk's original plan was to co-opt the ANC into his consociational reform agenda, now the shoe was on the other foot—henceforth, it was the NP that was to be co-opted into the ANC's majoritarian model. After ROU, the NP no longer fought for entrenched power sharing and protecting minority group rights; and when the NP still spoke of power sharing, it was no longer tied to consociational logic.

Buthelezi was incensed at what he perceived as an NP collapse. Worse, he believed ROU signaled that de Klerk had opted for an NP-ANC "elite pact" (i.e., abandoned an NP-IFP partnership).[56] Buthelezi clearly felt betrayed. In fact, the NP cabinet was split over the IFP issue between "non-racials" preferring an NP-ANC deal, and "consociationals" preferring an NP-IFP partnership.[57] The cabinet chose the NP-ANC pact. Buthelezi immediately opted to replicate ANC's mass-action tactics, leading a march of Zulus (armed with "traditional weapons") through Johannesburg's city center. This action signaled Buthelezi's defiance of the NP-ANC pact and demonstrated that ROU provisions on disarming Inkatha were unimplementable. A second bilateral "channel" was set up between Meyer and the IFP's Frank Mdlalose.[58] However, after ROU, Buthelezi's main concern was to disrupt implementation of any NP-ANC deal. He gathered together all those alarmed at the emerging outlines of a deal apparently excluding their constituencies—and U.S. Secretary of State Crocker warned: "a dangerous situation could emerge if you have a kind of unholy alliance that develops amongst those who see themselves as potential losers, not once, but forever."[59] Buthelezi created COSAG (Concerned South Africans Group), a loose alliance of Inkatha, the Bophuthatswana and Ciskei governments, and two Verwoerdian apartheid groups (the CP and *Afrikaner Volksunie*). When Buthelezi finally led COSAG members out of the Kempton Park talks, it threatened the very viability of these negotiations.[60] Effectively, after ROU, Buthelezi became the leader of those groups advocating minority group rights and consociationalism. In 1993, COSAG became the Freedom Alliance, which worked to oppose the NP-ANC constitutional deal.

The emergence of an ANC-NP deal was also facilitated by the "sunset clause," proposed by the SACP's Joe Slovo. In *The African Communist*, Slovo argued for a five-year coalition government. Although seemingly a concession in favor of the NP's power-sharing model, it was only for a five-year transitional period, so it did not serve the NP's original goal of long-term protection of minority rights. Slovo's sunset clause was a strategic masterstroke that bought off:[61]

- NP politicians by guaranteeing them participation in a transitional government (without conceding permanent minority vetoes or permanent power sharing),
- Afrikaner bureaucrats by agreeing to retain their services during the transitional period and offering good retirement benefits, and
- the security forces by agreeing to a general amnesty and offering good retirement benefits.

The NP naively believed it could negotiate (after the elections) to have this five-year sunset period extended into a permanent coalition arrangement;[62] although, for the ANC, it was clearly only a short-term strategic retreat that was not going to be allowed to obstruct the long-term goal of unbridled majority rule.[63]

The sunset clause and ROU transformed the negotiation process—the ANC dominated the Kempton Park negotiations.

Stage 5: Kempton Park Negotiations

On 1 April 1993, negotiations resumed in Kempton Park. They were more inclusive than Codesa because the white Right and PAC now participated.

However, on 10 April, white rightists tried to derail negotiations by assassinating the SACP leader, Chris Hani, who was killed by two Far Right immigrants—a Polish AWB member and an Anglo Rhodesian CP member. Because Hani was popular with township militants, his death threatened to unleash violence. ANC militants wanted the negotiations halted. However, Mandela successfully used television to calm the situation, and instead of derailing the negotiations, Hani's assassination strengthened the growing ANC-NP middle-ground partnership. In fact, they decided to speed up negotiations by fixing an election date and setting a one-year deadline for completing the interim constitution.

The white Right became exasperated by what they perceived as an NP sellout of minority rights, and in May, a "Committee of Generals" led by Constand Viljoen formed the *Afrikaner Volksfront*/AVF, which called for negotiations to stop until all political violence ceased. The white Right warned of civil war, and the ANC became concerned.[64]

The Kempton Park negotiations were fundamentally driven by ANC-NP bilateralism. Although many participated in plenary sessions, ultimately the negotiations revolved around three mechanisms:

- "The channel" between Ramaphosa and Meyer—where deals were agreed to before being taken to plenary sessions.
- The subcommittee, which brokered deals behind the scenes. This consisted of the ANC's Mac Maharaj, the NP's Fanie van der Merwe, and (until Inkatha walked out) Inkatha's Ben Ngubane. Because the subcommittee met in secret and kept no minutes, it ensured that the process kept moving. It became the "black box" steering negotiations[65]—the NP/ANC submitted proposals to the subcommittee, which identified points of agreement to take forward. Points of fundamental disagreement were identified to prevent a party locking itself into a position from which no retreat was possible. Van der Merwe was a civil servant and Maharaj operated like a civil servant rather than a politician. They coordinated a "technocratic brokering" service for Ramaphosa and Meyer. Because they were not in the limelight, they could get on with the job of drafting resolutions and letting Ramaphosa and Meyer take the political flak. The system worked because mutual confidence and trust grew up between Ramaphosa, Meyer, Van der Merwe, and Maharaj.[66]
- Bilateral (and some multilateral) meetings took place away from Kempton Park—in *bosberaads* ("bush meetings") when difficult issues needed to be resolved.[67]

As the process gathered momentum, the ANC and NP used the notion of "urgency" to bulldoze decision making through plenary sessions. COSAG's Mdlalose opposed "the galloping pace of negotiations" without guarantees on federalism and self-determination.[68] The white Right and IFP grew increasingly exasperated as the NP conceded point after point to the ANC. In June, AWB thugs lashed out and attacked the negotiating venue, which only served to strengthen the middle ground. In July, the IFP, KwaZulu government, and CP gave up, walking out on the negotiations. They never returned. The ANC, meanwhile, played the negotiations brilliantly—making the NP believe ANC-NP "elite bonding" was taking place, splitting the NP from its natural allies (COSAG), and using the media (and de Klerk) to "disrupt" securocrat networks. Imperceivably, power shifted from the NP government to the ANC. The first visible sign of this shift occurred when police antiterrorist units searched PAC premises and Ramaphosa summoned the police minister to the negotiating council for a dressing-down.[69] Significantly, as the NP systematically lost control (of the country and negotiations) so its black support base shrunk (from 14 percent in early 1992 to 3 percent by 1994),[70] thereby undermining de Klerk's Christian Democrat schemes.

In November, a final agreement was struck when "the channel" agreed on the "six-pack" deal. It was widely interpreted as an ANC victory. Ramaphosa claimed that NP negotiators "completely collapsed" during the last few days.[71] Once defeated, the NP shifted its focus to "symbolically" covering up its defeat.[72] Apartheid ended with a whimper.

Stage 6: Breaking Conservative Resistance

In December 1993, a Transitional Executive Council (TEC) met. Although the NP stayed in office until "one-person–one vote" elections, the TEC effectively meant it no longer ruled South Africa. As a joint NP-ANC executive (operating alongside the NP cabinet), the TEC now ran South Africa. It controlled the SADF, police, intelligence services, and state finances.[73] The Tricameral Parliament continued to meet, but now serviced the TEC rather than an NP cabinet. The ANC and its allies dominated the TEC[74] and Ramaphosa assumed something of a presidential role.

The TEC set itself the task of preparing South Africa for April '94 elections. In December 1993, it was unclear whether elections could be successfully held because the following players would not accept the Kempton Park deal:

- Inkatha saw the deal as a victory for ANC majoritarianism, which failed to protect minority group rights or grant sufficient federal autonomy to the "Zulu nation." The IFP became more alarmed when ANC leaders (including Mandela) began talking about "crushing" them.[75] IFP-aligned Zulu chiefs asked de Klerk for independence, saying the Zulus were a long-established nation with their own king and national territory: "We tolerated British rule. We tolerated rule by you [the Afrikaners]. We tolerated apartheid, but we will not tolerate rule by the Xhosas [many ANC leaders were Xhosa]. We demand our sovereignty."[76]

Analysts saw no possibility of holding fair elections in KwaZulu Natal, where a virtual IFP-ANC civil war raged. Zulu chiefs barred election activity in their areas, and when the IFP-ANC war spread to Johannesburg, elections there also looked threatened.[77] Inkatha warned the TEC they would have to send troops into KwaZulu to hold elections.[78] Buthelezi led the Freedom Alliance in concerted action to delay elections. The IFP announced its refusal to accept the ANC-NP deal and would not contest the elections. Given Inkatha's huge constituency, this would call into question the whole election process.

- The Bophuthatswana and Ciskei governments also refused to accept TEC authority, saying they were independent states and had no intention of allowing elections in their territory. Bophuthatswana's president, Mangope, said his homeland would resist reincorporation into South Africa and complained about Mandela's arrogance ("he thinks that he is God") in believing he had a right to simply unilaterally wipe Bophuthatswana from the map.[79] Ciskei had no real power base with which to resist the TEC, and quickly crumbled in the face of TEC pressure. However, Mangope (although he could not in the long run resist Pretoria's wishes) had a support base, and his homeland controlled enough economic resources (e.g., the world's largest platinum mine and major tourist infrastructures) to make some resistance possible.
- The white Right was fragmented. The AWB's neofascist militants had no realistic political program, but had some capacity to generate disruptive violence. The CP, traumatized by the speed of the NP's capitulation, had no plan. As a result, General Viljoen of the *Afrikaner Volksfront*/AVF came to the fore. The AVF demanded an Afrikaner homeland/*Volkstaat*. As an ex-SADF chief, Viljoen possessed the networks to mobilize real military resistance to elections and any future government. He was seen as easily capable of raising 50,000 soldiers and armed citizen force members.[80] The existing SADF chief warned the NP and ANC about Viljoen's plans to disrupt the elections; Viljoen was seen as a real threat.
- The PAC also rejected the deal because the ANC was seen to have sold out blacks by making too many concessions to whites. However, the PAC was not considered a substantive threat to the election process.

The ANC-dominated TEC moved to break conservative resistance. It ordered the South African police into KwaZulu (i.e., KwaZulu police jurisdiction) to "contain violence," thereby signaling TEC seriousness to Buthelezi. The TEC also vetoed a Development Bank loan to Bophuthatswana, signaling its capacity to financially strangle the homelands. The Ciskei, realizing it could not resist the TEC taking control of its territory, opted for reincorporation into South Africa in February 1994.

In March 1994, the ANC launched a revolt against the Bophuthatswana government (which was not permitting electioneering in its territory). Mangope called on his Freedom Alliance ally, General Viljoen, to help the Bophuthatswana army restore order. But before Viljoen could fully deploy his 3,000-strong paramilitary force in Bophuthatswana's capital, Mafikeng, AWB paramilitary thugs arrived and began an ill-disciplined shooting spree. This triggered a Bophuthatswana army mutiny. In the ensuing chaos, Bophuthatswana soldiers executed two AWB members who were seen on South African television (unsuccessfully) begging for their lives. Viljoen immediately withdrew his paramilitary force, and the TEC dispatched an armed column of SADF troops to take control of Bophuthatswana. On 12 March, a TEC delegation informed Mangope he had been deposed. As de Klerk noted, with Mangope's removal the last remnant of Verwoerd's grand apartheid plan was demolished.[81] A senior ANC member of the TEC said: "Two down, one to go."[82] Buthelezi hunkered down to resist the coming onslaught.

The televised execution of AWB members in Bophuthatswana brought home the reality of armed resistance and had a sobering effect on the white Right. In bilateral Viljoen-ANC talks, the ANC promised it would establish a council to examine creating an Afrikaner *Volkstaat* and Afrikaner self-determination. On the basis of this promise, Viljoen accepted the Kempton Park settlement, founded the Freedom Front Party, and was a (successful) candidate in the 1994 elections. The ANC established and then abolished the promised council.

Buthelezi was now without allies. On March 28, Inkatha staged a protest march on the ANC's Johannesburg head office. Sniper fire from the ANC building killed eight IFP marchers. Political violence in various parts of Johannesburg left more than 50 people dead that day. Meanwhile, the ANC-IFP civil war in KwaZulu Natal raged on, as did violence between Inkatha migrant hostel dwellers and ANC township residents in Johannesburg. The period between Mandela's release from jail and the 1994 elections generated intense political violence, as both sides fought to establish as much territorial authority as possible before the elections—that is, whereas 86 people were killed monthly in the mid-1980s (apartheid's most violent period), 230 were dying monthly during 1991–1994.[83] The prospects for successful elections consequently looked dim. In April 1994, the TEC declared a Natal state of emergency and dispatched troops, but it failed to halt the war.

Less than a week before the elections, Buthelezi agreed the IFP would participate due to a settlement brokered by a Kenyan mediator that saw the Zulu king and kingdom of KwaZulu constitutionally recognized. This deal preserved the Zulu feudal system, giving Zulu chiefs continued power and access to resources.[84] The IFP consequently retained a regional power base under the new constitution.

THE OUTCOME

The negotiations produced four key outcomes. First, South Africa became a majoritarian democracy. The NP's consociational reform agenda was defeated. This occurred partly because apartheid's legacy made it difficult for the NP to sell the notion of ethnic differentiation and minority-group rights.

The ANC simply had to create the conceptual link between "consociationalism" and "apartheid," and the NP's negotiation agenda became a nonstarter. Apartheid's repression came back to haunt the NP and its constituency. In this regard, the ANC also had a conceptual advantage over the NP when it came to winning support in Western liberal democracies (where majoritarian logic is largely taken for granted). But the consociational reform agenda was also defeated because the NP team negotiated poorly. As Giliomee says of De Klerk: "that he and his negotiators would manage to retain so little despite a position of relative strength places a serious question mark over his leadership abilities." De Klerk failed to deploy Huntington's advice about negotiating from strength (see chapter 4). Although he inherited a powerful military machine that could have been used as a trump card during negotiations, De Klerk refused to use it to bolster his negotiating position. This was one reason for the extraordinarily poor result NP negotiators produced for their constituency.[85] As General Meiring, chief of the SADF, said to de Klerk on the day Mandela became president: "You never used your strong base to negotiate from, you never used the military as a base of strength, which you had available to you, you never wanted to use it."[86]

Consequently, the ANC's majority-rule model won out,[87] and the NP constituency found its worst nightmares realized when the 1997 constitution was enacted and they were transformed into a politically powerless minority.

The second outcome was a brief transitional ("sunset") period, when Afrikaners shared power with the ANC. Although this was supposed to last five years, it actually ended when the NP walked out of the GNU in June 1996, after it became clear that the ANC intended to rewrite the constitution into a pure majoritarian model and had no intention of allowing permanent power sharing. The 1997 constitution had few changes from the interim constitution, but the changes made were significant—that is, the ANC removed from the new constitution all consociational and power-sharing provisions at national, provincial, and local levels.[88] An unbridled majoritarian model was the result. In addition, Afrikaans enjoyed some protection under the interim constitution thanks to a clause that no existing language rights could be abridged. The ANC removed this clause from the final constitution. Consequently, Afrikaans has been dropped as a bureaucratic language and dramatically wound back as a business, media, legal, and educational language.[89] The ANC government has also systematically pressurized Afrikaans schools and universities to shift to English language classes in order to give "access" to black students. The results have been dramatic—whereas in 1990 there were five Afrikaans medium universities and 1,800 white Afrikaans schools, by 2002, only 300 schools remained.[90] Further, the government compelled all Afrikaans universities to abandon Afrikaans uni-lingualism and provide classes in English.[91] Schools and universities consequently faced major Anglicization pressures, undermining the capacity for Afrikaners to culturally reproduce themselves. These changes were facilitated by the way Afrikaner political influence was purged from the system once the GNU collapsed—Afrikaners became conspicuously absent from positions of political influence after 1987. In the face of these developments, a sense of political powerlessness (that J.M. Coetzee calls "subjugation")[92] has manifested itself. Many Afrikaners have, as Mbeki noted, "migrated inwards"[93] into a state of "sullen resignation." Others have begun migrating outward to join the 1.6 million South Africans (mostly Anglos) who have already emigrated.

A third outcome was the survival of racial capitalism (albeit in a modified form). This was remarkable given that in 1990, the ANC, SACP, UDF, and Cosatu were all advocating a socialist future. The ANC's shift from socialism to neoliberalism was the result of a concerted early-1990s exercise undertaken by South Africa's corporate sector, the IMF, and diplomats to shift the ANC's economic policies. The corporate sector set up the Brenthurst Group (named after the Oppenheimer family home), which met periodically with Mandela and ANC leaders[94] to discuss policy options. Further, ANC leaders were invited to various economic forums, conferences, think tanks, workshops, seminars, briefings, and junkets (e.g., Western "familiarization tours") where persuasion and pressure were used to get them to adjust to the "realities" of globalized capitalism. A series of scenario workshops (run by Nedcor, Old Mutual, Sanlam, etc.) were designed to shift ANC economic thinking. The "slick packaging" of one such scenario workshop held at Mont Fleur in the Western Cape during 1992 apparently shifted the economic vision of key ANC leader Trevor Manuel,[95] while Mandela's economic vision was apparently changed at the 1992 Davos World Economic Forum.[96] Incrementally, ANC economic policy came to conform to the "Washington Consensus"[97] (which underpinned neoliberal globalization). Once this happened, the West felt comfortable with the notion of an ANC government, which meant de Klerk could no longer rely on Western support in the negotiation process. The ANC's shift to neoliberalism also comforted de Klerk, and the NP's negotiating position visibly softened following the ANC's 1992 abandonment of socialism.

A fourth outcome was a new set of winners and losers—the settlement's winners were South Africa's black middle class and (Anglo) big business, while the losers have been South Africa's black underclass, now (perhaps permanently) trapped in poverty, plus Afrikaners who face growing political and socioeconomic marginalization.

CHAPTER 8

The Emerging Postapartheid Society

In the 1980s, the African National Congress (ANC) and the National Party (NP) fought each other to a draw. The subsequent negotiations also produced an indeterminate outcome because it was based upon a balance of power requiring that all parties make substantive concessions. The 1990s settlement ultimately represented a compromise between three elites—the NP and ANC leaderships, plus the corporate sector.[1] It was a reformist deal originally conceptualized by the NP as an "elite pacting" exercise (i.e., building a consociational "grand coalition," where each elite "delivered" their constituency).

At heart, the negotiations were built upon a shared NP/corporate-sector need to find black partners able to end the political turmoil and violence that had taken hold during the 1980s. During the 1970s, the Urban Foundation/UF (corporate sector) proposed that the solution lay in building an urban black middle class with a vested interest in stabilizing capitalism. The UF had converted Botha to this vision,[2] thereby helping to kick-start his 1980s reforms. By 1989, it was clear that Botha had failed to find black political partners for his reform program, so de Klerk decided to try and co-opt "ANC-moderates" into a reformist deal on the assumption only they could control the Charterist Left and township youth.[3] De Klerk's reform plan involved securing three components—consociational democracy, neoliberal economics, and corporatism. The latter two were spelled out in the NP's 1993 Normative Economic Model (NEM).[4] Although the NP failed to secure its consociational model, it did secure neoliberalism, in addition to substantive elements of corporatism. However, the neoliberal success was due more to corporate-sector efforts than the NP—that is, the corporate sector engaged in an exercise of "super salesmanship,"[5] "propagandizing and myth-making"[6] to convert key ANC leaders. The result was a deal substantively stabilizing South Africa's socioeconomic order (racial capitalism), modifying the political structure (replacing partition/apartheid with majoritarian democracy), and initiating a process of replacing white faces with black faces in key political/economic positions as a UF-type exercise in stabilizing capitalism. As a result of this deal, "the ANC got its first prize—political control of South Africa—while the corporate sector got its first prize—continued control of the South African economy—in an even greater extent than before."[7] South Africa acquired a political system controlled by a black nationalist elite and an economic system controlled by a white (mostly Anglo) elite. Poor negotiation skills meant the NP ultimately failed to secure for itself (or its Afrikaner constituency) a long-term role in this new system. Because the NP failed to find a meaningful role for itself in the new political system, it rapidly lost most of its constituency from 1996 onwards (especially to the Democratic Party). This led to the NP being decimated in the 2004 elections. As a result, what was left of the NP opted not only to dissolve itself (in 2004), but to collapse itself into the ANC (for which the NP's leader was rewarded with a cabinet position).

THE MANDELA TRANSITION

Election day was peaceful, but the elections process was chaotic—irregularities and inadequate election machinery meant an accurate count became impossible. But a result was needed to prevent political violence, so the parties met and agreed to an outcome by "sufficient consensus."[8] In May 1994, an ANC/South African Communist Party (SACP)/Congress of South African Trade Unions (Cosatu) alliance became the government.

On becoming president, Mandela faced a problem—the ANC's black constituency had enormous (unrealistic) expectations about the delivery of "change." On the other hand, the white Right remained a threat, as did the danger of a skills exodus through white emigration. And since whites ran the economy, bureaucracy, and security apparatus, their capacity for disruption was substantial. The ANC apparently concluded that the potential white threat was more pressing than its own constituency's demands. Consequently, Mandela's presidency was characterized by his high-profile attempts to calm white fears. Mandela noted his "reconciliation" policy "stemmed from a realization that the ANC had not won the military struggle and that it had to find ways to neutralize white opposition."[9]

The ANC cleverly deployed Mandela as a "reconciler" and "bridge builder." Mandela's icon status became a huge asset, allowing him to effectively "float above" politics, "unencumbered by the realpolitik of his party,"[10] while the job of real politics and running the country was left to his deputy, Mbeki.[11] So, while Mbeki worked out how the ANC could get its hands on the levers of power, and tried to shore up the ANC's support base, Mandela was used in the public relations role of calming whites (though the symbolism of the "rainbow nation") and selling South Africa's "miracle transition" overseas in the hope of attracting foreign investment. Mandela performed his role brilliantly; a Mandela myth was constructed and used to stabilize a potentially volatile situation.[12]

The Mandela interregnum was also characterized by the fact that the ANC did not yet have its hands on the levers of power. Mandela's presidency involved a corporatism in which the ANC government, business sector, and trade unions negotiated deals behind closed doors through the Nedlac process.[13] Nedlac formally (and routinely) brought representatives of the trade unions, business and the state together within a structure that effectively pressured all to make compromises for the "national interest." This corporatist arrangement emerged as a much more powerful form of white minority influence on governance than did the parliamentary process.[14] Significantly, although corporatism gave the (mostly Anglo) white business political influence, it did not give other whites any political clout. The corporatist compromises clearly helped the government's stabilization requirements, but grew increasingly less beneficial to unions.[15] Not surprisingly, Mbeki's advocacy of business/labor/government corporatism saw him repeatedly attacked by the Charterist Left (SACP/Cosatu).

The era of joint ANC-NP rule lasted from the Transitional Executive Council's (TEC's) inauguration in December 1993 until June 1996, when the NP abandoned the Government of National Unity (GNU). During this period, the basic outlines of ANC hegemony emerged, as middle-class black nationalists became dominant within the Charterist movement and developed "working arrangements" with the white corporate sector. The ANC also used this period to familiarize itself with running the system, and systematically removed Afrikaners from influential positions, replacing them with ANC supporters.[16] By 1997, the ANC felt secure enough to shift away from calming white fears. The reconciliation bubble burst in December 1997, when Mandela slammed white attitudes;[17] the rainbow nation era was over.

Mbeki became president in 1999, which, some suggested, signaled reconciliation's end and the start of black empowerment and nationalism.[18] In reality, the Mandela and Mbeki eras exhibited great policy continuity[19]—except Mbeki's rule was stripped of the public relations veneer. The end of Mandela's "public relations presidency" exposed South Africa's racial fault lines. Mbeki did not create these fault lines; he merely exposed them through his assertive Africanism, his attacks on whites for their involvement in apartheid as a "crime against humanity"[20] (a theme then adopted by others), and his calls for whites to demonstrate their commitment to transformation. Under Mbeki, the ANC's nationalist mission and concern with "founding a new African nation" were certainly aggressively articulated,[21] and the ANC's Lembedian Africanist roots became ever clearer. Consequently, race relations worsened, and 1980s "nonracialism" began to look like a "temporary interlude" within Charterist history[22] as Africanism and Bikoism came to dominate ANC rhetoric.

Of course, realpolitik dictated that the era of calming white fears had to end eventually, if the ANC was to play its real role of stabilizing capitalism. At some point, Mbeki had to turn ANC attention back to its black constituency, if he was to retain their loyalty. But because of the negotiated compromise the ANC had agreed to, there was no way the ANC could now deliver substantive economic improvements to the majority of black South Africans. In the absence of economic delivery, Mbeki did the only thing he could—he turned to (nationalist) symbolic delivery as the mechanism for stabilizing South Africa's existing socioeconomic order of racial capitalism.

BLURRED RACIAL CAPITALISM

The foundations of the racial-capitalist (unified) state were laid under Anglo hegemony during the early twentieth century (see chapter 1). For 40 years, Afrikaner nationalists (unsuccessfully) tried to deconstruct this British-made unified racial-capitalist state through apartheid's partition model. When apartheid collapsed, South Africa's corporate sector (dominated by Anglos) worked hard to ensure (as the state was reunified) that as much of the racial-capitalist order was retained as possible—that is, the economic system remained capitalist, whites retained control of the economy, and blacks provided cheap labor. However, clearly, the old Milner system of white supremacy was untenable, and Milnerite racial capitalism was too starkly racist. To survive, racial capitalism needed modification to obscure (not remove) the racial dichotomy. Beginning in the 1970s, the corporate sector had advocated creating a black middle class as the solution. Now, with ANC moderates at the political helm, the project of stabilizing capitalism was begun in earnest—with stabilization to be achieved by multiracializing the middle and corporate classes. While the working and underclasses could remain black, the supervisory and ruling classes needed to become *visibly* multiracial. Mare suggests the result is a *multiracial capitalism*,[23] but the term *blurred racial capitalism* seems more appropriate given the persistence of an intense racial cleavage, and the way this cleavage is now obscured/blurred through "black window-dressing."

A mix of continuity and change characterizes blurred racial capitalism, as follows:

- The essence of the old (racial) capitalist economic order was retained and stabilized: First, the economic system remains mostly white-controlled. So, although the whites' share of wealth has dipped since 1994[24] (a decline originally initiated by Botha's NP), they remain mostly in society's top 30 percent and they still overwhelmingly own and manage the economy. Although a black middle class is growing, the overall post–1994 trend is for the black-white economic divide to actually widen[25] (as black poverty and unemployment worsen). Second, most of the blacks are concentrated in an (expanding) underclass, and appear trapped in poverty. Those in the black working class live in formal townships, effectively constitute a "labor aristocracy," and use trade unionism to protect their "privileged" status against the lumpen proletariat masses who congregate in (ever-expanding) shack-land slums now surrounding all South African cities. Since the ANC came to power, black unemployment has grown dramatically. In 1994, 28.6 percent of South Africans were unemployed; by 2001, 41.5 percent were unemployed.[26] Black unemployment has risen fastest.[27] Third, blurred racial capitalism is being stabilized around an affluent/nonaffluent cleavage of approximately 30–70 percent.[28] The 70 percent nonaffluent are almost all black—22 million people who are poorer today than they were under apartheid.[29] Blurred racial capitalism (like racial capitalism) is characterized by systemic exploitation, systemic exclusion, and systemic neglect of the underclasses.[30]

- The 1990s witnessed the rapid growth of a wealthy black elite. Although the Urban Foundation's (UF's) 1970s plan to create a black middle class produced significant 1980s results under Botha, this agenda was taken up with real vigor in the 1990s. During joint ANC-NP rule (1991–1996), the black middle class grew by 80 percent.[31] Currently, South Africa's black elite consists of about 10 million people (about 4 million a bourgeoisie and 6 million a petit bourgeoisie),[32] and will probably stabilize at that level. The income of the top 20 percent of black households is now some 40 times higher than the income of the lowest 20 percent of black households.[33] This black elite is profiting handsomely from blurred racial capitalism.

A defining feature of the postapartheid black elite is that at its core are ANC politicians who inherited the state in 1994. These politicians are central to the process of building what is called a "patriotic black bourgeoisie." The ANC is effectively at the center of an ethnic patronage system that distributes largesse and facilitates wealth transfer and opportunity creation for members of the black elite. This black patronage system is similar to the NP's 1950s–1960s system of Afrikaner patronage, but whereas the Anglo corporate sector opposed NP patronage, they now actively encourage ANC patronage because creating a black middle class and ANC-led "patriotic capitalism" manifestly serves their interests.[34] So, as with the NP before it, the ANC is now constructing a ruling elite grounded in racial solidarity and patriotism, and is also engaged in the politics of "catch-up nationalism," "ethnic reranking," and "modifying opportunity structures" (see chapter 2).

An important mechanism for creating job opportunities has been ANC "affirmative action"[35] and Black Economic Empowerment (BEE) legislation. This generated exceptionally rapid black career advancement in the civil service, parastatal corporations, and corporate sector. Creating spaces for black advancement has often necessitated culling white Afrikaner males (WAMs).[36] The BEE program of transferring wealth into black hands[37] is contributing to the rapid emergence of a black capitalist class, who by 1998 already controlled 20 percent of ("black chip") shares on the Johannesburg Stock Exchange.[38] The most successful BEE capitalists have been those with good lobbying powers within the government,[39] with a number of new capitalists being ex-ANC politicians, such as Cyril Ramaphosa, Tokyo Sexwale, and Mathews Phosa. Five types of black capitalists have emerged under the ANC:[40] (1) "activist capitalists" with ANC connections; (2) "overseas-educated exiles"; (3) "corporate sophisticates," who benefited from Sullivan Code–type initiatives; (4) "consultants of change," who marketed themselves as helpful to businesses that were anxious to understand the political changes; and (5) "conference circuit champions," who networked with white business, eager to be seen as BEE-friendly. Government support for small-to-medium black business is creating many companies with a high dependency on state fiat for survival.[41] The ANC's success with building black capitalists has, however, generated some internal ANC tensions, as businessmen like Ramaphosa push for privatizing state assets (into black ownership), while the Charterist Left (especially Cosatu) resists this.

Another interesting feature of this new elite is that the black middle classes created by the NP—the "homeland bourgeoisie" (homeland government functionaries and homeland capitalists) and the township middle classes—regarded as "apartheid collaborators" in the 1980s, have been rehabilitated and absorbed into the patriotic black bourgeoisie:

- A new power elite is emerging out of the compromise negotiated in the early 1990s. A white-controlled socioeconomic enclave (within a sea of black poverty) still sets the pace in South Africa. An ANC-led black elite has been incorporated into this enclave as junior partners,[42] and a symbiotic relationship between the mainly white corporate elite and the black political elite has emerged.[43] This new multiracial power elite has produced a "distributional coalition," which ensures that it benefits economically from blurred racial capitalism, to the detriment of the poorest 50 percent of black households and the less-wealthy coloreds, Indians, and whites (mainly Afrikaners).[44] This new multiracial power elite is held together by the ideology of neoliberalism, while Mbeki also uses Africanist ideology to steer his constituency.
- Despite its de facto neoliberal economic policies, the ANC denies its neoliberalism, and Mbeki[45] and the ANC[46] have even started criticizing neoliberalism. However, ANC economic policy and Mbeki's letters in *ANC Today* contradict such denials.[47] The ANC has, in fact, become somewhat schizophrenic in this regard, as it tries to reconcile advocacy for poverty alleviation and the Reconstruction and Development Program (RDP) with neoliberal policies and BEE. Mbeki

seems to reconcile this schizophrenia by conceptually applying differential policies to South Africa's "first economy" (developed) and "second economy" (underdeveloped).[48] But it is noteworthy that, beginning in 2002, Mbeki and the ANC noticeably adjusted their rhetoric to once again advocate the RDP,[49] state-led "development," uplifting the black underclass, eliminating poverty/underdevelopment,[50] and criticizing neoliberalism. This shift may have been triggered by prepublicity of Terreblanche's book[51] criticizing the ANC for selling out to the corporate sector and betraying the poor.[52]

- The political system has changed by eliminating the (Anglo) white supremacist model and the (Afrikaner) apartheid/partition model as options. Black majoritarianism is the new credo. Politically, Afrikaners have been rendered almost powerless, while the white (mostly Anglo) corporate sector retains political influence through corporatist mechanisms and membership of Mbeki's reference groups.[53]
- During the 1980s, Afrikaners dominated the sociocultural system; by the late 1990s, it was dominated by a multiracial "Anglo-Americanized" elite[54] comprised of Westernized urban blacks and white Anglos. Thanks to this new sociocultural elite, South Africa was effectively being Anglicized (despite the rhetoric of Africanism).
- A significant postapartheid shift has been the phenomenon of rapid urbanization. With the collapse of apartheid's migration policy, black people poured into the cities—a process beginning in the 1980s, but accelerating in the 1990s. The resultant mushrooming shack lands/slums around South Africa's cities have more than doubled the urban population, placing enormous strains on urban infrastructures and local governance and creating a huge pool of unemployed and desperate people who often turn to crime to survive. In a sense, South Africa's cityscapes have simply returned to the condition they were in at the end of World War II when uncontrolled urbanization had created slums and a pool of cheap labor conveniently accessible to the corporate sector.

THE MBEKI STATE

Mbeki replaced Mandela as ANC president in 1997, becoming South Africa's president in 1999. Between 1990 and 1997, Mbeki had consolidated his support base among returning ANC exiles, the Youth League, and the Women's League (led by Winnie Mandela),[55] but his key constituency became the growing black middle class.[56] Significantly, Mbeki ended his SACP membership.[57] Under Mbeki, the right wing of the Charterist movement became ascendant. Tensions between the Charterist Left and Right became more open after the 1998 SACP Congress, when Mbeki (and Mandela) told the Left to "toe the party line" or leave. Interestingly, today's ANC leadership core comprises people who resigned from the SACP.[58] However, despite the ANC's lurch to the Right, Mbeki still needs to mobilize some neosocialist "redistribution" language because most ANC voters remain a poverty-stricken underclass. Consequently, Mbeki still needs the Charterist Left (Cosatu/SACP) to help him manage the working and underclasses by holding out the promise of eventual ANC delivery of "a better life for all" (the ANC's 2004 election slogan). So, despite left-right Charterist tensions, the ANC/Cosatu/SACP alliance seems unlikely to crumble. Instead, Mbeki will continue to use patronage to co-opt left Charterists, and then use them to help prevent the underclasses from becoming a destabilizing force. In this regard, Mbeki is proving to be a competent political manager of blurred racial capitalism.

Mbeki's "two nations" speech[59] encapsulated his perception of the South African problem—namely, South Africa is a deeply divided society. Mbeki argued that South Africa consisted of two nations—one white and exhibiting the lifestyles of the developed world, the other black and subject to the same poverty and misery characterizing the underdeveloped world. The North-South divide ran through South Africa. To overcome this cleavage, socioeconomic upliftment of the underclass was needed. Without this, South Africa would remain characterized by high crime levels and face the potential that someone would eventually mobilize an underclass rebellion. Mbeki argued that upliftment was not happening because whites resisted underwriting an upliftment program; consequently, he questioned whether reconciliation should be continued.[60] Mbeki chose to blame whites for South Africa's problems. By choosing to focus on only the race dimension of the South African dilemma, he fell back upon the ANC's Africanist and anticolonial roots. As Mbeki has said, "our own 'oppressor nation' and 'ruling class' ceased to be foreign"[61] and remain within the country. This created for the ANC the challenge of how to destroy the old order, while having to continue to live within the same state as the "oppressor nation."[62] For Mbeki, the "enemy lies within,"[63] but the enemy is too powerful to be dislodged. The militarized stalemate of the 1980s and negotiations stalemate of the 1990s remain embedded in a contemporary postapartheid stalemate—a stalemate manifesting itself as blurred racial capitalism. As Mbeki stated, "the unwashed and the perfumed . . . are condemned to live together and interact with one another. Divorce is not possible."[64] Mbeki confronts a situation where both the black underclass and white elite have the capacity to destabilize society. Success means reconciling the irreconcilable—blacks demand more transformation, while whites believe too much has already been conceded.

However, Mbeki (as a black nationalist) has chosen to downplay the class dimension of his problem—that is, he is also "trapped" because his core constituency (the patriotic black bourgeoisie) has grown accustomed to the "good life" offered by blurred racial capitalism, and has effectively been co-opted into a corporatist "alliance" with the old order. With (modified) racial capitalism now successfully stabilized (by the ANC), it is difficult to see how the cleavages can be undone. Effectively, Mbeki's room for maneuver is limited by three phenomena, namely:

- his own middle-class constituency,
- globalization pressures (see chapter 9), and
- the ANC's "deal" with the white corporate sector, which denies him the resources to overcome the massive inequalities.

Reducing this all to "white selfishness" is both racist and disingenuous. Mbeki has specifically opted to explain the South African situation (plus the North-South divide) in racial rather than class terms.[65] By doing this, and conflating race and class, Mbeki caused the national debate to slide into a "race populism"[66] and potentially set up whites as future scapegoats. These are signals that Mbeki's solutions to South Africa's problems may eventually become racial (similar to Zimbabwe's land seizures).

To better understand the Mbeki state, his vision, governance style, and management of opposition are examined below.

Mbeki's Vision

Mbeki's project is being constructed around three themes. First, Mbeki has been influential in the process of shifting the ANC away from socialism toward nationalism. With the abandonment of socialism (associated with 1980s Charterism), the ANC's nationalist roots have come to the fore, and under Mbeki, Lembedian Africanism, and Bikoism have made a strong reappearance within the ANC. The resultant ANC nationalism bears some striking similarities to 1950s Afrikaner nationalism—that is, just as the NP rejected Afrikaner second-classness as encoded into racial capitalism's system of ethnic ranking (see chapter 2), so too did the ANC. Just as Afrikaner nationalists developed a form of catch-up nationalism to overcome the "pain" of being ranked badly, so too did Lembede and Biko. And Mbeki's own nationalism reveals a need to overcome the pain of bad ranking.[67] Just as the NP implemented a 1950–1960s ethnic reranking program, so too has the ANC during the 1990s–2000s. Consequently, a central feature of Mbeki's nationalist project has become black empowerment. Not surprisingly, as a catch-up nationalist project, BEE is reminiscent of Afrikaner *volkskapitalisme* (people's capitalism).

Mbeki's promotion of Africanism and nationalism serves a number of useful political purposes, that is, these ideologies:

- Provide the glue to bind together cross-class "black unity" and paper-over the cleavages within black South African society, for example, the enormous wealth disparities and continuing linguistic/tribal differences. Mbeki's project of building a new African state is fundamentally about integrating South Africa as a single unified nation. The vague and fuzzy discourses of "Africanism," "African Renaissance," "*ubuntu*," (African humanism) and "development" serve as Mbeki's tools to draw together a new ruling bloc.[68] Africanist/nationalist discourses help draw together a range of players and provides a new identity servicing Mbeki's nation-building project. For Mbeki-ites, this project is simply a continuation of the ANC's historic mission "to unite Africans for national liberation."[69] This "mission" requires conflating the state, civil society, and ANC into a single nationalist loyalty.[70] Political thought is "totalized," and "alternative thinking" becomes a threat to the nation-building project.[71] Mbeki-ism makes it possible for the ANC to justify (to themselves) "forcing" minority groups not comfortable with integration to join their new nation.

- Hide the reality that the patriotic black bourgeoisie (and their white corporate allies) are the real beneficiaries of Mbeki's state. Mbeki's race populism is highly functional because it appeals to the black underclasses—services their visceral dislike of white privilege, makes them feel "part" of the national project, and gives them hope that "their turn" will come, plus makes it possible for patriotic black bourgeois gains to be proclaimed a victory for *all* black people. Symbolic delivery replaces economic delivery.[72] Race populism also makes it easy to delegitimate opposition parties (e.g., Democratic Party) simply by labeling them "racist,"[73] as well as any criticism coming from nonblacks by simply tagging it as "racist." Debate is thus destroyed and replaced by a comfortable Africanist consensus. Mbeki's racializing of politics is thus highly functional—race is used as a shield against criticism.[74]
- Mean that the ANC can use its past "liberation credentials" to disguise the realities of its contemporary policies. At the same time, "Africanism" replaces "the antiapartheid struggle" as the ANC's unifying credo.[75]

Mbeki-ism has led to the growth of a black middle-class intellectual industry focused on developing the "African Renaissance." Echoes of Lembede's "Pan Africanism" and Biko's "black pride" can be heard strongly in this emergent black nationalism, as follows:

- The African Renaissance is conceptually tied to the "defeat" of white South Africa and the transfer of resources/land into black hands.[76]
- Identity is closely tied to "blackness" in the Garveyist sense of descent.[77] Hence, although the African Renaissance is rooted in Africa, the wider black diaspora is also regarded as part of this phenomenon, and "black identity" is defined as tied to the historical legacy of black repression associated with slavery, colonialism, and apartheid.[78] This sort of race-driven thinking underpinned Mbeki's 2004 state visit to Haiti to celebrate the bicentennial of the world's first black state.
- "Re-Africanizing" Africa is central to this project.[79] This involves undoing the impact of "Eurocentric culture" (brought to Africa during the colonial era) and replacing it with "Afrocentric culture."[80] The project has faced the dilemma of what to do about three "creolized cultures"[81] associated with Africa—namely, the black diaspora in America and Arabia, the Arabized population of North

Africa, and the Europeanized and Asianized populations of Southern and East Africa. The diasporic population is simply defined as "part" of "African culture" by virtue of racial descent. However, a different attitude is adopted toward white and Asian residents within Africa; they are only to be allowed into the African Renaissance project on condition they accept assimilation into African culture.[82] They are not to be allowed to retain their own separate cultural identities (as "nonintegrative impositions") in Africa,[83] but must "commit" (perhaps submit) to Africa and Africanization.[84] Many white South Africans have been alienated by this rhetoric of re-Africanization, Afrocentricism, and anti-Eurocentricism (which treats them as an unwelcome "other").

- Biko's notion of restoring black pride is a constant refrain. The project is about ethnic reranking as a means to overcome pain and the sense of inferiority created by colonialism, slavery, and apartheid.[85]

A second feature of Mbeki's project are neoliberal policies.[86] Mbeki's influence was significant in shifting the ANC away from its earlier (social democrat) RDP policy[87] toward the neoliberalism of Growth, Employment, and Redistribution (GEAR). For Mbeki, adjusting to globalization and attracting foreign capital is central to South African development; hence, GEAR focuses on attracting foreign investment by applying International Monetary Fund (IMF) criteria for good financial governance.[88] Ironically, GEAR is remarkably like the NP's Normative Economic Model, which the ANC had rejected in 1993. But by 1996, the Charterist Right (under Mbeki) was dominant within the ANC; therefore, when launching GEAR in June 1996, Mbeki could say without concern: "Just call me a Thatcherite."[89] Not surprisingly, Mbeki has become Washington's key partner in Africa.[90] South Africa's own corporate sector is more circumscribed in endorsing Mbeki because, although he has certainly stabilized blurred racial capitalism, he casts his (capitalist) solutions for South Africa in a racial framework, which rattles white corporate sector sensitivities.[91]

Interestingly, the Charterist Right are somewhat schizophrenic about their rapid shift from socialism into capitalism. They remain sensitive to suggestions that they are "Gucci comrades" who have been co-opted by the corporate sector, and serve as "black window dressing." And because so many of them were, until recently, members of a Soviet-aligned liberation movement fighting a guerilla war against "Western imperialism," many still exhibit embarrassment about being rich. Mbeki has lectured them on the need to abandon such embarrassment and get on with the job of ensuring blacks take control of South African capitalism.[92]

The neoliberal "alliance" between the Charterist Right and white corporate sector gave rise to an intellectual industry focused on developing the "*ubuntu*" concept.[93] Ubuntu focuses on building reconciliation on the basis of "African humanism" and mutual aid. It became an excellent fulcrum for promoting the notion of cross-class and multiracial cooperation within a framework acceptable to Africanists. Not surprisingly, it was embraced and promoted by South Africa's business sector.[94]

A third feature of Mbeki's project is its strong external focus—Mbeki wants to change the world.[95] Mbeki's Africanism is Pan-Africanist in scope—he wants to end what he calls "global apartheid," that is, a global system economically discriminating against Africans.[96] The African Renaissance program is about challenging this global system. This led to Mbeki's New Partnership for Africa's Development (NEPAD) plan, which seeks to reintegrate Africa into the globalizing world economy by ending Africa's conflicts and bringing good governance and the rule of law to Africa in order to end "Afro-pessimism."[97] NEPAD is Mbeki's African Renaissance concretized into a foreign policy; it now lies at the very heart of South Africa's foreign policy.[98] Of course, if neoliberal economic development is to be taken into Africa, it will be South Africa's corporate sector that does so—that is, NEPAD/African Renaissance represents a form of South African economic imperialism within Africa. It promises to turn South Africa into a regional power and deliver major profits for South African businesses. Mbeki's African Renaissance dream is consequently the best thing that has ever happened to South Africa's (still mostly white) corporate sector.[99]

The Executive and Parliament

As soon as Mbeki became president, he began restructuring governance by: creating a powerful presidency[100] (reminiscent of P.W. Botha's centralized president's office); clustering ministerial committees; making director generals accountable to him (and not their own ministers); and establishing a Policy Coordination Advisory Service (PCAS) under longtime trusted lieutenant, Joel Netshitenzhe. PCAS scrutinizes and vets all intended legislation to ensure presidential coordination and coherence. Mbeki's presidency engages in detailed policymaking/planning and day-to-day governance across all ministries. Mbeki has firm control of his cabinet and the legislative process. The presidency also established control over provincial governments (partly to try and stamp out the administrative chaos and corruption taking hold in many provinces).[101] A new intelligence ministry was created, reporting to the presidency. All government communications were brought directly under the presidency. Mbeki gathered into the presidency key allies (e.g., Essop Pahad and Frank Chikane) and an impressive collection of experts, turning his office into a significant power base—the fulcrum around which South African governance now revolves.

This centralization of power has been greatly facilitated by the nature of South Africa's legislative process. South Africa became a one-party dominant democracy,[102] that is, the ANC acquired overwhelming dominance, but not a monopoly of power. The ANC acquired this authority because South Africans have overwhelmingly voted in racial blocs, and the ANC learned to play the demographic game of mobilizing the black majority.[103] As long as voters remain loyal to their current racial/ethnic voting preferences, black majoritarianism guarantees the ANC electoral victory and continued dominance. Elections became a racial census, with the outcomes virtually predetermined. The result has been "low-intensity democracy" characterized by declining voter interest and decreased political competition.[104] Elections have become increasingly irrelevant as Parliament was reduced to the executive's rubber stamp (given that the presidency determines party career paths and is the dispenser of power, patronage, and largesse).

Managing Opposition

Mbeki is expert at using the presidency and one-party dominance to secure personal power—he mixes coercion, persuasion, and patronage to keep control[105] "through a combination of outright political intimidation, ideological mysticism and the co-option ('redeployment') of key ANC "trouble-makers' and Cosatu/SACP leaders into this governmental inner circle."[106] The SACP's Cronin argues that Mbeki's style derives from his exile years when top-down Stalinist centralization characterized the ANC.[107] Mbeki has proved skilled at silencing Charterist critics,[108] warning off potential enemies,[109] keeping the Charterist Left in line,[110] and controlling his party machinery and Charterist leaders.[111] This is generating an ANC leadership exhibiting signs of "political arrogance,"[112] strangely reminiscent of NP arrogance during the heyday of apartheid.

Mbeki faces four potential sources of dissatisfaction. First, the Charterist Left (Cosatu and SACP) have been showing signs of restiveness since 1998. Because of Mbeki's neoliberalism, there has been constant leftist talk of splitting away from the ANC to form a new left-wing political party. Mbeki is disparagingly dismissive of what he calls "the ultra-left."

Tensions between Mbeki and the Charterist Left were strained when Cosatu (supported by the SACP) launched general strikes (2000–2002) and mass actions against Mbeki's neoliberal policies. The resultant intra-alliance tension only eased after a series of meetings and the 2002 Charterist alliance summit, which slowed the pace of neoliberal reform. Ultimately, the ANC/Cosatu/SACP alliance has held together because:

- Mbeki is very skilled at using patronage (career paths) to co-opt "difficult" left-wingers.
- Cosatu is weak compared to its 1980s heyday because it has been stripped of its best leaders (who have co-opted into the ANC government, or have moved into businesses where "affirmative action"/BEE created excellent career paths.

- A leftist party is unlikely to unseat the ANC government, so opting out the alliance means relinquishing the (patronage) benefits of being inside government.
- Mbeki is a skilled political manager who makes sufficient concessions to the Left to keep them on board. Nonetheless, tensions continue, especially around the unbundling/privatizing of state assets (being promoted by ANC capitalists like Ramaphosa).

Second, the black underclass represents a potential threat to the Mbeki state. The ANC has simply not delivered to the black masses jobs, houses, electricity, land reform, and a functioning public school system. The government invested much into providing electricity, telephones, and clean water to millions of black households; however, most of the electricity and telephones were subsequently disconnected because people could not afford to pay for these services,[113] and millions have been evicted for nonpayment of rent/rates.[114] Delivery has fallen far short of government promises,[115] and dramatically short of 1994 ANC-driven expectations.

But it is the enormous growth of unemployment[116] posing the greatest challenge to Mbeki's government. Unemployment has consistently grown, as shown below:[117]

	1994	1995	1996	1997	1998	1999	2000	2001
Strict Definition	20.0	16.9	19.3	21.0	25.2	23.3	25.8	29.5
Broad Definition	28.6	26.5	34.9	38.9	37.5	36.2	35.9	41.5

Job losses in mining and farming have been especially dramatic—for example, 860,000 black farm workers became unemployed when government subsidies were withdrawn from (mostly Afrikaner) farmers.[118]

It is unclear who—if anyone—will succeed in mobilizing these unemployed and desperate people against ANC nondelivery. To date, Mbeki has successfully deployed ethnic mobilization to keep them loyal to the ANC. So although unemployment fuels a crime problem (which undermines investment), it has not yet generated a political problem for Mbeki. However, Calland and Jacobs suggest this constituency will eventually be successfully mobilized by a new generation of civics, unionists, intellectuals, and church leaders.[119] Mbeki denies that such a threat exists. He believes (probably correctly) the black masses will retain their (ethnic) loyalty to the ANC due to its "liberation credentials."[120]

Third, a large number of Afrikaners are alienated by strong Anglicization pressures, a sense of being a politically powerless minority, and by the way the ANC uses the "race card" to silence white criticism and even "linguistically disallow" Afrikaners from claiming their right to a separate identity. Under ANC rule, the use of Afrikaans as a bureaucratic/legal, business, media, and educational language has dramatically declined, causing considerable unhappiness and concern. In addition, Afrikaner poverty is reemerging.[121] However, except for a few extremists who planted bombs, Afrikaners have not resisted the ANC government. Instead, mainstream "resistance" has been limited to opposing government pressures to end Afrikaner-exclusive public schooling. (This is seen to deprive Afrikaners of the means to culturally reproduce themselves.)

The current mood among Afrikaners is a mixture of confusion, anger, lack of direction, and listlessness. Their loss of power was rapid—all the symbolisms of their "Afrikaner nationalist" republic were stripped away, Afrikaners have little public profile, Afrikaans has little "public presence" (for example, Afrikaans signage has been replaced, and Afrikaans has almost disappeared from television), and a high proportion of Afrikaner males lost their jobs in the "purchased revolution"[122] (financial payments being made to whites removed from their positions). The alienation and disaffection felt by many Afrikaners was exacerbated by the Truth and Reconciliation Commission (TRC), which referred to apartheid as "a crime against humanity" and effectively pointed a finger in the direction of Afrikaners, while ignoring other players. As political theatre, and a mechanism for cathartically releasing anguish, the TRC served its purpose by selectively exploring some abuses, while ignoring others. Ultimately, the TRC manufactured a "truth" conforming to the needs of the new elite[123] (comprising the ANC and corporate sector), with its decision not to examine Anglo business's role in building racial capitalism revealing much about its agenda.[124] Many Afrikaners saw the TRC as a witch-hunt run by commissioners (especially Anglos) with political scores to settle.[125] As a propaganda and myth-making machine, it helped destroy the NP,[126] disseminate the notion that the ANC fought a "just war," and create a "founding myth" for the new South Africa. The TRC served the ANC's nationalist nation-building project well,[127] but in the process, alienated many whites, especially Afrikaners. It did not bring about reconciliation.[128] Recognizing the growing alienation and threat to destabilizing race relations, the ANC government pragmatically relegated the TRC to a sideshow and implemented a de facto general amnesty.[129]

Most Afrikaners are not hostile to the new regime because they realize the ANC serves their interests by stabilizing society (through calming the black masses). However, because the price of this stabilization appears to be a radical downgrading of their culture/language, many Afrikaners have sunk into a state of disaffected resignation, with Mbeki noting that the "burden of despair" has been shifted from blacks to whites.[130] A majority of Afrikaners continue to think apartheid was a good idea, as revealed in a 2000–2001 Institute for Justice and Reconciliation survey,[131] as follows:

The Basic Idea of Apartheid Was Good?	True	Not True	Don't Know
Afrikaners	65	29	6
White Anglo	36	60	5
Xhosa	18	73	9
Zulu	25	65	10
Colored	38	65	7
All South Africans	39	55	7

As Mbeki has noted, many Afrikaners have not embraced the new South Africa, but have rather "migrated inwards."[132] The same could be said of many whites, Indians, and coloreds (WICs) alienated by affirmative action and triumphalist Africanism's devaluation of non-Afrocentric culture. But as long as Afrikaner (and WIC) alienation translates into "inward migration" or emigration, ANC governance is not threatened.

Fourth, although members of the white corporate sector are effectively Mbeki's corporatist partners and, on balance, have much to be pleased with about Mbeki's performance, business-sector support has been circumscribed because:

- Mbeki casts his (capitalist) solutions for South Africa in a racial framework that rattles white sensitivities.
- Investors are concerned about the collapse of South Africa's criminal justice system and police demoralization,[133] plus corruption, moral decay,[134] and rampant crime.
- An education system crisis—generating falling education outputs[135]—meant South Africa was not producing the skilled workforce needed to be globally competitive.
- A "culture of entitlement" generated widespread corruption and greed among newly appointed black staffers in the public and private sectors.[136] Overseas investors began to see South Africa's public sector as venal.[137]
- Rapid affirmative action meant 72 percent of civil servants were black by 2002. This, however, destroyed the civil service's experience base and institutional memory,[138] generating a "bureaucratic wobble," therefore weakening the state's capacity to deliver.
- High emigration rates among South Africa's most skilled people undermined the economy.
- Mbeki's handling of Zimbabwe's land seizures exacerbated South African racial tensions and generated concerns that the ANC might eventually turn to seizing white property.

Recognizing that these problems discouraged foreign investment and undermined NEPAD, Mbeki's government moved to correct them from 1999.[139] The resultant anticorruption mechanisms, plus attempts to rebuild the criminal justice system began producing some positive results from 2003. Further, a 2004 public relations campaign was launched to overcome WIC pessimism, in an attempt to encourage South Africa's diasporics to return home and also discourage South Africans at home and abroad from spreading stories undermining investor confidence.[140] By 2004, there were signs that Mbeki was securing the allegiance of the WIC business classes, and earlier corporate sector concerns were waning.

The ANC is better for business than the NP ever was.[141] Blurred racial capitalism has been stabilized based on a balance of power that locks all South Africans into making the negotiated compromise work. This has produced a rather schizophrenic country in which most seem to have grudgingly accepted the fact that they have to live with compromises they would rather not have made. Many do not like the outcome, but for the moment, the existing balance of forces has produced an ANC/corporate sector power elite that seems politically unchallengeable.

CHAPTER 9

Globalization and the New South Africa

Globalization emerged during the last two decades of the twentieth century as a new way of organizing wealth making and capital accumulation. Capitalism reinvented itself because of three opportunities. First, the 1970s/1980s information revolution created the means for constructing global communication networks (and instantaneous global communication), which facilitated globally organized production/distribution. Second, building global communication networks generated investment opportunities, which reinvigorated capitalism, and made the United States overwhelmingly dominant economically. Third, the Soviet collapse produced conditions for the Pax Americana's growth, that is, the United States became globally hegemonic. American dominance created opportunities for reconfiguring global trading systems with the United States at its heart.

From this emerged a new global business style that borrowed from the U.S. comprador approach of the center controlling the peripheries, in other words, local collaborators (compradors) are sought out and networked with those at the center.[1] Globalization as a new way of doing business involves:[2]

- Dispersing production. Globalized production became possible when the Soviet collapse turned the world into a single labor pool. Production is now scattered globally—factories are placed wherever efficient labor is cheapest. Components are then transported to "central" assembly sites. Products are marketed globally. This requires high-grade coordination/planning and analytical skills, as well as financing and negotiation skills. Global coordinators need high levels of cultural capital and tend to live in First World global cities.

- Restructuring work around information technologies (computers, internet communication), for example, computer-integrated manufacture. Conceptual, communication, and coordination skills become central to wealth making as the economy becomes "reflexive."[3]
- Liberalizing trade and capital flows, that is, capital and goods are made hypermobile.
- Reorganizing organizational structures away from bureaucratic hierarchies toward flexible formats.
- Reorganizing the state in ways reducing state autonomy/sovereignty (due to World Trade Organization/WTO pressures). The state's new role is to facilitate globalization.
- A new three-tiered geography of power is emerging. First, "wired" global cities (e.g., New York, London, Tokyo, Frankfurt, Hong Kong, Singapore) have emerged as globalization coordinating centers. Second, industrial production (involving "dirty," "monotonous" labor) is relocated to places where labor is cost-effective, a good work ethic exists, and regulations on pollution and work practices are lax, but an effective criminal justice system exists to create stability. This caused many U.S., European, and Australian cities to be deindustrialized, as production was shipped offshore to Southeast Asia, China, and Latin America. Third, those areas without appropriate cultural capital (to become coordination centers) and without efficient cheap labor (to become production centers) have fallen off the globalization map and become economically marginal. Much of the old Soviet Empire and Africa fall into this category. For postapartheid South Africa, this is proving a disaster.

SOUTH AFRICA'S DOUBLE TRANSFORMATION

When the African National Congress (ANC) came to power in 1994, it faced a double transformation—internal transformation involved the challenge of reconfiguring society following apartheid's demise, while external transformation involved meeting the challenges of globalization. Effectively, (external) global pressures limited the ANC's room for (internal) maneuver because the postapartheid state emerged into a context where if South Africa was to successfully reintegrate itself into the world economy and attract foreign investment, it had to perform in terms of criteria valued by the Pax Americana, as follows:

- States are encouraged to adopt ideals and institutions valued by Americans, for example, liberal democracy and individual rights.
- States are encouraged to adopt neoliberal economics and curtail state interventionism.
- Neoliberalism gives rise to great disparities in wealth distribution. But, for the stability of capitalism, it is important that disparities not be associated with ethnic/cultural differences.

- There is pressure for the free flow of capital and goods. The (WTO, International Monetary Fund/IMF) "Washington consensus" discourages tariff barriers and currency controls.
- There are pressures promoting global cultural homogenization associated with the use of English, cosmopolitanism, and materialist secularization.
- The United States prefers governing elites who facilitate the above. Politicians wishing to be successful need to take this into account.

At the same time, the ANC was confronted by their constituency's socialist and developmentalist demands and expectations. The problem was, the internal and global pressures clashed. Hence, choices had to be made, either offending ANC supporters or undermining South Africa's ability to attract foreign capital. Effectively, South Africa's new government had to navigate its way through the consequences of being an emerging "third wave democracy"[4]—its emergence tied to external pressure to conform to Pax Americana standards of political democratization and economic liberalization. Conforming to democratization demands had pressured the National Party (NP) pre-1994, while post-1994 neoliberal demands pressured the ANC. The new South Africa was born from this dual set of pressures/capitulations.

The result has been the creation of blurred racial capitalism administered by a modern secular state. This state is characterized by a balance of power that sees the ANC constrained by a (mostly white) internal corporate sector that is allied to the powerful external forces of globalized capitalism. This balance of power has resulted in the ANC placing globalization demands ahead of the wishes of its own constituency. This meant creating a political management structure that could circumvent (perhaps ignore) pressures from the underclasses. Hence, the South African state, although a formal constitutional democracy, is not a functioning liberal democracy. Instead, it is a one-party dominant democracy, characterized by corporatism and elite pacting.

Corporatism became an especially important feature of the Mandela presidency when the core problem was how to stabilize South Africa during its double transition, plus build "elite pacting" mechanisms. Corporatism became a crucial means for creating stability while the ANC learned how to govern and develop a route map for integrating South Africa into the globalized economy. Because integrating South Africa involved adopting neoliberal policies, the potential of mass (black) discontent was real. Corporatism became a "crisis response" of the "elite pact" (the emerging multiracial power elite) to this potential threat.[5] Under Mandela, the ideologies of "national unity" and "reconciliation" underpinned elite collaboration between the ANC/Congress of South African Trade Unions (Cosatu)/South African Communist Party (SACP), the NP, and the corporate sector. An interesting feature of this corporatism was how Cosatu/SACP were ensnared in ways demobilizing their workerist constituencies.[6] After the NP left the Government of National Unity (GNU) and Mbeki became president, "neoliberal" ideology became the glue binding the ANC and corporate sector. Growing Cosatu/SACP unhappiness about neoliberalism saw corporatist mechanisms decline in importance (but not disappear), and the presidency emerge as the key "elite pact" coordinating fulcrum. Mbeki's office became the nodal point for organizing South Africa's transition, via:

- Keeping the corporate sector on board.
- Building a black bourgeoisie as the core of a new ruling elite.
- Creating a black-run civil service (i.e., removing whites), both as a means to secure control of the state and as a form of ANC patronage (creating black middle-class loyalty to the ANC).
- Keeping Cosatu/SACP on board and/or demobilizing their resistance.
- Ensuring Parliament functions as a compliant rubber stamp (i.e., managing a "low-intensity democracy"[7]).
- Finding ways to keep the black masses loyal to the ANC and demobilizing any moves to build resistance.
- Managing "negative fallouts" derived from government policies. Mbeki's management strategy involved two features—first, substituting symbolic delivery for real delivery (e.g., Africanism, African Renaissance, blaming "apartheid's legacy" or "blaming whites," and promising delivery sometime in the future). Second, constructing an intelligence ministry to monitor potential dissidents (the black underclasses, Afrikaners, and Muslims[8]).

To date, corporatism and the presidency have proved effective mechanisms for steering South Africa's double transformation—managing to keep all parties on board and keeping the masses passive despite very high unemployment levels and the ANC's failure to meet "delivery" expectations. The outcome has been an ANC radically transformed since 1990. The ANC's adjustment to globalization (and neoliberalism) has been nothing short of remarkable.

SHIFTING INTO GEAR

In 1989, the ANC/SACP alliance was a Soviet-supportive liberation movement. In 1990, the ANC still advocated socialism, with Mandela stating that the ANC intended to nationalize banks, mines, and industry.[9] The ANC believed in state interventionism, developmentalism, and socialism, and their Reconstruction and Development Program (RDP) policy proposed economic growth through redistribution.[10] Redistributing wealth from the (white) rich to the (black) poor lay at the heart of ANC policy and rhetoric. They planned to create a modernist developmentalist state to achieve this. The ANC were, in effect, modernists—products of the NP's apartheid project in modernist social engineering and rationalist planning. The heart of the NP plan had been to build a modern industrial nation in "white" South Africa, surrounded by ten black nations (the homelands). But what apartheid's modernizers achieved was (contrary to their plan) not a white African modern industrial state, but rather an industrialized society dependent upon a black working class. The NP inadvertently created Africa's largest (black) working class, plus a smaller (black) middle class; these thoroughly modern people were to become the heart of the ANC's constituency. Significantly, they acquired from the NP an unshakable modernist faith in nation building, rational planning, industrialism, and state interventionism/developmentalism. Unfortunately, these were all beliefs that did not mesh well with a globalizing (neoliberal) world.

The ANC and its constituency did not seem well placed to manage South Africa's transition into globalization, so South Africa's corporate sector, the IMF, World Bank, and diplomats launched a concerted exercise (of think tanks, workshops, seminars, conferences, forums, briefings, and junkets) to "adjust" the ANC to the "realities" of globalized capitalism and shift their economic policies. The benefits of market economics, export-led growth, and trickle-down economics were promoted.[11] The proselytizing exercise worked—the ANC was converted to the "Washington consensus,"[12] and abandoned the development state[13] and socialism. The start of the ANC's entrapment into neoliberalism occurred in 1993, when the Congress, in addition to the NP and corporates, signed a secret economic policy protocol encoding the Washington consensus.[14] It ended with the 1996 adoption of Growth, Employment, and Redistribution (GEAR), which cemented the ANC's co-option into neoliberalism.[15] In 1996, the RDP ministry was closed. The ANC excused this radical shift by claiming it was being "forced" to change by the GNU.[16] The "change industry" of scenario planning also shifted white South African opinion,[17] which contributed to a growing (multiracial) elite consensus.

The 1996 adoption of GEAR represented the ANC's complete conversion to globalization logic and IMF thinking. GEAR looked like the NP's 1993 Normative Economic Model,[18] advocating redistribution through growth. Growth was to be achieved by attracting foreign investment (through fiscal discipline) into the manufacturing sector and promoting export-led growth.[19] GEAR looked like a desperate attempt to attract foreign investment.[20] For the local Anglo corporate sector, it was a dream come true—apartheid had interfered with their profit making, isolated them from the world's economy, and trapped their capital within South Africa where investment opportunities were becoming exhausted.[21] With the ANC's conversion to neoliberalism, South African Anglo corporates were free to reintegrate themselves with their international brethren. South Africa's largest corporations (Anglo America, De Beers, Old

Mutual, SA Breweries, Didata, and Gencor/Billiton) took advantage of this, and in 2001, "reintegrated" themselves into the global economy by moving their financial headquarters from Johannesburg to London[22]—representing massive capital disinvestment from South Africa.

The ANC's conversion to neoliberalism reflected its weak position. It had not won its liberation war, but had been invited into an elite pact on terms set by the old white establishment. To make matters worse, the ANC came to power at a historically inopportune moment—just as globalization removed its room for maneuver.[23] Whereas Afrikaner nationalists and Malay nationalists were able to capture the state and use it to facilitate ethnic redistribution,[24] the ANC found itself constrained by a world economic system penalizing state economic interventionism and developmentalism. The ANC's original economic model had proposed a type of Afrikaner ethnic reranking/affirmative action or Malaysian *bumiputra* (a policy of affirmative action favoring ethnic-Malays), but globalization pressures constrained them.[25]

Finding itself checkmated by the power of globalized capital and the white establishment, the ANC abandoned plans to uplift the black masses through state interventionism. Instead, it opted to uplift *some* black people by promoting black capitalism. Having replaced public provision with privatized provision,[26] the ANC apparently decided that if they could not have 100 percent, they'd settle for 30 percent in the form of state interventionism to enrich some blacks through Black Economic Empowerment (BEE). This would have the added benefit of creating some *visible* black progress—providing successful black people who could be trotted out to demonstrate that the ANC was delivering change.[27] Once the process of creating a patriotic black bourgeoisie was initiated, it took on a life of its own—the black bourgeoisie mushroomed. With Mbeki's patronage, this bourgeoisie became the ANC Right, who increasingly influenced ANC policy to promote their own interests.

THE ANC'S DILEMMAS

The ANC's acceptance of neoliberalism and globalization has created five dilemmas for the organization. First, the black underclasses still constitute the majority of ANC supporters, and neoliberalism/globalization is not delivering them any benefits. This underclass expects economic delivery at some stage and remains emotionally committed to developmentalism and state interventionism geared to transferring wealth into their hands. If the ANC does not eventually deliver real benefits, it will face a voter backlash. When Zimbabwe's government faced such a backlash, it turned to seizing white farms (which destroyed Zimbabwe's economy).

Second, South Africa's uneven development means that whites, Indians, and coloreds (WICs) are generally skilled and blacks generally unskilled.

Most black South Africans lack the requisite cultural capital/skills to function in a globalized world—global capital can find more productive and cost-effective labor elsewhere. WICs, however, possess the required cultural capital/skills to prosper in a globalizing environment. This presents the ANC with a dilemma—if it adopts policies promoting unfettered WIC prosperity, it faces a likely black voter backlash. However, if it curtails WIC opportunities (e.g., affirmative action, BEE) it stimulates WIC emigration, which squanders cultural capital and undermines economic growth.[28] It also creates white negativity, which deters foreign investors (because Anglos are well connected overseas), thereby undermining economic growth. Lack of economic growth, in turn, generates crime, which fuels capital flight and the emigration of skilled people. The ANC has not solved this chicken-and-egg quandary.

Third, the ANC has discovered that it cannot rerank its poor black constituency as initially envisaged. Originally, the ANC intended to copy the NP's successful ethnic reranking of Afrikaners. However, the NP's program involved only a small percentage of the total population (making it achievable), whereas the ANC confronts a black underclass of 30 million. Furthermore, the NP was not constrained by globalization pressures and therefore could deploy state interventionism and agricultural subsidies, and stimulate industrialization through tariff protection.[29] The ANC came to power just as globalization foreclosed these options. The problem is that pre-1994, the ANC promised its constituency an ethnic upgrading program. Now unable to deliver, the ANC must substitute "symbolic delivery" for material improvements. But Mbeki is aware there is a time limit on nondelivery (as the Zimbabwe fiasco demonstrates).

Fourth, the shift to GEAR generated a Left Charterist revolt. Mbeki, however, needs to keep Cosatu/SACP in the alliance as his main communication conduits with the black masses. The longer he can retain the SACP/Cosatu as allies, the longer he can substitute "symbolic delivery" for real delivery. However, this alliance comes at a cost, because Cosatu/SACP have extracted policy concessions from Mbeki. On balance, the ANC Right wins more policy battles than the ANC Left, but the combination of wins and losses generates unhelpful policy mixes, for example, promoting trade liberalization without labor market reforms cuts across Mbeki's attempts to attract foreign capital and therefore increases unemployment.[30]

Fifth, neoliberalism has clearly not delivered what the corporate sector/IMF claimed it would.

- GEAR has not attracted large-scale foreign investment, and what limited investment arrived was short-term "speculative money." Essentially, South Africa (like the rest of Africa) is regarded as a bad investment bet due to Afro-pessimism—in other words, Africa's workforce is seen as unskilled with low productivity relative to cost, there are no significant internal markets, and Africa is seen as politically unstable/violent, with poor criminal justice systems. Globalization is effectively channeling capital to "chosen locations";[31] however, Africa, is not one of these locations,[32] and is instead becoming economically marginalized.[33] So instead of neoliberalism attracting foreign investment to South Africa, foreign exchange liberalization actually produced disinvestment/capital flight, sparking a collapse in the value of South Africa's currency.[34]

- GEAR was supposed to deliver export-oriented economic growth, grounded in a growing manufacturing sector (based on the Asian model). Because of South Africa's weak export competitiveness,[35] it did not.[36] Also, unlike the Asian cases, South Africa's state played no interventionist role.[37]
- Far from creating economic growth, neoliberalism and South Africa's rapid reinsertion into a globalized economy generated massive increases in unemployment, and per capita living standards sank to lows last seen in the early 1960s.[38]

Despite the ANC's failure to solve its dilemmas and deliver material improvements to the black masses, it has retained the loyalty of black South Africans, receiving 69 percent of the vote in the 2004 elections, thereby confirming South Africa's status as an entrenched one-party dominant democracy. Because most South Africans vote in racial blocs, Mbeki can rely on the "ethnic loyalty" of black voters. Also ANC voters responded positively to Mbeki's black nationalist rhetoric, his deployment of ANC "national liberation" credentials, his promises of "future" economic delivery, and his skillful use of "victimhood discourses" (blaming apartheid, colonialism, and local and global white racism for continued black poverty).

MBEKI'S FOCUS: BEE AND NEPAD

Constrained by the internal balance of power and globalization pressures, the ANC government is unable to solve the above dilemmas. Consequently, Mbeki looked for areas where he could have an impact. The result has been the ANC's focus on BEE and the New Partnership for Africa's Development (NEPAD).

The ANC's core dilemma is that it cannot rerank its black constituency as originally planned (in the manner achieved by Malays and Afrikaners). However, if the ANC simply accepts the status quo, it will remain trapped within the existing balance of power. The only way to break out of this existing unfavorable balance (wherein white corporates are so powerful) is to promote capital transfer into black hands. If achieved, such a capital transfer would wind back the white corporate sector's stranglehold over policy options. This has led to Mbeki's Black Economic Empowerment policies, which have remarkable echoes of Afrikaner *Volkskapitalisme*.

Mbeki's "patriotic capitalism" has become a form of substitutism—BEE's uplifting of a minority of blacks into a capitalist class enables the

ANC to claim it is meeting its transformatory pledges.[39] In truth, the ANC is unable to meet its original pledges because during the Kempton Park negotiations, it agreed to be co-opted into the role of stabilizing racial capitalism, and is now trapped in this role. This only leaves the ANC government one realistic option—promoting black capitalism so its black constituency can capture as much capitalist power as possible. Hence, BEE is geared to redistributing wealth upward into the hands of a patriotic black bourgeoisie in contradistinction to the RDP plan of distributing wealth downward to the black masses. Such redistribution is perfectly acceptable (indeed desirable) to those administering the Washington consensus, and so Mbeki has become the United States' key African ally.[40] Unfortunately for Mbeki, BEE alienates WICs, feeding skilled emigration and capital flight. It also annoys the Charterist Left, who accuse him of abandoning promises to lift the black masses out of poverty.

Ultimately, Mbeki's BEE policies are driven by the same logic as those of Malaysia's Mahathir (and Mbeki has clearly been influenced by Mahathir's thinking). Both have sought to ethnically rerank their constituencies, and create "patriotic capitalism" through ethnic patronage and rearranging society's opportunity structures. However, Mahathir has been luckier than Mbeki because he began his *Bumiputera* (Malay affirmative action) project before globalization imposed limitations of state interventionism. When globalization struck, Mahathir had already substantially constructed his "patriotic capitalist" class. Postglobalization, he successfully maintained his *Bumiputera* project by privatizing state assets into Malay hands and attracting Japanese capital, which provided continued resources for maintaining the Malay patronage system.[41] Mbeki, however, had to build his black bourgeoisie within the limitations imposed by both globalization and an inability to attract foreign capital. This leaves Mbeki with only three options:

- privatizing state assets into black hands,
- finding mechanisms to force the transfer of white assets into black hands, or
- only awarding state procurement contracts to black-owned businesses.

Mbeki has started using land redistribution legislation to transfer white farms into black hands, and BEE legislation to force the transfer of white capital into black hands. The process of "unbundling" white companies and transferring the unbundled "pieces" to black empowerment companies began during the 1990s,[42] with BEE legislation geared to speeding up this capital transfer process. The BEE program also means state procurement contracts go to business with black ownership. The issue of privatizing state assets is proving to be a problem for Mbeki because Left Charterists are slowing down the process to the annoyance of the patriotic black bourgeoisie within the Charterist Right.

A second feature of Mbeki's presidency has been a shift away from a local focus toward an international focus. Finding himself constrained internally by the local and global balance of power, Mbeki has increasingly focused on foreign affairs under the rubric of NEPAD. Under Mbeki, "the global replaces the national as a primary 'site of struggle' while, at the same time, functioning as an alibi for [failed domestic policies]."[43] Mbeki has effectively transferred his "antiapartheid struggle" to the international context—global capitalism is the new enemy. For Mbeki, just as South Africa is divided into rich white and poor black parts, so too is the world.[44] Mbeki sees the world as divided into a rich white North and a poor black South. Within his "black victimhood" cosmology,[45] these divisions (South African and global) are caused by white racism. According to Mbeki, it's time for the world's black "have-nots"[46] to challenge the white "haves," and claim what is their rightful economic due.[47] Hence, the black South needs to see globalization as an opportunity[48] within which to grab its rightful share of global wealth by using the same methods the ANC deploys inside South Africa—that is, mobilizing political pressure to force whites to transfer wealth to blacks. The white North is to be shamed[49] (by reminding it of its "slavery, colonialism and racism") and told it cannot defend itself against a "starving South."[50] In this regard, Mbeki has come to see himself as a global leader representing a black global constituency. South Africa's foreign policy reflects this Mbeki cosmology.

Mbeki sees Africa as having a particular problem—that is, Africa is being economically marginalized within globalization. NEPAD is Africa's response to globalization,[51] emerging from Mbeki's engagement with the G-8 (USA, UK, Japan, Germany, France, Italy, Canada, Russia).[52] NEPAD lies not just at the heart of Mbeki's foreign policy, but ultimately underpins his domestic policy. At some point, the ANC has to overcome South Africa's massive unemployment crisis and deliver some economic benefits to the black masses. There is a time limit to how long the ANC can rely on nationalist rhetoric and symbolic delivery to appease its poor black constituency. Failure to deliver will see the ANC eventually face a political backlash of the sort Zimbabwe's Mugabe faced. For Mbeki's domestic policy (GEAR) to work, South Africa needs foreign investment to deliver economic growth/jobs. But as long as Africa is seen as a bad investment bet, South Africa will also face economic marginalization. All of Africa must therefore conform to the Washington consensus if South Africa's GEAR policy is to succeed. Therefore, Mbeki's NEPAD aims to deliver a new kind of Africa,[53] conforming to the Washington consensus, which includes:

- Democratic governance
- Functioning criminal justice systems
- Functioning national states/bureaucracies (not characterized by corruption)

- Well-maintained infrastructures (transport, communication, health, services, etc.)
- Improved education (to create the necessary cultural capital)
- Market access and privatized economies
- An end to wars and warlordism
- Constructing an African peacekeeping force

NEPAD represents Mbeki's attempts to overcome Afro-pessimism. Both GEAR and NEPAD are geared to the same Mbeki project of building a black South African middle class. The ideological glue for this project is African Renaissance. This middle class is to form the heart of South Africa's new ruling elite and function as the "coordinating hub" for all Africa within the globalized world economy (i.e., South Africa's black middle class will be networked with middle-class ruling elites across Africa). Ultimately, this is simply compradorism[54] rearticulated into a globalized framework.

If Mbeki succeeds, his black middle-class constituency—as neocolonial agents[55]—will reap handsome rewards. His problem is that African instability continues to feed Afro-pessimism, and foreign investment continues to avoid Africa.[56] Unless Mbeki can turn this problem around and attract substantial capital inflow into South Africa, the ANC will be unable to deliver economic improvements to the country's poverty-stricken underclass. At some point in the future, "blaming apartheid" will presumably no longer work to deflect attention away from the ANC's lack of delivery and the increasingly extravagant lifestyle of the "patriotic black bourgeoisie." If that happens, the ANC could face a backlash. That is when the ANC Right (using Africanist ideology) would be most likely to turn to scapegoating white South Africans. When Zimbabwe's African National Union-Patriotic Front (ZANU-PF) government faced a similar crisis, it turned to confiscating white wealth.

For the moment, however, Mbeki has created a stable (albeit weak) postapartheid state, and stabilized (blurred) racial capitalism. Further, he has a coherent plan to make globalization work for his black middle-class constituency, which will also supposedly deliver "trickle-down" benefits to the black underclasses. Only time will tell if his plan works.

Notes

PREFACE

1. E. A. Walker, *A History of Southern Africa* (London: Longman, 1957); C.W. De Kiewiet, *A History of South Africa* (Oxford: Clarendon, 1941); I.D. Macrone, *Race Attitudes in South Africa* (Oxford: Oxford University Press, 1937); L. Van den Berghe, *South Africa: A Study in Conflict* (Westport, CT: Greenwood, 1965); R. De Villiers, "Afrikaner Nationalism," in M. Wilson and L. Thompson, *The Oxford History of South Africa* (Oxford: Oxford University Press, 1971); and L. Thompson, *The Political Mythology of Apartheid* (New Haven, CT: Yale University Press, 1985). Thompson's book is the most sustained liberal attempt to decode Afrikaner nationalism. Although it includes some insightful deconstructions of Afrikaner mythology, Thompson fails to recognize and deconstruct his own Anglo liberal mythology (which reveals itself in his emphases and de-emphases, exaggerations, and omissions). Ironically, the book says as much with regard to Anglo liberal mythology as it does about Afrikaner nationalist mythologies.

2. H. Wolpe, "Capitalism and Cheap Labour Power," *Economy and Society* 1 (4); M. Legassick, "South Africa: Capitalist Accumulation and Violence," *Economy and Society* 3 (3); J. Slovo, "South Africa—No Middle Road," in B. Davidson, J. Slovo, and A.R. Wilkinson, *Southern Africa: The New Politics of Revolution* (Harmondsworth: Penguin Books, 1976); R. Davies, *Capital, State and White Labour in South Africa, 1900–1960* (Sussex: Harvester and Davies, 1979); B. Bozzoli, *The Political Nature of a Ruling Class: Capital and Ideology in South Africa 1890–1933* (London: Routledge and Keagan Paul, 1981); and D. Yudelman, *The Emergence of Modern South Africa* (Westport, CT: Greenwood Press, 1983).

3. H. Wolpe, *Race, Class and the Apartheid State* (Paris: Unesco, 1988), 32; S. Dubow, *Racial Segregation and the Origins of Apartheid* (Oxford: MacMillan, 1989), 3.

4. M. Lipton, *Capitalism and Apartheid* (Aldershot, England: Wildwood House, 1986).

5. M. O'Dowd, "The O'Dowd View: The Stages of Economic Growth and the Future of South Africa," in L. Schlemmer and E. Webster, *Change, Reform and Economic Growth in South Africa* (Johannesburg: Ravan, 1978).

6. Lipton, *Capitalism*, 365.

7. B. Freund, "Some Unasked Questions on Politics," *Transformation* 1: 124.
8. D. O'Meara, *Volkskapitalisme* (Johannesburg: Ravan, 1983).
9. D. Posel, *The Making of Apartheid 1948–1961* (Oxford: Clarendon Press, 1997).
10. H. Giliomee, *The Afrikaners* (London: Hurst & Company, 2003).

CHAPTER 1: MILNER'S MODEL OF SETTLER CAPITALISM

1. J. Benyon, *Proconsul and Paramountcy in South Africa* (Pietermaritzburg, South Africa: University of Natal Press, 1980), 279–287.
2. In building this racial-capitalist state, Milner drew upon, systematized, and reconfigured Southern Africa's long race-based labor relations legacy. S. Terreblanche, *A History of Inequality in South Africa, 1652–2002*. (Pietermartzburg, South Africa: University of Natal Press, 2003) sketches out this legacy.
3. Gellner has noted that states are functional for industrial society. See A.D. Smith, *Nationalism and Modernity* (London: Routledge, 1998), 35–36.
4. J. Habermas, *The Philosophical Discourse of Modernity* (Cambridge, UK: Polity Press, 1987).
5. L. Van Vucht Tijssen, J. Berting, and F. Lechner, *The Search for Fundamentals: The Process of Modernization and the Quest for Meaning* (Dordrecht, Netherlands: Kluwer Academic, 1995), 21.
6. J. Locke, *Second Treatise of Government* (Oxford: Basil Blackwell, 1966).
7. T. O'Brein, *Milner* (London: Constable, 1979), chapter 3.
8. Holland's Cape Colony was established in 1652.
9. Afrikaners emerged as a self-conscious community in the eighteenth century. They grew from a fusion of Dutch, German, and French settlers at Cape Town and its hinterland, who came to see themselves as Africans ("Afrikaners") rather than Europeans. The first recorded use of the term was in 1707, when a Stellenbosch man in conflict with the Dutch authorities exclaimed, "I am an Afrikaner." H. Giliomee, *The Afrikaners* (London: Hurst & Company, 2003), 22. For this he was banished into exile, and died in Australia.
10. B. Roberts, *Kimberley: The Turbulent City* (Cape Town: David Philip, 1976).
11. In South Africa, "colored" refers to mixed-race people, the majority of whom speak Afrikaans. The Griquas are a colored people who constituted the first pioneer wave of Western migration out of the Cape Colony and into the interior.
12. Cecil Rhodes (1853–1902) migrated to South Africa at the age of 17 and joined the 1871 diamond rush to Kimberley. Rhodes, who founded the De Beers diamond mining company, became one of the Cape Colony's wealthiest men. Further, as founder of the Goldfields of South Africa mining company, Rhodes later became a powerful Johannesburg mine-owner. In addition, Rhodes established the British South Africa Company (BSAC) that he used to simultaneously expand his own financial interests and the British Empire across Southern Africa. Through the BSAC Rhodes established a virtual fiefdom over Bechuanaland (Botswana), Southern Rhodesia (Zimbabwe) and Northern Rhodesia (Zambia). He also became Prime Minister of the Cape Colony and the most powerful man in British-Africa. Oxford University's Rhodes Scholarship scheme was his creation.
13. R. Turrell, *Capital and Labor on the Kimberley Diamond Fields 1871–1890* (Cambridge: Cambridge University Press, 1987).

14. Boer means "farmer."

15. J.F.W. Grosskopf, *The Poor White Problem in South Africa: Rural Impoverishment and Rural Exodus* (Stellenbosch, South Africa: Pro Ecclesia-Drukkery, 1932), 6.

16. J.G. McDonald, *Rhodes* (London: Chatto and Windus, 1941).

17. D.H. Houghton, "Economic Development 1863–1965," in M. Wilson and L. Thompson, eds., *The Oxford History of South Africa, Vol. II* (Oxford: Oxford University Press, 1971), 1–8.

18. D. Innes, *Anglo: Anglo American and the Rise of Modern South Africa* (Johannesburg: Ravan, 1984), 50.

19. Afrikaner colonization of the Boer Republics was a neofeudal affair. The original goal of the *voortrekkers* (pioneers) was to occupy lands depopulated by the genocidal 1820s *Difaqane* (carried out by Zulus and Matabele). The *voortrekkers*, however, also came to claim sovereignty over large swathes of the Highveld interior after they defeated the Ndebele in 1837, and the Ndebele relocated to Zimbabwe. Therefore, although the Boer Republics were built upon lands depopulated by the *Difaqane* and Ndebele exodus, Afrikaner sovereignty extended beyond their own settlements because they became the heirs to Ndebele power over subject tribes. The Boer relationship to their tribes was one of neofeudal overlordship—they lived alongside these tribes, but never integrated with them.

20. J.A.L. Agar-Hamilton, *The Native Policy of the Voortrekkers* (Cape Town: Maskew Miller, 1928).

21. P. Delius, *The Land Belongs to Us* (Johannesburg: Ravan, 1983), 183.

22. B. Bozzoli, *The Political Nature of a Ruling Class: Capital and Ideology in South Africa 1890–1933* (London: Routledge and Keagan Paul, 1981), 45.

23. Innes, *Anglo*, 58–59.

24. Bozzoli, *Political*, 43, 48–60.

25. Ibid., 60.

26. G.B. Pyrah, *Imperial Policy and South Africa 1902–10* (Oxford: Oxford University Press, 1955), 98.

27. Terreblanche, *Inequality*, 9–10, notes that the 1880s saw the closing of the settlement frontier. Until then, South Africa had always possessed empty land suitable for agriculture. With the closure of the settlement frontier came competition over land and hence, for the first time, the emergence of classes among Afrikaners. Landless (and therefore poor) Afrikaners emerged—some were rural *bywooners (poor white squatters)*, while others moved to the towns, so initiating the birth of an Afrikaner proletariat.

28. Bozzoli, *Political*, 44.

29. Ibid., 41–51.

30. Ibid., 40.

31. W. Nimocks, *Milner's Young Men: The "Kindergarten" in Edwardian Imperial Affairs* (Durham, NC: Duke University Press, 1968).

32. C. Headlam, ed., *The Milner Papers, Vol. II* (London: Cassell & Company, 1933), 300.

33. E.A. Walker, *A History of Southern Africa* (London: Longman, 1957), 501.

34. L.S. Amery, *My Political Life, Vol. I* (London: Hutchinson, 1953), 174.

35. J. Marlowe, *Milner, Apostle of Empire* (London: Hamish Hamilton, 1976), 136–140; and O'Brein, *Milner*, 197–219.

36. O'Brein, *Milner*, 198–199.
37. Headlam, *Papers*, 501.
38. Ibid., 308.
39. Bozzoli, *Political*, 44.
40. Headlam, *Papers*, 297.
41. Ibid., 311.
42. Ibid., 384.
43. Ibid., 307.
44. Ibid., 299.
45. Ibid., 459.
46. Pyrah, *Imperial*, 149.
47. Headlam, *Papers*, 238.
48. Ibid., 283.
49. Ibid., 284.
50. Ibid., 285.
51. Pyrah, *Imperial*, 198.
52. Headlam, *Papers*, 547.
53. Ibid., 468.
54. Ibid., 469.
55. Ibid.
56. Ibid., 467.
57. Ibid., 511.
58. Ibid., 511–512.
59. Ibid., 512.
60. Milner had wanted Rhodesia as part of a unified South Africa, but Rhodesian voters (overwhelmingly Anglos) rejected joining South Africa because of fears of Afrikaner domination.
61. J.R.T. Wood, *The Welensky Papers: A History of the Federation of Rhodesia and Nyasaland* (Durban: Graham Publishing, 1983).
62. Headlam, *Papers*, 242–243.
63. O'Brein, *Milner*, 205.
64. Headlam, *Papers*, 424.
65. Ibid., 280–281.
66. Pyrah, *Imperial*, 202.
67. Ibid., 83.
68. W.K. Hancock, *Smuts* (Cambridge: Cambridge University Press, 1962), 174.
69. Ibid., 176.
70. Headlam, *Papers*, 515.
71. J.C. Steyn, *Tuiste in eie taal* (Cape Town: Tafelberg, 1980), 183.
72. In the Cape Colony, blacks and coloreds were enfranchised (since 1854) if they met the "standards" of British civilization, that is, Westernized and middle class. Because the numbers were small, the Cape's political system remained effectively "white."
73. Terreblanche, *Inequality*, 246.
74. Under Anglo imperial hegemony, this northern "rural aristocracy" was consolidated into a class of Afrikaner agrarian capitalists. It was the shift of their support from Smuts's United Party (UP) to Malan's National Party (NP) that gave the NP victory in 1948 and ended the Anglo imperial hegemony.

75. W. Beinhart, *Twentieth Century South Africa* (Oxford: Oxford University Press, 1994), 71.

76. Hertzog was not enthusiastic about the empire, and viewed Botha and Smuts's enthusiastic acceptance of South Africa's role in the empire as a betrayal. See K. Ingham, *Jan Christian Smuts* (London: Weidenfeld and Nicolson, 1986), 64.

77. T.J. Keegan, *Rural Transformations in Industrializing South Africa.* (Johannesburg: Ravan, 1986), 109, 198.

78. Grosskopf, *Poor*, xxi.

79. Terreblanche, *Inequality*, 266–267, notes that a number of factors contributed to the emergence of a large impoverished Afrikaner working class. Afrikaner proletarianization started with the 1880s closure of the settlement frontier, was strengthened by the rinderpest epidemic (1896–1897), and massively intensified by Britain's victory in the Boer War.

80. D. Yudelman, *The Emergence of Modern South Africa* (Westport, CT: Greenwood Press, 1983), 131–132.

81. W.A. de Klerk, *The Puritans in Africa* (Harmondsworth: Penguin Books, 1975), 90–91.

82. See Yudelman, *Emergence.*

83. Ibid., 40.

84. Ibid., 128.

85. Ibid., vii.

86. Grosskopf, *Poor.*

87. N. Herd, *1922* (Johannesburg: Blue Crane Books, 1966).

88. The *vierkleur* had been the ZAR's flag and subsequently became an Afrikaner nationalist symbol.

89. Yudelman, *Emergence*, 63.

90. De Klerk, *Puritans*, 109–110.

91. Ibid., 105.

92. Houghton, *Economic*, 36.

93. Anonymous, *The Atlantic Charter.* A full text of the joint Declaration of the President of the United States of America and the Prime Minister of Great Britain, 12 August (London: Whitcombe & Tombs Ltd., 1941).

94. Giliomee, *Afrikaners*, 481.

CHAPTER 2: THE THEORY OF APARTHEID

1. T. Nairn, "Nationalism and the Uneven Geography of Development," in D. Held, ed., *States and Societies* (Oxford: Martin Robertson, 1983), 195–196.

2. An Afrikaner pejorative term for Anglo South Africans is "*soutpiele*" (pickled penis) derived from the perception that Anglos are "foreigners" with one foot in Africa and one foot in Britain, resulting in the penis becoming pickled in seawater.

3. W.A. De Klerk, *The Puritans in Africa* (Harmondsworth: Penguin Books, 1975), 104.

4. In 1934, Verwoerd—then still a social work professor—argued that Afrikaner poverty was caused by unfair competition from black migrants, and that ending this migration would end the poverty. H.F. Verwoerd, "Die bestryding van armoede en die herorganisasie van welvaartswerk (The Ending of Poverty and the

Reorganization of Welfare Work)," in P. Du Toit, *Report of the People's Conference on the Poor White Problem*, Kimberley, 2–5 October 1934, 31. In 1937, during testimony to a Commission of Enquiry into Cape Coloureds (UG54/1937, Vol. 3, 3163-3171), Verwoerd reiterated his view that black migrants were an economic threat to poor whites and coloreds and should be deported.

5. Ibid., 107.

6. P.J. Meyer became the head of the South African Broadcasting Corporation.

7. It is impossible to adequately translate Reddingsdaadbond. It loosely means "Rescue Association" but also encodes the idea of an "act of redemption." This organization sought to mobilize the Afrikaner petit bourgeoisie to work to overcome the poverty/economic subjugation of the Afrikaner underclass.

8. SABRS was the precursor to SABRA (South Africa Bureau for Racial Affairs), established in 1948.

9. Eiselen (who became a key architect of apartheid) explicitly repudiated racist thinking—see W.W.N. Eiselen, "The Meaning of Apartheid," *Race Relations* 15, no. 3 (1948): 71–72—and he told a Potchefstroom University graduating class the idea that some races were inferior was incorrect. W.W.M. Eiselen, "Ons Jeug en ons Rasse-aangeleenthede," *Journal of Racial Affairs* 4, no. 3 (1953): 22.

10. N. Diederichs, *Nasionalisme as lewensbeskouing en sy verhouding tot internasionalisme* (Bloemfontein: Nasionale Pers, 1936), 29–30, also explicitly rejected race, blood, or descent as the basis for nationalism (29–30), saying a nation is based upon a "shared culture" and identity (36–38).

11. Giliomee, *Afrikaners*, 465.

12. Diederichs, *Nasionalisme*.

13. In Holland, Kuyper's ideas led to "pillarization" (*verzuiling*)—an ultrapluralist division of society into "autonomous" religious and secular blocks, each with its own political cultural organizations. In Indonesia (a former Dutch colony), Kuyperian pluralism led to *pancasila*—enforced religious pluralism blocking majoritarianism/Islamicization. D. Ramage, *Politics in Indonesia* (London: Routledge, 1995), 18. In South Africa, Kuyperian pluralism led to apartheid.

14. De Klerk, *Puritans*, 204.

15. Diederichs, *Nasionalisme*, 22–23.

16. Ibid., 27–36.

17. Ibid., 22–24.

18. Significantly, Cronje was professor of sociology and social work at Pretoria University, the same position Verwoerd had occupied at Stellenbosch University. Both displayed the same social work concerns for dealing with the negative impacts of racial capitalism upon Afrikaners. Cronje was the only apartheid theorist who used explicitly racist logic.

19. G.A. Cronje, *In Tuiste vir die Nageslag: Die blywende Oplossing van Suid-Afrika se Rasse-Vraagstukke* (Stellenbosch: Pro Eccleasia-Drukkery, 1945).

20. G.A. Cronje, W. Nicol, and E. Groenewald, *Regverdige Rasse-apartheid* (Stellenbosch: Christen-Studenteverenigingmaatskappy van Suid-Afrika, 1947).

21. Cronje, *Tuiste*, 55.

22. Ibid., 40.

23. Ibid., 115.

24. Giliomee, *Afrikaners*, 475.

25. E.G. Jansen, "Die Volkskongres oor die Rassebeleid van die Afrikaner," *Inspan* 4, no. 1 (October 1944).

26. B.I.C. Van Eeden and N. Olivier, "Die Rassevraagstuke van Ons Land," *Inspan* 6, no. 7 (April 1947), and no. 8 (May 1947).

27. Eiselen, *Meaning*, 76.

28. Eiselen, *Meaning*, 76, 79; and Cronje, *Tuiste* , 117.

29. Eiselen, *Meaning*, 85.

30. The term "verticalization" was coined by L.J. du Plessis, "Problems of Nationality and Race in Southern Africa," *International Studies* 13 (1949).

31. L.J. Du Plessis, "Die Naturellevraagstuk in Suid-Afrika," *Koers* 8, no. 1 (1940): 5.

32. A. Hepple, *Verwoerd* (Harmondsworth: Penguin Books, 1967), 57.

33. D. O'Meara, *Volkskapitalisme* (Johannesburg: Ravan, 1983), 52.

34. Giliomee, *Afrikaners*, 477, argues that academics, church ministers, professionals, and journalists led the Afrikaner nationalists' movement. This is in contradistinction to O'Meara's *Volkskapitalisme* argument that businessmen and farmers were dominant.

35. These nationalists also opposed Anglo capitalism's importation of Indian laborers, and advocated that South African Indians should be returned to India.

36. De Klerk, *Puritans*, 114.

37. B. Anderson, *Imagined Communities* (London: Verso, 1991).

38. Drawing on the work of Afrikaner historian and journalist Gustav Preller.

39. A.D. Smith, *National Identity* (Reno: University of Nevada Press, 1991), 64–65.

40. O'Meara, *Volkskapitalisme*, 76.

41. J. Lochner, *Taal en Hegemony: Die ontwikkeling van Afrikaans as uitsaaitaal, 1923–1948* (South Africa: Potchefstroom University, 2002).

42. G. Cronje, "'n Sociologiese beskouing oor die Westerse kultuurproblematiek in Suid-Afrika," *Hertzog-annale van die Suid-Afrikaanse Akademie vir Wetenskap en Kuns* 12, no. 16 (December 1963): 26–42.

43. J.J. Van Rooyen, *Die Nasionale Party* (Cape Town: Cape National Party, 1956), 263.

44. D.F. Malan, *Afrikaner-Volkseenheid en ervarings op die pad daarheen* (Cape Town: Nasionale Boekhandel, 1959).

45. However, Malan recognized the need for the NP to find "common ground" with Anglos concerning a policy toward blacks in order to "make South Africa safe" for "white Christian civilization." See "Drie Mikpunte" speech in D.F. Malan, *Glo in u volk* (Cape Town: Tafelberg, 1964).

46. Van Rooyen, *Nasionale*, 263.

47. De Klerk, *Puritans*, 119; and O'Meara, *Volkskapitalisme*, 75.

48. M. Dia, *The African Nations and World Solidarity* (London: Thames & Hudson, 1962), 34.

49. The post-1994 African National Congress (ANC) government faced a similar problem as a growing white South African diaspora (of 1.6 million by 2002) spread negative stories about "black rule."

50. Giliomee, *Afrikaners*, 492.

51. F.W. de Klerk notes that his father was punished for speaking English in one of Milner's schools. F.W. de Klerk, *The Last Trek—A New Beginning* (London: MacMillan, 1998), 12.

52. There are striking parallels between Afrikaner anti-imperialist rhetoric of the first half of the twentieth century and post–World War II black anti-imperialist rhetoric. See N. Sithole, *African Nationalism* (Oxford: Oxford University Press, 1959), 20–23.

53. Cronje, *Tuiste*, 17.

54. O'Meara, *Volkskapitalisme*, 61.
55. Ibid., 65.
56. Ibid., 55.
57. Hepple, *Verwoerd*, 77.
58. Malan, *Volkseenheid*, 178–179.
59. Robert's Heights became *Voortrekkerhoogte* (Voortrekker Heights).
60. L.J. Du Plessis, "Liberalistiese en Calvanistiese Naturelle-politiek," in FCSSA, *Koers in die Krisis, Vol. 2* (Stellenbosch: Pro Ecclesia, 1940), 226–227.
61. Ibid., 226–227.
62. Cronje, *Regverdige*, 168.
63. De Wet was addressing a 1912 protest meeting in Pretoria. The meeting was held next to President Paul Kruger's statue, which (because it was a republican symbol) Milner had relocated to Prince's Park. De Wet, unable to find a platform, stood on the only raised area—a dung heap. His dung-heap speech became a rallying cry for Afrikaner nationalists.
64. Van Rooyen, *Nasionale*, 7.
65. O'Meara, *Volkskapitalisme*, 176.
66. Hepple, *Verwoerd*, 68.
67. The importance of religion within Afrikaner nationalism derives from the fact that the three Dutch reformed churches became virtually the only Afrikaans-language institutions to survive the Boer War and Milnerism intact. Further, the speed with which Afrikaners were urbanized after the Boer War produced tremendous cultural dislocation and poverty. During this period of dislocation, Calvinist churches became the only familiar touchstone and/or refuge within a world that was both foreign (Anglo) and brutal.
68. The *Gereformeerde Kerk* was the most Kuyperian.
69. Cronje, *Tuiste*; *Regverdige*; and Diederichs, *Nasionalisme*.
70. O'Meara, *Volkskapitalisme*, 152–153.
71. Sachs was successful in unionizing Afrikaner workers.
72. Giliomee, *Afrikaners*, 488–489, notes that by 1948, Afrikaners had put poverty behind them. However, the memory of recent poverty and the fact that most Afrikaners remained working-class meant that anti–Anglo capitalist rhetoric still resonated.
73. L. Pretorius, "The Head of Government and Organized Business," in R. Schrire, ed., *Malan to De Klerk* (New York: St. Martin's Press, 1994) 232.
74. Hoggenheimer encapsulated the general anti-imperialist and anticapitalist sentiment of Afrikaner workers, together with their specific hostility to the Oppenheimer family, who dominated gold and diamond mining.
75. De Klerk, *Puritans*, 281.
76. O'Meara, *Volkskapitalisme*, 107–116.
77. Verwoerd, *Bestryding*, 31.
78. Hepple, *Verwoerd*, 25–27, 35, 59, 67.
79. Verwoerd, *Bestryding*, 30.
80. D. Horowitz, *Ethnic Groups in Conflict* (Berkeley: University of California Press, 1985), 184.
81. Ibid., 170–171.
82. J. Jesudason, "The Ethnic Factor in Development," in J. Ravenhill, ed., *Singapore, Indonesia, Malaysia, the Philippines and Thailand, Vol. II* (Aldershot, UK: Elgar Reference, 1995), 7.

83. See Sithole, *African*, 28–29, 32.
84. Horowitz, *Ethnic*, 165.
85. The *Ossewabrandwag* (OB) threatened Malan's dream of "Afrikaner unity" because the OB's stress on the "socialism" in National Socialism threatened to drive Afrikaner capitalists and affluent farmers away from nationalism. O'Meara, *Volkskapitalisme*, 131.
86. In the 1948 election, B.J. Vorster (who would one day become NP prime minister) was debarred from running as an NP candidate because of his *Ossewabrandwag* membership.
87. J. Hatch, *A History of Post-War Africa* (London: Methuen, 1965), 209.
88. W.W.N. Eiselen, "Harmonious Multi-community Development," *Optima* (March 1959).
89. Jansen, *Volkskongres*.
90. J.D. Du Toit, "Die Godsdienstige basis van ons rasse-belied," *Inspan* 3, no. 4 (December 1944). Du Toit—like Diederichs—saw Afrikaner nationalism as God-ordained.
91. The religious distinction was especially important in the early Dutch colony. Hence, the origins of the South African pejorative term for blacks, "kaffir," refer to those who do not believe in God. The term "kaffir" (nonbeliever) was brought to Cape Town by Muslim Malays. These Malays (who have always formed an important component of the Cape population) shared with whites a distain for the animistic religions of Africa. For the Cape colonists, "nonbeliever," "heathen," "primitive," and "dark-skins" all became enmeshed into a single distained "otherness."
92. Canada gave the vote to Native Americans in 1960; the United States removed restrictions preventing black people from voting in 1964–1966; and Australia enfranchised aboriginals in 1967.
93. Van Rooyen, *Nasionale*, 274.
94. D. Prinsloo, *Stem uit die Wildernes* (Mosselbaai, South Africa: Vaandel-Uitgewers, 1997), 238.
95. Giliomee, *Afrikaners*, 464.
96. Ibid., 466.
97. Ibid., 447.
98. Constant references were made to Afrikaners as *'n klein volkie* (a small people).
99. For this reason, Afrikaners never saw Anglo South Africans as fully reliable partners—because Anglos were seen to have options not available to Afrikaners, namely, migration to places (e.g., Britain or Australia) where they did not have to change their language/culture.
100. Although a majority of Afrikaners probably did see blacks as "inferior" and "less developed."
101. Giliomee, *Afrikaners*, 470.
102. Giliomee, *Afrikaners*, 472, describes Louw as a liberal nationalist.
103. N. Van Wyk Louw, *Versamelde Prosa* (Cape Town: Tafelberg, 1986), 460–463.
104. Ibid., 505.
105. Cronje, *Tuiste*, 24.
106. Cronje feared that cross-racial miscegenation in these slums threatened the survival of Afrikaners as a separate ethno-national group.
107. D. Posel, *The Making of Apartheid 1948–1961* (Oxford: Clarendon Press, 1997) argues there was no apartheid "grand plan" when the NP came to power

and that the apartheid-as-partition model was only developed at the end of the 1950s after the defeat of the NP's pragmatists. Posel's thesis, although correctly identifying different apartheid stages, underestimates the pragmatism and flexibility of their two-stage model.

108. Apartheid eventually created ten nonwhite universities: Fort Hare (Xhosa), Transkei (Xhosa), Zululand (Zulu), University of the North (Pedi/Sotho), Venda, Bophuthatswana (Tswana), Vista (urban blacks), Medical University of South Africa (black), Durban-Westville (Indians), and Western Cape (colored). Separate universities were created for Anglos and Afrikaners—Anglos: Witwatersrand; Cape Town, Natal; and Rhodes. Afrikaners: Stellenbosch, Pretoria, Potchefstroom, Free State, and Rand Afrikaans. Two universities operated in both English and Afrikaans, namely, the University of South Africa and Port Elizabeth.

109. Resistance stirred up by the United Party (UP) government's 1943 "national unity" proposal to make all Afrikaans schools bilingual only served to promote the National Party (NP) and its vision of "own-ness." See J. Steyn, *Tuiste in Eie Taal* (Cape Town: Tafelberg, 1980), 209.

110. W. Beinart, *Twentieth-Century South Africa* (Oxford: Oxford University Press, 1994), 154.

111. H. Giliomee and C. Simkins, *The Awkward Embrace* (Amsterdam: Harwood, 1999).

112. Jesudason, *Ethnic*, 7.

113. Unlike the NP, the ANC's "affirmative action" program is not based upon building separate parallel infrastructures. Instead, it involves taking control of *existent* socioeconomic structures and replacing white people with black people.

114. The NP's success in upgrading Afrikaners can be seen in the following figures from H. Adam and H. Giliomee, *The Rise and Crisis of Afrikaner Power* (Cape Town: David Philip, 1979), 174:

Ratio of Income of Afrikaners to English, 1946–1976

Year	Personal Income	Per capita Income
1946	40:60	100:211
1960	47:53	100:156
1976	50:50	100:141

115. O'Meara, *Volkskapitalisme*, 158–160.

116. Verwoerd, *Bestryding*, 31.

117. O'Meara, *Volkskapitalisme*, 162.

118. Eiselen, *Meaning*, 84, refers to apartheid as migration control.

119. B.I.C. Van Eeden and N. Olivier, "Die Fagan Verslag," *Inspan* 7, no. 1 (August 1948): 25.

120. Hepple, *Verwoerd*, 114.

121. Ibid., 121.

122. Dubow argues that apartheid was a form of segregation. W. Beinart and S. Dubow, *Segregation and Apartheid* (London: Routledge, 1995).

123. Ibid., 6.

124. G. Cronje, *Voogdyskap en Apartheid* (Pretoria: Van Schaiks, 1948).

125. Afrikaner nationalists also argued that they were giving to black people what they wanted for themselves, namely, "own-ness" and sovereignty.

126. Swaziland, Lesotho, and Botswana were part of early 1940s apartheid theorizing. Apartheid theorists inherently questioned the arbitrariness of imperial boundary drawing, and argued these territories were part of South Africa's economic migration zone and therefore should be part of the partition solution.

127. De Klerk, *Last*, 16.

128. Van Rooyen, *Nasionale*, 266.

129. The ANC government has retained as part of South Africa's post-1994 legal framework the racial/ethnic categories first codified by the NP in 1950.

130. Verwoerd saw the generally low level of black education/skills as an obstacle to building viable self-governing black homelands; hence, his advocacy of increased spending on Bantu Education and black universities. Ironically, in building this expanded black education system, Verwoerd created a major locus of antiapartheid resistance from the mid-1970s onward.

131. Davenport argues that the NP did increase black productivity by ending Milner's system of importing peasant labor to the cities, ending rural sharecropping, and providing education. T. Davenport, *South Africa: A Modern History* (Johannesburg: MacMillan, 1977).

132. Eiselen regarded mother-tongue education as the best way to anchor people in their own culture.

133. Beinart *Twentieth*, 153.

134. The UP represented Anglo capitalists.

135. Hepple, *Verwoerd*, 105.

136. De Klerk, *Last*, 53–54.

137. During the 1960s/1970s, an ever-increasing percentage of wealth was transferred into black hands. Adam and Giliomee, *Rise*, 175.

138. J. Western, *Outcast Cape Town* (Cape Town: Human & Rousseau, 1981), chapters 3 and 4.

139. During World War II, Smuts had purged the civil service of *Broederbonders*. During the 1948 election, Smuts symbolically lost his own parliamentary seat to an NP candidate who had been fired from the civil service for being a *Broederbonder*.

CHAPTER 3: APARTHEID IN PRACTICE

1. Anonymous, *The Atlantic Charter* (London: Whitcombe & Tombs Ltd., 1941).

2. For example, communism and postcolonial nation-building "development" projects.

3. L. Berger, *Pyramids of Sacrifice* (Harmondsworth: Penguin Books, 1977), 20–22.

4. D. Posel, *The Making of Apartheid 1948–1961* (Oxford: Clarendon Press, 1997).

5. W.W.N. Eiselen, "The Meaning of Apartheid," *Race Relations* 15, no. 3 (1948): 82–84.

6. South Africa's corporate sector has on two occasions successfully tamed (and ultimately co-opted) political movements they deemed threatening to their interests. On coming to power, both the NP and ANC had to learn to be "practical," and adjust their ideals (partition and socialism) to suit "economic realities."

7. Posel, *Making*, 112, notes that the UP and business lobbying extracted urban black Section 10 rights from the NP—a modification of the original apartheid model that was to severely undermine apartheid's implementation.
8. Represented by the anticapitalist/Hoggenheimer sentiments.
9. See D. O'Meara, *Volkskapitalisme* (Johannesburg: Ravan, 1983).
10. Verwoerd changed the Department of Native Affairs to "Bantu Affairs" because he said Afrikaners were also natives of Africa. Bantu means "people" in Zulu/Xhosa.
11. H.F. Verwoerd, "Die bestryding van armoede en die herorganisasie van welvaartswerk," in Du Toit, *Report*, 31.
12. W. Beinart, *Twentieth-Century South Africa* (Oxford: Oxford University Press, 1994), 143.
13. Once apartheid was ended, many coloreds switched political allegiance, and in the 1994 elections, a majority of coloreds voted for the NP.
14. S. Dreyer, "Die filosofiese grondslag van die beleid van afsonderlike ontwikkeling," *Journal of Racial Affairs* 22, no. 4 (October 1971): 152.
15. S. Terreblanche, *A History of Inequality in South Africa* (Pietermartizburg: University of Natal Press, 2003), 266.
16. Because the Malan-Strijdom period was so different from Verwoerdian apartheid, Posel, *Making*, developed a thesis that there was no apartheid "grand plan" in the early 1950s. An examination of the extensive writings of the apartheid theorists refutes this. Posel is correct that the NP camp was not unified and the party succumbed to external pressures. However, a clear apartheid model did exist in 1948, perhaps best summed up by Eiselen, *Meaning*, 80–84, who spelled out an unfolding process of handing over ever-larger amounts of land to blacks in order to create viable black states. Interestingly, Eiselen, *Meaning*, 84, stated unambiguously in 1948 that it would take some time to prepare the ground for real partition, and that during the transition period/lead-up to partition, the Fagan (segregation) plan would be a suitable policy.
17. J.J. Van Rooyen, *Die Nasional Party* (Cape Town: Cape National Party, 1956), 275.
18. D. Welsh, "The Executive and the African Population," in R. Schrire, ed., *Malan to De Klerk* (New York: St Martin's Press, 1994), 144.
19. When Afrikaans church leaders called for "total apartheid" (partition) at a 1950 conference, Malan said this ran counter to NP policy. H. Giliomee, *The Afrikaners* (London: Hurst & Company, 2003), 484.
20. Segregation emerged in various parts of the British Empire and the United States as a response to the way capitalism erased feudalism's identities (based on "social ranking" differences) while simultaneously drawing together people from a wide diversity of backgrounds, and placing them in close proximity to each other in urban centers where they were economically integrated into a single workforce. In many of these contexts, new identities (often based on race or ethnicity) became salient, and these new identities became encoded into patterns of spatial segregation.
21. W. Beinart and S. DuBow, *Segregation and Apartheid* (London: Routledge, 1995), 6.
22. *South Africa (1955) Report of the Commission for the Socio-Economic Development of the Bantu Areas within the Union of South Africa*, UG61-1955.
23. Welsh, *Executive*, 150–151.

24. Verwoerd's refusal is strange given the conceptualization that he and other apartheid theorists had expounded on homeland development—A.N. Pelzer, ed., *Verwoerd Speaks: Speeches 1948–1966* (Johannesburg: APB Publishers, 1966), 17–18; Eiselen, *Meaning*, 78; and J.L. Sadie, "The Industrialization of the Bantu Areas," *Journal of Racial Affairs* 11, no. 2 (1960): 59.

25. The way that black education was neglected prior to the NP is revealed by the fact that in 1952 there were only 8,488 blacks with Matric qualifications; see Giliomee, *Afrikaners*, 507.

26. Beinart, *Twentieth*, 154.

27. In 1928, the South African Communist Party's official policy became the creation of a "native republic."

28. M.C. De Wet Nel, "Waarom die beleid van apartheid," *Journal of Racial Affairs* 11, no. 4 (1960): 172.

29. About the size of Maryland.

30. T. Malan and S. Hattingh, *Swart Tuislande in Suid-Afrika* (Pretoria: Africa Institute, 1975), 25.

31. D. O'Meara, *Forty Lost Years* (Athens: Ohio University Press, 1996), 159.

32. A. Hepple, *Verwoerd* (Harmondsworth: Penguin Books, 1967), 191.

33. For example, the Physical Planning Act (1967).

34. These thrived because gambling was allowed in the TBVC (Transkei, Bohhuthatswana, Venda, Ciskei) states but banned in South Africa by Calvinist-inspired laws.

35. L. Pretorius, "The Head of Government and Organized Business," in R. Schrire, ed., *Malan to De Klerk* (New York: St Martin's Press, 1994), 218.

36. Ibid., 218.

37. N. Worden, *The Making of Modern South Africa* (Oxford: Blackwell, 2000), 127.

38. However, ethnic tension was still a feature of Anglo-Afrikaner relationships in the 1980s.

39. B. Pottinger, *The Imperial Presidency* (Johannesburg: Southern, 1988), 55.

40. L. Platzky and C. Walker, "Review of Relocation," in South African Research Service, *South African Review 1* (Johannesburg: Ravan, 1983), 87.

41. Beinart, *Twentieth*, 188–191.

42. Ibid., 191.

43. Mechanisms to stop new black migration to "white" cities.

44. Beinart, *Twentieth*, 172–173.

45. Terreblanche, *Inequality*, 355.

46. Ibid.

47. D. O'Meara, *Forty Lost Years* (Athens: Ohio University Press, 1996), 120.

48. Beinart, *Twentieth*, 230.

49. Worden, *Making*, 138.

50. D. Prinsloo, *Stem uit die Wildernes* (Mosselbaai, South Africa: Vaandel-Uitgewers, 1997), 243–245.

51. Giliomee, *Afrikaners*, 473–474.

52. F.A. Van Jaarsveld, *Die Evolusie van Apartheid* (Cape Town: Tafelberg, 1979), 23.

53. Prinsloo, *Stem*, 207.

54. S. Huntington, *Political Order in Changing Societies* (Yale University Press, 1968), and "Reform and Stability in a Modernizing Multi-Ethnic Society," *Politikon* 8, no. 2 (1981).

55. Prinsloo, *Stem*, 208.
56. A. Lijphart, *Democracy in Plural Societies* (New Haven: Yale University Press, 1977).
57. Prinsloo, *Stem*, 209–210.
58. Ibid., 222–224.
59. Ibid., 226.
60. Ibid.
61. Prinsloo, *Stem*, 236.
62. M. Sutcliffe, "Managing the Cities," in C. Murray and C. O'Regan, *No Place to Rest* (Cape Town: Oxford University Press, 1990), 88.
63. Beinart, *Twentieth*, 138.
64. N. Mandela, *Long Walk to Freedom* (Randburg, South Africa: Macdonald Purnell, 1994), 525–527.
65. H. Adam, *Modernizing Racial Domination* (Berkeley: University of California Press, 1971), 45.
66. Ibid., 46.
67. F. Wilson and M. Ramphele, *Uprooting Poverty* (Cape Town: David Philip, 1989); Surplus People Project, *Forced Removals in South Africa, 5 Vols.* (Cape Town: Surplus People Project, 1983).
68. A. Stadler, *The Political Economy of Modern South Africa* (Cape Town: David Philip, 1987), 14.
69. L. Platzky and J. Walker, *The Surplus People: Forced Removals in South Africa* (Johannesburg: Ravan, 1985), 10.
70. Platzky and Walker's 3.5 million estimate includes 1.1 million farm evictions (i.e., retrenched farm workers told to leave the property).
71. A. Claassens, "Rural Land Struggles in the Transvaal in the 1980s," in Murray and O'Regan, *Place*, 31.
72. Ibid., 40.
73. Wilson and Ramphele, *Uprooting*, 216–217.
74. C. Bundy, "Land, Law and Power," in Murray and O'Regan, *Place*, 9.
75. Beinart, *Twentieth*, 197–202.
76. T. Davenport, *South Africa: A Modern History* (Johannesburg: MacMillan, 1977), 364–366.
77. Beinart, *Twentieth*, 151–152.
78. Truth & Reconciliation Commission, *Final Report, Vol. 2*, 1998, chapter 1, p. 3.
79. J. May, "The Migrant Labour System," in N. Nattrass and E. Ardington, *The Political Economy of South Africa* (Cape Town: Oxford University Press, 1990), 177.
80. Beinart, *Twentieth*, 153.
81. Ibid., 198–205; and Wilson and Ramphele, *Uprooting*, 100–101.
82. Beinart, *Twentieth*, 190.
83. Wilson and Ramphele, *Uprooting*, 124.
84. Beinart, *Twentieth*, 256.
85. These warlords generally began their careers as shack-lords (i.e., renting shacks in informal settlements). The 1980s trade in firearms from Mozambique made it possible for these shack-lords to build armed militias and therefore transform themselves into warlords. Much of South Africa's crime is run out of these shack lands, which are effectively beyond the reach of the central government.
86. Although, as Stadler notes, this generated a vibrant cultural life. Stadler, *Political*, 111.

87. Ibid., 159, 213–215.

88. F. Wilson, "Poverty, the State and Redistribution," in Nattrass and Ardington, *Political*, 235–236.

89. M. Marks, *Young Warriors* (South Africa: University of Witwatersrand Press, 2001).

90. Initially proposed by Sampie Terreblanche. C. McCarthy, "Apartheid Ideology and Economic Development," in Ibid., 45.

91. M. McGrath, "Economic Growth, Income Distribution and Social Change," in M. Marks, *Young Warriors* (South Africa: University of Witwatersrand Press, 2001), 98.

92. J. Hofmeyer, "Black Wages: The Post-War Experience," in Ibid., 129.

93. Wilson and Ramphele, *Uprooting*, 196.

94. Ibid., 195–196.

95. Terreblanche, *Inequality*, 387–391.

96. F. Auerbach and D. Welsh, "Education," in S. Van der Horst, ed., *Race Discrimination in South Africa* (Cape Town: David Philip, 1981), chapter 4.

97. By the 1970s, two-thirds of black high schools were in the homelands. Beinart, *Twentieth*, 208.

98. Traditional African culture foregrounds collectivism; plus a "spiritual" role for ancestors, "curses" and "shamans" in determining good or bad fortune.

99. Western culture foregrounds individualism, materialism, secularism, rationalism, and private initiative.

100. McCarthy, *Apartheid*, 49.

101. Wilson and Ramphele, *Uprooting*, 164–165.

102. B. Streek and R. Wicksteed, *Render unto Kaiser* (Johannesburg: Ravan, 1981).

103. Stadler, *Political*, 138.

104. Wilson and Ramphele, *Uprooting*, 213–214.

105. McCarthy, *Apartheid*, 47.

106. Beinart, *Twentieth*, 245.

107. Truth & Reconciliation Commission, *Final Report, Vol. 2*, 1998, chapter 1, p. 8.

108. Ibid., 3.

CHAPTER 4: APARTHEID IN CRISIS AND MILITARIZED REFORM

1. W.W.N. Eiselen, "The Meaning of Apartheid," *Race Relations* 15, no. 3 (1948).

2. H. Giliomee, *The Afrikaners* (London: Hurst and Company, 2003), 608.

3. D. Prinsloo, *Stem uit die Wildernes* (Mosselbaai, South Africa: Vaandel-Uitgewers, 1997), 227.

4. Giliomee, *Afrikaners*, 595.

5. A. Du Toit, *Die sondes van die vaders* (Cape Town: Rubicon, 1983).

6. Botha first signaled his lack of interest in protecting Afrikaner workers during a 1979 strike.

7. A. Lijphart, *Democracy in Plural Societies* (Yale University Press, 1977); S. Huntington, "Reform and Stability in a Modernizing Multi-Ethnic Society," *Politikon* 8, no. 2 (1981); A. Beaufre, *An Introduction to Strategy* (London: Faber, 1963).

8. J.J. Scholtz, *Vegter en hervormer: Grepe uit die toesprake van W. Botha* (Cape Town: Tafelberg, 1988); and D. Prinsloo, *Stem uit die Wildernes* (Mosselbaai, South Africa: Vaandel-Uitgewers, 1997).

9. Hansard, 29 April 1979, Cols. 5072–5073.

10. Huntington, *Reform*, 19.

11. Ibid., 20.

12. Ibid.

13. Many similarities exist between the National Security Management System (NSMS) that Botha constructed in the 1980s and the homeland security system built by George Bush after September 11, 2001.

14. Huntington, *Reform*, 17.

15. E. Rhoodie, *P.W. Botha: The Last Betrayal* (Johannesburg: SA Politics, 1989), 134.

16. B. Pottinger, *The Imperial Presidency* (Johannesburg: Southern Book Publishers, 1988), 79.

17. Malan also served under Beaufre in Algeria, while on secondment to the French army.

18. H. Frankel, *Pretoria's Praetorians* (Cambridge: Cambridge University Press, 1984), 46.

19. Beaufre, *Introduction*, 125.

20. Frankel, *Pretoria's*, 56.

21. Ibid., 42.

22. Pottinger, *Imperial*, 416.

23. The Afrikaans press and South Africa Broadcasting Corporation produced messages appropriate to securocrat needs.

24. Censorship never prevented liberal or left-wing criticism of the government.

25. Pottinger, *Imperial*, 426–427.

26. K.W. Grundy, *The Militarization of South African Politics* (London: Tauris, 1986), 37.

27. Ibid., 38.

28. J. Selfe, "South Africa's National Management System," in J. Cock and L. Nathan, *War and Society* (Cape Town: David Philip, 1989), 155.

29. Ibid., 151.

30. M. Swilling and M. Phillips, "The Emergency State: Its Structure, Power and Limits," in G. Moss et al., *South African Review 5* (Johannesburg: Ravan, 1989), 83–87.

31. By 1988, more than 65 percent of South Africa's operational soldiers were "people of color." C. Cooper, *Race Relations Survey 1988/89* (Johannesburg: SAIR, 1989), 521.

32. L. Nathan, "Troops in the Townships 1984–1987," in J. Cock and L. Nathan, *War*, 70.

33. J. Cock, "Introduction" in Ibid., 5–6.

34. Grundy, *Militarization*, 46.

35. F. Bridgland, *The War for Africa* (Johannesburg: Ashanti Publishing, 1990).

36. Giliomee, *Afrikaners*, 603.

37. M. Mann, "The Giant Stirs: South African Business in an Age of Reform," in P. Frankel et al., *State Resistance and Change in South Africa* (Johannesburg: Southern Books, 1988).

38. Pottinger, *Imperial*, 255.

39. H. Barrell, *MK: The ANC's Armed Struggle* (Harmondsworth: Penguin, 1990), 51.

40. Ibid., 64.

41. Pottinger, *Imperial*, 275.

42. J.J. McCuen, *The Art of Counter-Revolutionary War* (London: Faber, 1966).
43. M. Swilling and M. Phillips, "State Power in the 1980s," in J. Cock and L. Nathan, *War*, 143.
44. N. Worden, *The Making of Modern South Africa* (Oxford: Blackwell, 2000), 147.
45. F. Meer, *Resistance in the Townships* (Durban: Madiba Publications, 1989), 241–242.
46. Swilling, *Emergency*, 75.
47. Ibid., 77.
48. Ibid., 78.
49. Swilling, *State*, 145.
50. J. Seekings, *The UDF* (Cape Town: David Philip; Oxford: James Currey; Athens: Ohio University Press, 2000), 202.
51. Ibid., 144.
52. Ibid., 286.
53. Ibid., 300.
54. Truth & Reconciliation Commission, vol. 2, no. 3 (1999): 53.
55. Catholic Institute for International Relations, *Now Everyone is Afraid* (London: CIIR, 1988), 9.
56. Ibid., 14.
57. Black Sash, *Greenflies: Municipal Police in the Eastern Cape* (Cape Town: Black Sash, 1988), 21.
58. The now-restored urban black councils employed the municipal police. Many councilors were businessmen created by Botha's drive to create a black middle class.
59. S. Bekker, *Capturing the Event: Conflict Trends in the Natal Region 1986–1992* (Durban: Indicator, 1992), 8.
60. Seekings, UDF, 207.
61. P. Frankel, "Beyond Apartheid: Pathways for Transition," in Frankel et al., *State*, 280.
62. N. Mandela, *Long Walk to Freedom* (Johannesburg: MacDonald Purnell, 1994), 522.
63. R. Harvey, *The Fall of Apartheid* (Basingstoke, England: Palgrave, 2001), 127.
64. Giliomee, *Afrikaners*, 637.
65. F. W. de Klerk, *The Last Trek* (London: MacMillan, 1998), 263–265.
66. Ibid., 265.

CHAPTER 5: THE STRUGGLE AGAINST APARTHEID: EVOLVING VISIONS

1. D. Welsh, "The Growth of Towns," in M. Wilson and L. Thompson, *The Oxford History of South Africa* (Oxford: Oxford University Press, 1971), 210.
2. Until 1936, a small group of Westernized middle-class blacks who had been enfranchised in the Cape Colony were deemed to be part of the core (white) state. But they were removed from the "white" voter roll in 1936.
3. G.M. Gerhart, *Black Power in South Africa* (Berkeley: University of California Press, 1978), 5–6.

4. Buthelezi Commission Report, *The Requirements for Stability and Development in KwaZulu and Natal* (Durban: H&H, 1982).
5. Gerhart, *Black*, 34.
6. P. Walshe, *The Rise of African Nationalism in South Africa* (London: C. Hurst, 1970), 38.
7. Ibid., 38.
8. N. Mandela, "Whither the Black Consciousness Movement?" in M. Maharaj, ed., *Reflections in Prison* (Cape Town: Zebra, 2001), 49.
9. N. Mandela, "Clear the Obstacles and Confront the Enemy," in Maharaj, *Reflections*, 17.
10. Whites outside the Cape Province—because of demographic considerations—rejected extending the Cape franchise. Except for the area east of the Fish River, the Cape Province had no indigenous black population, and blacks were not a "demographic threat" to Cape whites. In the other three provinces, enfranchising blacks created the possibility of black voters exerting real political influence.
11. Walshe, *Rise*, 158–160.
12. Ibid., 163.
13. G.M. Carter, "African Concepts of Nationalism in South Africa," in H. Adam, *South African Sociological Perspectives* (Oxford: Oxford University Press, 1971), 104.
14. Walshe, *Rise*, 340.
15. F. Meli, *A History of the ANC: South Africa Belongs to Us* (Bloomington: Indiana University Press, 1988), 54.
16. L. Kuper, "African Nationalism in South Africa," in Wilson and Thompson, *Oxford*, 430.
17. Walshe, *Rise*, 264, 268.
18. To which the Inkatha Freedom Party (IFP) traces its roots.
19. W. Beinart, *Twentieth-Century South Africa* (Oxford: Oxford University Press, 1994), 99–100.
20. Walshe, *Rise*, 244.
21. Ibid., 249.
22. Ibid., 258.
23. Beinart, *Twentieth*, 263.
24. Meli, *History*, 94–96.
25. M. Ballinger, *From Union to Apartheid* (Johannesburg: Juta, 1969), 111.
26. Walshe, *Rise*, 276.
27. Kuper, *African*, 454.
28. Gerhart, *Black*, 94.
29. Kuper, *African*, 459.
30. Sisulu, Mandela, and Lembede had originally been the most ardent proponents of racially exclusivist nationalism. Walshe, *Rise*, 356.
31. Walshe, *Rise*, 328.
32. Ibid., 353; N. Mandela, *The Struggle Is My Life* (London: International Defence & Aid Fund for Southern Africa, 1986), 20–30; Meli, *History*, 117.
33. Meli, *History*, 109.
34. A.M. Lembede, "Policy of the Congress Youth League," in T. Karis and G.M. Carter, *From Protest to Challenge: Documents, Vol. 2* (Stanford: Hoover Institute Press, 1973), 317.

35. Gerhart, *Black*, 58.
36. Ibid., 62.
37. Lembede, *Policy*, 318.
38. However, for the ANC Youth League (ANCYL), coloreds were outside the "black nation," as seen by the fact that African nationalism defined the start of its struggle as the Eastern Cape (black-white) border wars rather than the earlier Western Cape (KhoiSan-white) struggle. Mandela, *Struggle*, 23.
39. Walshe, *Rise*, 353–354.
40. N. Ndebele, "The African National Congress and the Policy of Non-Racialism: A Study of the Membership Issue," *Politikon* 29, no. 2 (2002): 134.
41. Lembede, *Policy*, 317–318.
42. Gerhart, *Black*, 80.
43. Meli, *History*, 117.
44. Ibid., 116; Walshe, *Rise*, 356–358.
45. H. Wolpe, *Race, Class and the Apartheid State* (Paris: Unesco, 1988), 32; S. Dubow, *Racial Segregation and the Origins of Apartheid* (Oxford: MacMillan, 1989), 29–30.
46. B. Freund, "Some Unasked Questions on Politics: South African Slogans and Debates," *Transformation* 1 (1986): 122.
47. Ibid., 128.
48. Walshe, *Rise*, 288.
49. Mandela, *Obstacles*, 17, notes this influence.
50. T. Lodge, *Black Politics in South Africa since 1945* (London: Longman, 1983), 46–47.
51. Carter, *African*, 113.
52. Mandela, *Struggle*, 55.
53. Gerhart, *Black*, 119.
54. Beinart, *Twentieth*, 125.
55. Mandela, *Struggle*, 74.
56. Gerhart, *Black*, 173–175.
57. Lodge, *Black*, 281.
58. Ibid., 266–284.
59. Gerhart, *Black*, 159.
60. M. Motlhabi, *Black Resistance to Apartheid* (Johannesburg: Skotaville, 1984), 46.
61. Ibid., 91.
62. R.M. Sobukwe, "Future of the Africanist Movement," in Karis and Carter, *From Protest, Vol. 3*, 508.
63. Ibid., 508.
64. Gerhart, *Black*, 196.
65. Ibid., 147.
66. Ibid., 206.
67. Ibid., 206.
68. Ibid., 187.
69. Ibid., 247.
70. N. Mandela, *Long Walk to Freedom* (Johannesburg: MacDonald Purnell, 1994), 259.
71. Ibid., 258.
72. S.M. Davis, *Apartheid's Rebels* (Johannesburg: A.D. Donker, 1987), 13.

73. Mandela, *Struggle*, 40.
74. Davis, *Apartheid's*, 13.
75. Mandela, *Long*, 262.
76. Davis, *Apartheid's*, 16.
77. Mandela, *Struggle*, 122.
78. Davis, *Apartheid's*, 17.
79. Mandela, *Struggle*, 169.
80. Davis, *Apartheid's*, 16.
81. Ibid., 21.
82. Gerhart, *Black*, 253.
83. Lodge, *Black*, 309–310.
84. Ibid., 317.
85. Ndebele, *African*, 137.
86. H. Barrell, "The Turn to the Masses: The ANC's Strategic Review of 1978–79," *Journal of Southern African Studies* 18, no. 1 (1991): 70.
87. Ibid., 71.
88. Ibid.
89. Ibid., 69.
90. Ibid.
91. Lodge, *Black*, 300.
92. Barrell, *Turn*, 67.
93. Ibid., 68.
94. Ibid., 69.
95. Lodge, *Black*, 296.
96. Mandela, *Obstacles*, 14.
97. Ibid., 15.
98. Ibid., 16.
99. W. Sisulu, "We Shall Overcome," in Maharaj, *Reflections*, 80.
100. Meli, *History*, 167.
101. Barrell, *Turn*, 72.
102. Meli, *History*, 167–169.
103. The 1960s experience of nonracial solidarity among London-based South African exiles played a role in this shift. Ndebele, *African*, 142.
104. Ibid., 170.
105. L. Wilson, "Bantu Stephen Biko: A Life," in B. Pityana et al., *Bounds of Possibility* (Cape Town: David Philip, 1991), 23.
106. S. Buthelezi, "The Emergence of Black Consciousness: An Historical Appraisal," in Pityana, *Bounds*, 112.
107. Ibid., 113.
108. Ibid.
109. C. Halisi, "Biko and Black Consciousness Philosophy," in Pityana, *Bounds*, 103.
110. Buthelezi, *Emergence*, 118.
111. S. Biko, *I Write What I Like* (Harmondsworth: Penguin Books, 1988), 31–40.
112. Ibid., 38.
113. Ibid., 55.
114. Ibid., 60
115. Ibid., 39.
116. Ibid., 36.

117. Ibid., 79.
118. Gerhart, *Black*, 269.
119. Ibid., 294.
120. Halisi, *Biko*, 104.
121. The Non-European Unity Movement (NEUM) was founded in 1943 to promote the idea of a unified nonwhite struggle based on the principle of boycott politics and noncollaboration with the white system. The Unity Movement (UM), which grew out of NEUM, has always been a significant force in Western Cape radical "colored" politics. UM's "Trotskyism" and opposition to "multiracialism" placed it in opposition to the African National Congress (ANC)/South African Communist Party (SACP) alliance and the United Democratic Front (UDF). Neville Alexander is a key UM theorist.
122. Halisi, *Biko*, 105.
123. Biko, *Write*, 9.
124. Ibid., 50.
125. Biko, *Write*, 51.
126. Biko's opposition to such acculturation overlapped with the National Party's (NP's) perspective.
127. Biko, *Write*, 70.
128. Ibid., 89.
129. Ibid., 63.
130. D. Horowitz, *Ethnic Groups in Conflict* (Berkeley: University of California Press, 1985), 184.
131. Wilson, *Bantu*, 29.
132. Many Biko statements were lifted straight out of F. Fanon, *The Wretched of the Earth* (New York: Grove Press, 1968).
133. Buthelezi, *Emergence*, 126.
134. Halisi, *Biko*, 100.
135. Biko, *Write*, 42.
136. Halisi, *Biko*, 101.
137. Biko, *Write*, 43.
138. Halisi, *Biko*, 102.
139. Halisi, *Biko*, 109.
140. Wilson, *Bantu*, 35.
141. Biko, *Write*, 42.
142. Ibid., 88.
143. Ibid., 139.
144. Motlhabi, *Black*, 121.
145. Biko, *Write*, 149.
146. Ibid., 39.
147. Motlhabi, *Black*, 111.
148. Biko, *Write*, 84.
149. Motlhabi, *Black*, 134.
150. Lodge, *Black*, 328.
151. Barrell, *Turn*, 74.
152. Ibid.
153. Ibid., 75.
154. Ibid., 79.

155. Ibid.
156. Ibid., 75–77.
157. Meli, *History*, 200.
158. Davis, *Apartheid's*, 58.
159. Ibid., 61–62.
160. Ibid., 66.
161. In 1990, Mhlaba said two-thirds of the ANC executives were SACP members. T. Lodge and B. Nasson, *All, Here, and Now* (Cape Town: David Philip, 1991), 175.
162. Barrell, *Turn*, 80–81.
163. Ibid., 82.
164. Ibid., 85.
165. Ibid., 81.
166. Ibid.
167. Ibid., 89.

CHAPTER 6: THE STRUGGLE AGAINST APARTHEID: THE 1980s UPRISING

1. J. Seekings, *The UDF* (Cape Town: David Philip; Oxford: James Currey; Athens: Ohio University Press, 2000), 11.
2. Ibid.
3. I. Van Kessel, *Beyond Our Wildest Dreams* (Charlottesville: University Press of Virginia, 2000), 51.
4. M. Marks, *Young Warriors* (South Africa: University of Witwatersrand Press, 2001), 35.
5. M. Swilling, "The UDF and Township Revolt," in W. Cobbett and R. Cohen, *Popular Struggles in South Africa* (London: James Currey, 1988), 93.
6. Seekings, UDF, 61.
7. Ibid., 311.
8. Ibid., 14.
9. Ibid., 32.
10. Marks, *Young*, 56.
11. Seekings, UDF, 218.
12. J. Grobbelaar et al., *Vir Volk en Vaderland: A Guide to the White Right* (Durban: Indicator, 1989).
13. T. Lodge and B. Nasson, *All, Here, and Now: Black Politics in South Africa in the 1980s* (Cape Town: David Philip, 1991), 188.
14. Ibid., 181.
15. Ibid., 183.
16. H. Barrell, *MK: The ANC's Armed Struggle* (Harmondsworth: Penguin Books, 1990), 64.
17. S.M. Davis, *Apartheid's Rebels* (Johannesburg: A.D. Donker, 1987), 132.
18. S. Friedman, *Building Tomorrow Today* (Johannesburg: Ravan, 1987), 406.
19. A. Erwin, "The Question of Unity in the Struggle," in *South African Labour Bulletin* 11, no. 1 (1985).
20. Seekings, UDF, chapter 8.

21. Van Kessel, *Beyond*, 2.
22. Lodge and Nasson, *All*, 34.
23. Ibid., 35.
24. Ibid., 143.
25. Alexander opposed multiracialism as a form of racism, and saw the United Democratic Front's (UDF's) nonracialism as a form of multiracialism. Alexander advocated antiracism. N. Alexander, *Sow the Wind* (Johannesburg: Skotaville, 1985), 45–46.
26. Lodge and Nasson, *All*, 143.
27. Ibid., 144.
28. The Western Cape's UDF leadership was strongly influenced by the Unity Movement's (UM's) noncollaborationist position, or what Allan Boesak called "the politics of refusal" (Seekings, UDF, 98); in fact, there was always a subcurrent of Alexander/UM ideas in Cape UDF politics (Seekings, UDF, 80–81).
29. Lodge and Nasson, *All*, 212.
30. T. Lodge, *South African Politics since 1994* (Cape Town: David Philip, 1999), 12.
31. Lodge and Nasson, *All*, 153.
32. Ibid., 155.
33. Ibid., 167.
34. UDF leaders criticized this. Journal of the UDF, *Isizwe* 1, no. 2 (March 1986): 8.
35. Lodge and Nasson, *All*, 168.
36. Ibid.
37. Ibid.
38. Ibid., 168–169.
39. Ibid., 169.
40. Seekings, UDF, 44.
41. Ibid., 41.
42. Ibid., 67.
43. Ibid., 43.
44. Ibid., 9.
45. Ibid., 22.
46. Ibid., 45–48.
47. A. Boesak, *Black and Reformed* (Johannesburg: Skotaville, 1984), 120–132.
48. Ibid., 168–176.
49. Seekings, UDF, 22.
50. Ibid., 71.
51. Ibid., 314.
52. The National Forum (NF)/Azanian People's Organization (AZAPO) was similarly dominated by the middle-class Indian/colored intelligentsia.
53. Ibid., 123.
54. Ibid., 72.
55. Ibid., 73.
56. Ibid., 62.
57. Ibid., 63.
58. Ibid., 123.
59. Ibid., 184, 185.
60. Ibid., 125.

61. The UDF opposed populism. *Isizwe* 1, no. 2 (March 1986): 16–25.
62. Marks, *Young*, 119.
63. Ibid., 82.
64. Ibid., 25, 29, 55.
65. Ibid., 60.
66. Ibid., 83.
67. Ibid., 88.
68. Van Kessel, *Beyond*, 68.
69. Marks, *Young*, 62.
70. Ibid., 101.
71. Ibid., 52.
72. Seekings, UDF, 124, 128.
73. Ibid., 162.
74. Ibid., 160.
75. Ibid., 158.
76. Ibid.
77. Ibid., 125.
78. Conscientizing was a term widely used by the South African Left. It meant creating a "revolutionary consciousness" in which people believed they could successfully rise up against the state.
79. Ibid., 126.
80. Ibid., 128.
81. Ibid., 130.
82. Ibid., 186.
83. Ibid., 187.
84. Ibid., 132.
85. Ibid., 143.
86. Ibid., 133.
87. Anonymous, "Lekota on UDF," *Work in Progress* 30 (February 1984): 8.
88. Lodge and Nasson, *All*, 76.
89. Davis, *Apartheid's*, 89.
90. Seekings, UDF, 175.
91. Ibid., 144.
92. Davis, *Apartheid's*, 94.
93. Ibid., 91.
94. Seekings, UDF, 158, 169–174.
95. I. Obery, "People's Education: Creating a Democratic Future," *Work in Progress* 42 (May 1986), 8.
96. Van Kessel, *Beyond*, 69.
97. Seekings, UDF, 190.
98. Ibid., 193.
99. Lodge and Nasson, *All*, 135–140.
100. Seekings, UDF, 194.
101. Ibid., 194.
102. Davis, *Apartheid's*, 90.
103. C.A. Crocker, *High Noon in Southern Africa* (Johannesburg: Jonathan Ball, 1992), 258.
104. Ibid., 254–260.
105. J.J. McCuen, *The Art of Counter-Revolutionary War* (London: Faber, 1966).

106. Seekings, UDF, 196.
107. Ibid., 210.
108. Ibid., 215.
109. Ibid., 216.
110. Ibid., 227.
111. Ibid., 216.
112. Ibid., 207–208.
113. Ibid., 216.
114. Ibid., 314.
115. Ibid., 225.
116. Ibid.
117. Ibid.
118. Ibid., 226.
119. Ibid., 233.
120. Ibid., 235.
121. A. Borraine, "Building Broad Alliance: The Unity and the Contradictions," *South African Labour Bulletin* 13, no. 8 (1989), 34–36.
122. Seekings, UDF, 229.
123. Ibid., 241.
124. Ibid.
125. Ibid., 244.
126. Ibid., 190.
127. Ibid., 194.
128. Ibid., 237.
129. Ibid., 238–239.
130. Ibid., 252.
131. Ibid., 265.
132. Ibid., 261–265.
133. Ibid., 308.
134. Van Kessel, *Beyond*, 64.
135. Lodge and Nasson, *All*, 129.
136. Seekings, UDF, 143.
137. *Isizwe* 1, no. 1 (November 1985): 11.
138. Seekings, UDF, 315.
139. Ibid., 296.
140. Lodge and Nasson, *All*, 131.
141. Seekings, UDF, 295.
142. Van Kessel, *Beyond*, 70.
143. Journal of the UDF, *Isizwe* 1, no. 2 (March 1986): 2–4.
144. Ibid., 71; and Lodge and Nasson, *All*, 297.
145. Lodge and Nasson, *All*, 131.
146. Van Kessel, *Beyond*, 69; Seekings, UDF, 295.
147. Lodge and Nasson, *All*, 133.
148. Van Kessel, *Beyond*, 69.
149. R. Suttner and J. Cronin, *Thirty Years of the Freedom Charter* (Johannesburg: Ravan, 1986).
150. Seekings, UDF, 313.
151. Van Kessel, *Beyond*, 56.
152. Seekings, UDF, 22.

153. Ibid., 22.
154. Ibid., 193.
155. Van Kessel, *Beyond*, 57.
156. Seekings, UDF, 291.
157. Ibid., 22.
158. K.G. Tomaselli and P.E. Louw, *The Alternative Press in South Africa* (London: James Currey, 1991); P.E. Louw, "The Emergence of a Progressive Alternative Genre of Media Practice in South Africa with Reference to Grassroots," *Communicatio* 15, no. 2 (1989).
159. Van Kessel, UDF, 56.
160. Seekings, UDF, 93.
161. Van Kessel, *Beyond*, 4.
162. Seekings, UDF, 71–72.
163. Ibid., 88.
164. Ibid., 310–312.
165. Ibid., 79.
166. Ibid., 75–76.
167. Ibid., 77.
168. Ibid., 74.
169. Ibid., 83.
170. Ibid., 122.
171. Ibid., 144, 312.
172. Ibid., 98.
173. Ibid., 308.
174. Ibid., 220.
175. Van Kessel, *Beyond*, 65.
176. Ibid., 65.
177. Ibid., 63.
178. Seekings, UDF, 221.
179. Ibid., 207.
180. Ibid., 166.
181. *Isizwe* 1, no. 2 (March 1986): 17.
182. Van Kessel, *Beyond*, 60.
183. Marks, *Young*, 59.
184. Van Kessel, *Beyond*, 69.
185. Truth and Reconciliation Commission, *Final Report, Vol. 2*, 1998, chapter 1, p. 3.
186. Seekings, UDF, 294.

CHAPTER 7: NEGOTIATING A SETTLEMENT TO END APARTHEID

1. R. Spitz, *The Politics of Transition* (South Africa: Witwatersrand University Press, 2000), 14.
2. H. Giliomee, *The Afrikaners* (London: Hurst and Company, 2003), 625.
3. T. Lodge, "People's War or Negotiation? ANC Strategies in the 1980s," in G. Moss et al., *South African Review 5* (Johannesburg: Ravan, 1989), 47.
4. N. Mandela, *Long Walk to Freedom* (Johannesburg: MacDonald Purnell, 1994), 562.

5. S. Ryklief, "Does the Emperor Really Have No Clothes?" in S. Jacobs and R. Calland, *Thabo Mbeki's World* (Pietermaritzburg, South Africa: University of Natal Press, 2003), 108.

6. Lodge, *People's*, 48.

7. R. Harvey, *The Fall of Apartheid* (Basingstoke: Palgrave, 2001), chapters 12–15.

8. C. Landsberg, "Directing from the Stall?" in S. Friedman and D. Atkinson, *South African Review 7* (Johannesburg: Ravan, 1994), 296.

9. F.W. de Klerk, *The Last Trek* (London: MacMillan, 1998), 291, stated his own preference was for a consociational model similar to the Belgian or Swiss systems.

10. Spitz, *Politics*, 16.

11. Mandela, *Long*, 598, rejected power sharing because it represented a white minority veto over the black majority.

12. Spitz, *Politics*, 16, 89.

13. Ibid., 16.

14. Ibid.

15. Ibid.

16. Ibid., 24.

17. Ibid., 23.

18. Ibid.

19. Ibid.

20. Ibid., 24.

21. Mandela, *Long*, 544, rejected ethnic group rights because this would undermine black majority rule and entrench continued white minority power.

22. In the original NP model, senators represented federated states and "ethnic groups"—each ethnic group would have 10 senators (i.e., Afrikaans, Anglo, Indian, and nine black ethnic groups). A later model allocated the same number of seats to all parties with over 10 percent support.

23. Spitz, *Politics*, 23, 27.

24. Ibid.

25. Ibid., 22.

26. Mandela, *Long*, 508.

27. Ibid., 508.

28. Spitz, *Politics*, 21.

29. Ibid.

30. Ibid., 19.

31. Ibid.

32. Ibid., 17.

33. Ibid.

34. Ibid., 21.

35. R. Humphries et al., "The Shape of the Country," in Friedman and Atkinson, *South*, 158.

36. Spitz, *Politics*, 21.

37. Humphries et al., "The Shape," 158.

38. Ibid., 163–164.

39. Mandela, *Long*, 509.

40. Ibid., 508.

41. Ibid., 545.

42. Ibid., 510–511.

43. Ibid., 518.
44. De Klerk, *Last*, 173.
45. Giliomee, *Afrikaners*, 631.
46. D. O'Meara, *Forty Lost Years* (Athens: Ohio University Press, 1996), 408.
47. Giliomee, *Afrikaners*, 632–633.
48. J. Collinge, "Launched on a Bloody-Tide," in Moss et al., *South*, 23.
49. Mandela, *Long*, 594.
50. O'Meara, *Forty*, 407.
51. Spitz, *Politics*, 28.
52. O'Meara, *Forty*, 412.
53. Meyer appears to have come to the conclusion that the NP had no bargaining power (Giliomee, *Afrikaners*, 639). The ANC assessed the situation quite differently (639–640).
54. Giliomee, *Afrikaners*, 642.
55. Spitz, *Politics*, 32.
56. Ibid., 30.
57. D. Atkinson, "Brokering a Miracle?" in Friedman and Atkinson, *South*, 14.
58. Ibid., 17.
59. Landsberg, *Directing* , 291.
60. Ibid., 32.
61. Spitz, *Politics*, 31.
62. De Klerk, *Last*, 257.
63. Spitz, *Politics*, 31.
64. Atkinson, *Brokering*, 27.
65. Ibid., 24.
66. Spitz, *Politics*, 52.
67. Ibid., 53.
68. Atkinson, *Brokering*, 29.
69. Spitz, *Politics*, 39.
70. Giliomee, *Afrikaners*, 642.
71. D. Atkinson, "Principle Born of Pragmatism?" in Friedman and Atkinson, *South*, 106.
72. Giliomee, *Afrikaner*, 645.
73. I. Sarakinsky, "Rehearsing Joint Rule: The TEC," in Friedman and Atkinson, *South*, 74–76.
74. Ibid., 87–88.
75. De Klerk, *Last*, 305.
76. Ibid., 305.
77. Atkinson, *Brokering*, 38.
78. Ibid., 33.
79. De Klerk, *Last*, 284.
80. Giliomee, *Afrikaners*, 646.
81. De Klerk, *Last*, 315.
82. Atkinson, "Brokering," 36.
83. H. Marais, *South Africa: Limits to Change* (London: Zed, 2001), 134.
84. Ibid., 40.
85. C. Louw, *Boetman en die swanesang van die verligtes* (Cape Town: Human and Rousseau, 2001) is similarly damning in his critique of the NP team's negotiating abilities.

86. Ibid., 641.

87. There were local government consociational provisions in the interim constitution, largely due to the fact that the Conservative Party (CP) played a major role in negotiating these sections of the constitution (Spitz, *Politics*, 183–185).

88. Ibid., 423.

89. P.E. Louw, "Political Power, National Identity and Language: The Case of Afrikaans," *International Journal of the Sociology of Language* (2004): 170.

90. Giliomee, *Afrikaners*, 658.

91. The Gerwel Report proposed allowing two universities to remain Afrikaans-medium, but the cabinet rejected this. J. Jansen, "The State of Higher Education in South Africa," in J. Daniel et al., *State of the Nation* (Pretoria: Human Sciences Research Council, 2003), 306.

92. J.M. Coetzee, *Disgrace* (London: Vintage, 2000), 159.

93. T. Mbeki, Address on Acceptance of an Honorary Doctorate from the University of Stellenbosch, 20 February 2004 (http://www.anc.org.za/ancdocs/history/mbeki/2004/tm0220.html).

94. S. Terreblanche, *A History of Inequality in South Africa* (Pietermaritzburg, South Africa: University of Natal Press, 2003), 141.

95. P. Bond, *Elite Transition* (London: Pluto Press, 2000), 70–71.

96. A. Sampson, *Mandela: The Authorized Biography* (Johannesburg: Jonathan Ball, 1999), 434–435.

97. Marais, *South*, 138–139.

CHAPTER 8: THE EMERGING POSTAPARTHEID SOCIETY

1. S. Terreblanche, *A History of Inequality in South Africa* (Pietermaritzburg, South Africa: University of Natal Press, 2003), 96.

2. Ibid., 76–77, 330.

3. S. Jacobs and R. Calland, "Thabo Mbeki: Myth and Context," in S. Jacobs and R. Calland, *Thabo Mbeki's World* (Pietermaritzburg, South Africa: University of Natal Press, 2002), 9.

4. Ibid., 83.

5. Ibid., 98.

6. Ibid., 101.

7. Ibid., 102.

8. S. Friedman and L. Stack, "The Magic Moment: The 1994 Election," in S. Friedman and D. Atkinson, *South African Review 7* (Johannesburg: Ravan, 1994), 327.

9. X. Mangeu, "The State of Race Relations in Post-Apartheid South Africa," in J. Daniel et al., *State of the Nation* (Pretoria: Human Sciences Research Council, 2003), 105.

10. H. Marais, *South Africa: Limits to Change* (London: Zed, 2001), 299.

11. Jacobs and Calland, *Thabo*, 13.

12. Marais, *South*, 299.

13. National Economic Development Labour Council.

14. H. Adam et al., *Comrades in Business* (Cape Town: Tafelberg, 1997) .

15. S. Buhlungu, "The State of Trade Unionism in Post-Apartheid South Africa," in Daniel et al., *State*, 201.

16. The South African Broadcasting Corporation was the first organization "restaffed" by the African National Congress (ANC). See P.E. Louw, *New Voices Over the Air: The Transformation of the South African Broadcasting Corporation in a Changing South Africa* (Cresskill, NJ: Hampton Press, 2005).
17. N. Mandela, *Report by the President of the ANC to ANC National Conference*, Mafikeng, South Africa, 16 December 1997 (http://www.anc.org.za/ancdocs/history/mandela/1997/sp971216.html).
18. A. Habib et al., "Introduction," in Daniel et al., *State*, 3.
19. Ibid.
20. The UN General Assembly declared apartheid a crime against humanity in 1973. This resolution, promoted by the Soviet and African blocs, was never ratified by Western countries.
21. G. Mare, "The State of the State," in Daniel et al., *State*, 42.
22. Mangeu, "The State," 110–111.
23. Mare, "The State," 37.
24. Marais, *South*, 201.
25. Habib et al., "Introduction," 11.
26. M. Altman, "The State of Employment and Unemployment in South Africa," in Daniel, *State*, 160.
27. Ibid., 161.
28. Marais, *South*, 5, 274.
29. Terreblanche, *Inequality*, 133.
30. Ibid., 423.
31. Marais, *South*, 200.
32. Terreblanche, *Inequality*, 133.
33. Ibid.
34. H. Marais, "The Logic of Expediency," in Jacobs and Calland, *Thabo*, 96–97.
35. Employment Equity Act, 1998; Promotion of Equality and Prevention of Unfair Discrimination Act, 2000.
36. Louw, *New*, chapter 4.
37. Black Economic Empowerment Commission, *A National Integrated Black Economic Empowerment Strategy* (Johannesburg: Skotaville, 2001).
38. T. Lodge, *South African Politics since 1994* (Cape Town: David Philip, 1999), 9.
39. Mare, "The State," 44.
40. D.J. Randall, "Prospects for the Development of a Black Business Class in South Africa," *Journal of Modern African Studies* 34, no. 4 (1996): 666–669.
41. Marais, *South*, 193.
42. Terreblanche, *Inequality*, 422.
43. Ibid., 423.
44. Ibid., 38.
45. *ANC Today* 3, no. 33 (August 2003); *ANC Today* 4, no. 1 (January 2004).
46. Statement by the National Executive Council of the ANC on the 92nd anniversary of the ANC, 8 January 2004 (http://www.anc.org.za/ancdocs/pr/2004/pr0108.html).
47. *ANC Today* 3, no. 22 (June 2003).
48. *ANC Today* 3, no. 33 (August 2003); *ANC Today* 3, no. 43 (October 2003).
49. *ANC Today* 4, no. 11 (March 2004).

50. *ANC Today* 2, nos. 5 and 8 (February 2002); *ANC Today* 2, no. 29 (July 2002); *ANC Today* 3, no. 50 (December 2003).
51. Terreblanche, *Inequality*.
52. *ANC Today* 2, no. 50 (December 2002), criticizes Terreblanche.
53. W. Gumede, "Down to Business, but Nothing to Show," in Jacobs and Calland, *Thabo*, 202–203.
54. Ibid., 422.
55. Jacobs and Calland, *Thabo*, 10.
56. Ibid., 11.
57. Ibid., 10.
58. H. Sheehan, Interview with Jeremy Cronin, 2002 (http://www.comms.deu.iw/sheehanh/za/cronin02.htm).
59. T. Mbeki, Statement at the Opening of the Debate in the National Assembly on "Reconciliation and Nation Building," Cape Town, 29 May 1998 (http://www.anc.org.za/ancdocs/history/mbeki/1998/sp980529.html).
60. Ibid.
61. T. Mbeki, "Where Are They Now?" Second National Institute for Economic Policy, Oliver Tambo Lecture, Johannesburg, 11 August 2000 (http://www.anc.org.za/ancdocs/history/mbeki/2000/tm0811.html).
62. Ibid.
63. Calland and Jacobs, "Conclusion," in Jacobs and Calland, *Thabo*, 264.
64. S. Ryklief, "Does the Emperor Really Have No Clothes?" in Jacobs and Calland, *Thabo*, 113.
65. T. Mbeki, *Africa Define Yourself* (Cape Town: Tafelberg, 2003), 136.
66. Mare, "The State," 38.
67. Mbeki, *Africa Define*, 71, 92–93, 130–131, 134, 140.
68. S. Buhlungu, "From 'Madiba Magic' to 'Mbeki Logic,'" in Jacobs and Calland, *Thabo*, 179–180.
69. Mare, "The State," 42.
70. Ibid., 43.
71. Buhlungu, "From 'Madiba,'" 197.
72. Marais, *South*, 235.
73. R. Southall, *Opposition and Democracy in South Africa* (London: Frank Cass, 2001), 277.
74. Mangeu, "The State," 117.
75. Marais, *South*, 248.
76. B.M. Magubane, "The African Renaissance in Historical Perspective," in M.W. Makgoba, *African Renaissance* (Johannesburg: Mafube, 1999), 34.
77. K.K. Prah, "African Renaissance or Warlordism?" in Makgoba, *African Renaissance*, 57.
78. Ibid., 41.
79. P. Ntuli, "The Missing Link between Culture and Education," in Makgoba, *African Renaissance*, 188.
80. Prah, "African Renaissance," 60.
81. M. Mamdani, "There Can Be No African Renaissance without an Africa-Focused Intelligentsia," in Makgoba, *African Renaissance*, 128–129.
82. Prah, "African Renaissance," 39.
83. Ibid., 38.

84. Ibid., 39.
85. L. Teffo, "Moral Renewal and African Experience(s)," in Makgoba, *African Renaissance*, 165; J. Netshitenzhe, "The Media in the African Renaissance," in Makgoba, *African Renaissance*, 385. Mbeki's "Letter from the President" in *ANC Today* also frequently talks about this.
86. Associated with occasional criticisms of neoliberalism.
87. African National Congress, *The Reconstruction and Development Programme* (Johannesburg: ANC, 1994).
88. Marais, *Thabo*, 86–90.
89. P. Bond, *Elite Transition* (London: Pluto Press, 2000), 83.
90. Jacobs and Calland, *Thabo*, 5.
91. Ryklief, "Does the Emperor," 114.
92. T. Mbeki, Speech at National Conference of Black Management Forum, 20 November 1999 (http://www.anc.org.za/ancdocs/history/mbeki/1999/tm1120.html).
93. Lodge, *South*, 100.
94. Marais, *South*, 250.
95. Jacobs and Calland, *Thabo*, 14.
96. P. Vale et al., "Thabo Mbeki: South Africa and the Idea of an African Renaissance," in Jacobs and Calland, *Thabo*, 130.
97. Ibid., 140.
98. Ibid., 125.
99. Ryklief, "Does the Emperor," 116.
100. F. Chothia and S. Jacobs, "Remaking the Presidency," in Jacobs and Calland, *Thabo*.
101. Lodge, *South*, 14–16.
102. R. Southall, "The South African Election of 1994: The Re-making of a Dominant Party State," *Journal of Modern African Studies* 32, no. 4 (1994); H. Giliomee et al., "Dominant Party Rule: Opposition Parties and Minorities in South Africa," in R. Southall, *Opposition*.
103. P.E. Louw, "South Africa's Second Post-Apartheid Elections." *Australian Journal of International Affairs* 54, no. 2 (2000).
104. R. Southall, "The State of Party Politics," in Daniel et al., *State*, 74–75.
105. Buhlungu, "From 'Madiba,'" 193.
106. D. McKinley, "Democracy, Power and Patronage," in Southall, *Opposition*, 200.
107. Southall, "The State," 55.
108. Chothia and Jacobs, "Remaking the Presidency," 155.
109. Southall, "The State," 59.
110. Ibid., 61–63.
111. Marais, *South* , 252–254.
112. Southall, "The South," 68.
113. Marais, *South*, 190.
114. A. Habib, "State-Civil Society Relations in Post-Apartheid South Africa," in Daniel et al., *State*, 236.
115. Marais, *South*, 190–192.
116. Altman, "The State of Employment."
117. Ibid., 160.

118. Lodge, *South*, 33.
119. Calland and Jacobs, *Thabo*, 270–271.
120. *ANC Today* 2, no. 40 (October 2002).
121. Terreblanch, *Inequality*, 38.
122. H. Giliomee, *The Afrikaners* (Hurst and Company, 2003), 657.
123. Terreblanche, *Inequality*, 126.
124. Marais, *South*, 302; Terreblanche, *Inequality*, 126–129.
125. Giliomee, *Afrikaners*, 654.
126. M. Fullard and N. Rousseau, "An Imperfect Past," in Daniel et al., *State*, 82.
127. Ibid., 81.
128. Mangeu, "The State," 107.
129. Fullard and Rousseau, "An Imperfect Past," 93.
130. T. Mbeki, State of the Nation Address, Parliament, 6 February 2004 (http://www.anc.org.za/ancdocs/history/mbeki/2004/tm0206.html).
131. Giliomee, *Afrikaners*, 655.
132. T. Mbeki, Address on Acceptance of Honorary Doctorate from the University of Stellenbosch, 20 February 2004 (http://www.anc.org.za/ancdocs/history/mbeki/2004/tm0220.html).
133. Until 1994, the ANC repeatedly attacked the police. Black policemen (and teachers) were attacked as "sellouts." They were unable to simply forget these attacks and put aside their resultant demoralization and paranoia when the ANC came to power in 1994—the South African police and black school systems became dysfunctional.
134. *ANC Today* 2, no. 16 (April 2002).
135. L. Chisolm, "The State of Curriculum Reform in South Africa," in Daniel et al., *State*; J. Jansen, "The State of Higher Education in South Africa," in Daniel et al., *State*.
136. Mare, "The State," 44–45.
137. Lodge, *South*, 56.
138. Policy Co-ordination and Advisory Service, *Towards a Ten-Year Review* (Pretoria: The Presidency, 2003), 12, 106.
139. Ibid., 15.
140. Mbeki has expressed outrage at how whites and businessmen "badmouth" South Africa—*ANC Today* 1, no. 41 (November 2001); *ANC Today* 2, no. 9 (March 2002).
141. Terreblanche, *Inequality*, 111.

CHAPTER 9: GLOBALIZATION AND THE NEW SOUTH AFRICA

1. P.E. Louw, *The Media and Cultural Production* (London: Sage, 2001), 127.
2. Ibid., chapter 6.
3. S. Lash and J. Urry, *Economies of Signs and Space* (London: Sage, 1994), 61.
4. S. Huntington, *The Third Wave: Democratization in the Late Twentieth Century* (Norman: University of Oklahoma Press, 1991).
5. J. Van der Westhuizen, *Adapting to Globalization* (Westport, CT: Praeger, 2002), 113.
6. Ibid., 112.

7. R. Southall, "The State of Party Politics," in J. Daniel et al., *State of the Nation* (Pretoria: Human Sciences Research Council, 2003) 74–75.

8. Far Right Afrikaners (*Boeremag*) and Muslim dissidents (*Pagad*) have engaged in antistate terrorism.

9. S. Terreblanche, *A History of Inequality in South Africa* (Pietermaritzburg, South Africa: University of Natal Press, 2003), 86.

10. N. Nattrass, "Politics and Economics in ANC Economic Policy," *African Affairs* 93 (1994), 353.

11. Terreblanche, *Inequality*, 424–425.

12. Van der Westhuizen, *Adapting*, 116.

13. Ibid., 116.

14. Terreblanche, *Inequality*, 96–98.

15. Ibid., 428.

16. Van der Westhuizen, *Adapting*, 118.

17. Ibid., 102.

18. Ibid., 106.

19. Terreblanche, *Inequality*, 115.

20. Ibid., 114.

21. H. Marais, *South Africa: Limits to Change* (London: Zed, 2001), 155.

22. Terreblanche, *Inequality*, 122.

23. H. Marais, "The Logic of Expediency," in S. Jacobs and R. Calland, *Thabo Mbeki's World* (Pietermaritzburg, South Africa: University of Natal Press, 2002), 84.

24. Van der Westhuizen, *Adapting*, chapters 2 and 3.

25. Ibid., 129.

26. Ibid., 4.

27. S. Ryklief, "Does the Emperor Really Have No Clothes?" in Jacobs and Calland, *Thabo*, 118.

28. N. Nattrass, "The State of the Economy," in Daniel et al., *State*, 151.

29. Van der Westhuizen, *Adapting*, chapter 3.

30. Nattrass, "The State," 150.

31. Marais, *South*, 111.

32. Ibid., 147.

33. P. Bond, "Thabo Mbeki and NEPAD," in Jacobs and Calland, *Thabo*, 54.

34. Ibid., 59–60.

35. Marais, *South*, 114–115.

36. The only export successes have been assembled cars.

37. Terreblanche, *Inequality*, 119.

38. Bond, "Thabo," 61.

39. H. Marais, "The Logic of Expediency," in Jacobs and Calland, *Thabo*, 97.

40. S. Jacobs and R. Calland, "Thabo Mbeki," in Jacobs and Calland, *Thabo*, 4.

41. Van der Westhuizen, *Adapting*, chapter 4.

42. Ibid., 134–137.

43. Marais, "The Logic of Expediency," 100.

44. *ANC Today* 1, no. 29 (August 2001).

45. T. Mbeki, *Africa Define Yourself* (Cape Town: Tafelberg, 2003), 134.

46. *ANC Today* 1, no. 39 (October 2001).

47. T. Mbeki, Speech at the Launch of the African Renaissance Institute, Pretoria (October 1999).

48. Ibid., 136.
49. Mbeki's attempt to promote this agenda through his 2001 World Conference Against Racism was spurned by Western governments.
50. Mbeki Speech, 136–137.
51. *ANC Today* 2, no. 23 (June 2002).
52. Bond, "Thabo," 62–64.
53. *ANC Today* 2, no. 26 (July 2002).
54. Bond, "Thabo," 53.
55. P. Bond, *Elite Transition* (London: Pluto Press, 2000), 196.
56. Except for Nigeria and Angola's oil economies.

Selected Bibliography

Adam, H. 1971. *Modernizing Racial Domination*. Berkeley: University of California Press.

Adam, H., and H. Giliomee. 1979. *The Rise and Crisis of Afrikaner Power*. Cape Town: David Philip.

Adam, H., K. Moodley, and F. Van Zyl Slabbert. 1997. *Comrades in Business*. Cape Town: Tafelberg.

Alexander, N. 1985. *Sow the Wind*. Johannesburg: Skotaville.

Barrell, H. 1990. *MK: The ANC's Armed Struggle*. Harmondsworth: Penguin.

———. 1991. "The Turn to the Masses: The ANC's Strategic Review of 1978–79." *Journal of Southern African Studies* 18 (1).

Beaufre, A. 1963. *An Introduction to Strategy*. London: Faber.

Beinart, W. 1994. *Twentieth-Century South Africa*. Oxford: Oxford University Press.

Beinart, W., and S. Dubow, 1995. *Segregation and Apartheid*. London: Routledge.

Biko, S. 1988. *I Write What I Like*. Harmondsworth: Penguin Books.

Boesak, A. 1984. *Black and Reformed*. Johannesburg: Skotaville.

Bond, P. 2000. *Elite Transition: From Apartheid to Neoliberalism*. London: Pluto Press/Pietermaritzburg: University of Natal Press.

Bozzoli, B. 1981. *The Political Nature of a Ruling Class: Capital and Ideology in South Africa 1890–1933*. London: RKP.

Catholic Institute for International Relations. 1988. *Now Everyone Is Afraid*. London: CIIR.

Cock, J., and L. Nathan. *War and Society*. Cape Town: David Philip.

Crocker, C.A. 1992. *High Noon in Southern Africa*. Johannesburg: Jonathan Ball.

Cronje, G.A. 1945. *'n Tuiste vir die Nageslag: Die blywende Oplossing van Suid-Afrika se Rasse-Vraagstukke*. Stellenbosch: Pro Eccleasia-Drukkery.

Cronje, G.A., W. Nicol, and E.P. Groenewald. 1947. *Regverdige Rasse-apartheid*. Stellenbosch: Christen-Studenteverenigingmaatskappy van Suid-Afrika.

Daniel, J., A. Habib, and R. Southall. 2003. *State of the Nation*. Pretoria: Human Sciences Research Council.

Davenport, T.R.H., and C. Saunders. 2000. *South Africa: A Modern History*. New York: St Martin's Press.

Davies, R. 1979. *Capital, State and White Labour in South Africa, 1900–1960*. London: Harvester.

Davis, S.M. 1987. *Apartheid's Rebels: Inside South Africa's Hidden War*. Johannesburg: A.D. Donker.

De Klerk, W.A. 1975. *The Puritans in Africa: A Story of Afrikanerdom*. Harmondsworth: Penguin Books.

Diederichs, N. 1936. *Nasionalisme as lewensbeskouing en sy verhouding tot internasionalisme*. Bloemfontein: Nasionale Pers.

Dubow, S. 1989. *Racial Segregation and the Origins of Apartheid*. Oxford: MacMillan.

Eiselen, W.W.N. 1948. "The Meaning of Apartheid." *Race Relations* 15 (3).

———. 1953. "Ons Jeug en ons Rasse-aangeleenthede." *Journal of Racial Affairs* 4 (3).

Frankel, P.H. 1984. *Pretoria's Praetorians*. Cambridge: Cambridge University Press.

Frankel, P., M. Swilling, and N. Pines. 1988. *State Resistance and Change in South Africa*. Johannesburg: Southern Books.

Friedman, S. 1987. *Building Tomorrow Today: African Workers in Trade Unions 1970–1984*. Johannesburg: Ravan.

Friedman, S., and D. Atkinson. *South African Review 7*. Johannesburg: Ravan.

Gerhart, G.M. 1978. *Black Power in South Africa*. Berkeley: University of California Press.

Giliomee, H. 2003. *The Afrikaners*. London: Hurst & Company.

Grosskopf, J.F.W. 1932. *The Poor White Problem in South Africa: Rural Impoverishment and Rural Exodus*. Stellenbosch: Pro Ecclesia-Drukkery.

Grundy, K.W. 1986. *The Militarization of South African Politics*. London: Tauris.

Headlam, C., ed. 1933. *The Milner Papers*. Vol II. London: Cassell & Company.

Hepple, A. 1967. *Verwoerd*. Harmondsworth: Penguin Books.

Horowitz, D. 1985. *Ethnic Groups in Conflict*. Berkeley: University of California Press.

Huntington, S.P. 1981. "Reform and Stability in a Modernizing Multi-Ethnic Society." *Politikon* 8 (2).

Jacobs, S., and R. Calland. 2002. *Thabo Mbeki's World*. Pietermaritzburg: University of Natal Press/London: Zed.

Keegan, T.J. 1986. *Rural Transformations in Industrializing South Africa*. Johannesburg: Ravan.

Klerk, F.W. 1998. *The Last Trek—A New Beginning*. London: MacMillan.

Legassick, M. 1974. "South Africa: Capitalist Accumulation and Violence." *Economy and Society* 3 (3).

Lijphart, A. 1977. *Democracy in Plural Societies*. New Haven: Yale University Press.

Lipton, M. 1986. *Capitalism and Apartheid*. Aldershot (England): Wildwood House.

Lodge, T. 1983. *Black Politics in South Africa since 1945*. London: Longman.

———. 1999. *South African Politics since 1994*. Cape Town: David Philip.

Lodge, T., and B. Nasson. 1991. *All, Here, and Now: Black Politics in South Africa in the 1980s*. Cape Town: David Philip.

Louw, P.E. 2000. "South Africa's Second Post-Apartheid Elections. *Australian Journal of International Affairs* 54 (2).

Maharaj, M., ed. 2001. *Reflections in Prison*. Cape Town: Zebra & Robben Island Museum.

Makgoba, M.W., ed. *African Renaissance*. Johannesburg: Mafube/Cape Town: Tafelberg.

Malan, D.F. 1959. *Afrikaner-Volkseenheid en ervarings op die pad daarheen*. Cape Town: Nasionale Boekhandel.
Mandela, N. 1986. *The Struggle Is My Life*. London: International Defence & Aid Fund.
———. 1994. *Long Walk to Freedom*. Johannesburg: MacDonald Purnell.
Marais, H. 2001. *South Africa: Limits to Change*. London: Zed/Cape Town: University of Cape Town Press.
Marks, M. 2001. *Young Warriors*. Johannesburg: University of Witwatersrand Press.
Mbeki, T. 2003. *Africa Define Yourself*. Johannesburg: Mafube/Cape Town: Tafelberg.
McCuen, J.J. 1966. *The Art of Counter-Revolutionary War*. London: Faber.
Meli, F. 1988. *A History of the ANC: South Africa Belongs to Us*. Bloomington: Indiana University Press/London: James Currey.
Moss, G., and I. Obrey, eds. 1990. *South African Review 5*. London: Hans Zell.
———. 1992. *South African Review 6*. Johannesburg: Ravan.
Murray, C., and C. O'Regan, eds. 1990. *No Place to Rest*. Cape Town: Oxford University Press.
Nattrass, N., and E. Ardington, eds. 1990. *The Political Economy of South Africa*. Cape Town: Oxford University Press.
Ndebele, N. 2002. "The African National Congress and the Policy of Non-Racialism: A Study of the Membership Issue." *Politikon* 29 (2).
Nimocks, W. 1968. *Milner's Young Men: The "Kindergarten" in Edwardian Imperial Affairs*. Durham, NC: Duke University Press.
O'Meara, D. 1983. *Volkskapitalisme: Class, Capital and Ideology in the Development of Afrikaner Nationalism*. Johannesburg: Ravan
———. 1996. *Forty Lost Years*. Athens: Ohio University Press/Johannesburg: Ravan.
Pelzer, A.N., ed. 1966. *Verwoerd Speaks: Speeches 1948–1966*. Johannesburg: APB Publishers.
Pityana, N.B., M. Ramphele, M. Mpumlwana, and L. Wilson, eds. 1991. *Bounds of Possibility*. Cape Town: David Philip.
Posel, D. 1997. *The Making of Apartheid 1948–1961*. Oxford: Clarendon Press.
Pottinger, B. 1988. *The Imperial Presidency*. Johannesburg: Southern Books.
Prinsloo, D. 1997. *Stem uit die Wildernes*. Mosselbaai (South Africa): Vaandel-Uitgewers.
Pyrah, G.B. 1955. *Imperial Policy and South Africa 1902–10*. Oxford: Oxford University Press.
Schrire, R., ed. 1994. *Malan to De Klerk*. New York: St Martin's Press.
Seekings, J. 2000. *The UDF*. Athens: Ohio University Press/Cape Town: David Philip/London: James Currey.
Southall, R. 2001. *Opposition and Democracy in South Africa*. London: Frank Cass.
Spitz, R. 2000. *The Politics of Transition*. Johannesburg: Witwatersrand University Press.
Steyn, J.C. 1980. *Tuiste in eie taal*. Cape Town: Tafelberg.
Surplus People Project. 1983. *Forced Removals in South Africa*. 5 Vols. Cape Town: Surplus People Project.
Suttner, R., and J. Cronin. 1986. *Thirty Years of the Freedom Charter*. Johannesburg: Ravan.
Terreblanche, S. 2003. *A History of Inequality in South Africa, 1652–2002*. Pietermaritzburg (South Africa): University of Natal Press.

Truth and Reconciliation Commission. 1998. *Final Report.* http://www.inc.co.za/online/trc.

Van der Westhuizen, J. 2002. *Adapting to Globalization: Malaysia, South Africa and the Challenge of Ethnic Redistribution with Growth.* Westport, CT: Praeger.

Van Kessel, I. 2000. *Beyond Our Wildest Dreams.* Charlottesville: University Press of Virginia.

Verwoerd, H.F. 1934. "Die bestryding van armoede en die herorganisasie van welvaartswerk." In P. Du Toit, *Report of the People's Conference on the Poor White Problem*, Kimberley, South Africa, 2–5 October.

Walker, E.A. 1957. *A History of Southern Africa.* London: Longman.

Walshe, P. 1970. *The Rise of African Nationalism in South Africa.* London: C. Hurst.

Wilson, F., and M. Ramphele. 1989. *Uprooting Poverty.* Cape Town: David Philip.

Wilson, M., and L. Thompson. 1971. *The Oxford History of South Africa.* Oxford: Oxford University Press.

Wolpe, H. 1972. "Capitalism and Cheap Labour Power." *Economy and Society* 1 (4).

———. 1988. *Race, Class and the Apartheid State.* Paris: Unesco.

Worden, N. 2000. *The Making of Modern South Africa.* Oxford: Blackwell.

Yudelman, D. 1983. *The Emergence of Modern South Africa.* Westport, CT: Greenwood Press.

Index

About the Author

P. ERIC LOUW is Director of Communication Programs at the University of Queensland. During the 1980s, Louw was a United Democratic Front anti-apartheid activist. His previous books include *The Media and Cultural Production* (2001), *South Africa Media Policy* (1993), and *The Alternative Press in South Africa* (1991).